Evidence
of
Innocence

By
Edward R. Clark

Cadmus Publishing
www.cadmuspublishing.com

Copyright © 2022 Edward R. Clark

Published by Cadmus Publishing
www.cadmuspublishing.com
Port Angeles, WA

ISBN: 978-1-63751-102-2
Library of Congress Control Number: 2021923578

All rights reserved. Copyright under Berne Copyright Convention, Universal Copyright Convention, and Pan-American Copyright Convention. No part of this book may be reproduced, stored in a retrieval system, or transmitted in any form, or by any means, electronic, mechanical, photocopying, recording or otherwise, without prior permission of the author.

Preface

My sources include notes taken before and during the trials as well as transcripts, appeal briefs, court exhibits, letters, and newspaper clippings-some without complete dates or source information. I have included as much documentation as has been available to me.

I have altered spelling and punctuation in quotes for clarity, consistency, and easier reading. The titles of appeal references are truncated to main words. The names of those providing court testimonies are sometimes presented with their titles so as to help the reader. Not all of the testimony of these cases is pertinent to the arguments of this volume-ellipses indicate breaks in the testimony; extraneous words and repetitions have also been deleted for brevity and readability.

To my son Jeff, who is ever more on my mind.

To my publisher, Cadmus Publishing. My heartfelt appreciation for your innovative services and expertise.

Contents

Introduction 1
Part I: My Story 3
Chapter 1: Encountering Hitchhikers, 1974 4
Chapter 2: The Hitchhiker Murders 9
Chapter 3: The Arrest 23
Part II: The Michael Jiminez Case 48
Chapter 4: Pretrial Events 49
Chapter 5: The Case for the Prosecution 60
Chapter 6: The Case for the Defense 91
Chapter 7: Closing Arguments and Verdict 122
Part III: The Barbara Jiminez Case 126
Chapter 8: Imprisoned, Preparing for the Second Trial 127
Chapter 9: Eavesdropping - Motion to Dismiss 138
Chapter 10: Pretrial Events 157
Chapter 11: The Case for the Prosecution 161
Chapter 12: The Case for the Defense 252
Chapter 13: Prosecution's Closing Statement 282
Chapter 14: Defense's Closing Statement 294
Chapter 15: Judge's Instructions, Jury Deliberations, Sentence 309
Part IV: Exculpatory Evidence 313
Chapter 16: Discovery 314
Epilogue 330
Appendix 340

INTRODUCTION

"This is the biggest event to hit our town since we hung the Indians on Main Street!" remarked the deputy sheriff to his partner while transporting me to the courthouse for the first of two murder trials. He referred to the hanging of 39 Native Americans following the Dakota Wars of 1862 (or Sioux Uprising), 112 years before.

An editorial in the local newspaper referred to my case as the latest of "14 or 15 drug-related murders . . . killed in gangland style." Fueling the rumors, the local movie theater brought back a two-year-old film about a contract killer. Adding more fuel to the fire, the judge publicly announced that the court reporter had been killed.

Ensuring that I would not receive a fair trial, my court-appointed attorney, among his other disservices, left it to me to decide on the jurors, who were from a local population to whom I was a stranger. Such a task required the expertise of an experienced trial lawyer. Among the prospective jurors were two women stating that, because of the news coverage, they had already decided I was guilty. Another said she was too nervous to serve, and still another said she was afraid. The newspaper published a list of the jurors after they were impaneled, identifying them by name and occupation. A juror who subsequently complained of harassment was not excused. The trial nevertheless retained its venue.

Learning I was not in the state when the murders took place, investigators threatened a witness who could testify to that fact. Through illegal eavesdropping on attorney-client conferences, the authorities learned about which evidence of my innocence to suppress and which court documents to alter so as to impeach my key defense witness.

After I was found guilty of the first murder in the first degree, the judge sentenced me to life in prison. A public defender assigned to represent me in the second trial (in the death of a second victim) warned me against pleading not guilty. If I were found guilty, he said, a second life sentence would run consecutive to the first.

Many people facing the possibility of spending the rest of their lives in prison would plead guilty regardless of their innocence, but that was something I would not do. Now, even after spending nearly five decades in prison, I do not regret my decision. As documented here, evidence surfaced much later as to the identity of the killers and their motive. Investigative reports, trial transcripts, appeal briefs, and newspaper articles further attest to the story that follows.

The National Institute of Justice, reporting on its independent, comprehensive, nationwide study of convictions, in 1996 noted: "Reasonably credible estimates are [that] up to 10 percent of our national prison population may be factually innocent of the crimes of which they were convicted." With a prison population of more than two million, more than 200,000 Americans now behind bars may be innocent.

If there is a lesson here for the reader, it is "There, but for the grace of God, go I!"

Part I

My Story

Chapter 1: Encountering Hitchhikers, 1974

Saturday, April 20

I had driven into the Sierra Nevada Mountains around Lake Tahoe, along the California/Nevada border, a couple of days before starting the long drive back to my home in Michigan.

My initial trip to the Sacramento area had been in preparation for moving my family to the West Coast, as my wife yearned to move back to her home state and we wanted a fresh start after closing down our auto-repair business. Even though the business had a good reputation and brought in customers from across the Detroit metro area, my partners had not lived up to their end of our agreement. They had promised to relieve me of some of the administrative duties requiring that I work 12 to 16 hours a day, seven days a week.

In closing down the business, I had underestimated the malice of my former partners: They filed a lawsuit that froze our bank account and placed a lien on our home, which held up the closing of its sale. They also hired a private investigator to locate me in California, so as to serve a summons. The investigator harassed my wife's parents, who lived in the Sacramento area.

On my attorney's advice I remained scarce while he prepared my case. My stay on the West Coast had lasted longer than anticipated, and I couldn't take being away from my family any longer. On Saturday morning I started the long drive back to Michigan, having no idea that a never-ending nightmare would dwarf my preoccupation with the lawsuit.

Sunday, April 21

After driving more than 1,600 miles in 34 hours on just a few hours sleep at Lake Tahoe, I reached the outskirts of Des Moines, Iowa, around 6 P.M. The gas gauge on the Ford Bronco read almost empty, so I took an exit ramp off the expressway where Interstates 80 and 35 run together around Des Moines.

At the service station, three hitchhikers-two men and a woman, apparently in their early twenties-noticed my Michigan license plates and asked whether I was "going east".

Normally I didn't pick up hitchhikers, but if someone was stranded during inclement weather or having car trouble, I tried to be a Good Samaritan. The trio was clean-cut and friendly, and with one of them a woman, I didn't see any risk in giving them a ride. Having had no sleep and with fatigue setting in, I considered that one of them might do some of the driving. When I asked whether any of them had a driver's license, one of the men nodded. He got into the driver's seat, and the others got into the back. I sat in the front passenger seat and shortly dozed off.

Later that evening I awoke to the sound of idling diesel engines, a sure sign we were at a truck stop. The driver said we needed gas. This was in the midst of the 1974 energy shortage, and there was a line at the pumps. I was hungry and suggested we get something to eat in the restaurant during the wait. The driver didn't respond, and the couple sitting in the back whispered to one another. Since they were hitchhiking, I assumed they didn't have much money. Uncomfortable at the thought of eating while they just sat in my vehicle, I offered to treat them to a meal. The couple followed me into the restaurant, and the driver headed for the rest room. After the waitress took our order, I went out to take the Bronco to the gas pump. After filling up, I moved the vehicle to where I would be able to see it from the restaurant. The hitchhiker who had been driving returned from the rest room to the Bronco, and I went back to the restaurant. By that time my meal was cold, so I ate only half of my "hot" roast-beef sandwich.

I paid for the meal and gas with a traveler's check. On returning to the Bronco, I felt chilled from the night air and poured myself a cup of coffee from a thermos lying between the front, bucket seats. After drinking one cup, I felt nauseated, which I attributed to my lack of sleep. I quickly dozed off as the vehicle began to move, assuming we were still heading east. Because I had paid for the gas and meal with a traveler's check, the truck stop later was determined to be located off of Interstate 35-we were heading north!

Monday, April 22

I awoke the next morning, alone in the Bronco on a rural gravel road. I could make out farms in the distance, silhouetted against the early morning dawn. The vehicle wasn't running, but the ignition switch was on. The gas gauge read empty. I assumed the driver, looking for a service station, had exited the Interstate before he found one. Apparently the three hitchhikers had simply gone their way.

"If only they had awakened me," I thought, "That extra five gallons of gas in the car-top carrier would have saved them a lot of trouble!"

After pouring the gas into the fuel tank, I drove around the area looking for the trio and for a service station. Finding neither, I headed back to the place where I had awakened. Passing it, I went up, then down, the other side of an incline, to where the gravel road intersected with a paved highway. A sign identified it as a roadway in *Minnesota!* This placed me a couple hundred miles north of Interstate 80, where I had expected to be.

I instinctively pulled over to check the contents of my vehicle, including the gun case containing my rifle, which I had used for target practice in the Sierra Nevada Mountains. The case was partly unzipped, but to my relief the gun was inside. I was, however, missing a suitcase containing a sports coat and slacks. A well-worn brown suede jacket lay across the contents of a box I used for trash. Apparently one of the hitchhikers had helped himself to my clothes, in exchange for the jacket. As the trash box was full and would serve only to remind me of their deceit, I discarded the box.

About ten miles north of the Iowa border I stopped for gas, and then headed in a southeasterly direction through Wisconsin. I arrived in the Belvidere, Illinois area, for gas and phoned my wife to say I expected to be home around 11 o'clock that night. Her tone, eager for my return, reaffirmed my feelings for her as well as my sadness at our being apart for what had turned out to be weeks instead of days. Our conversation gave me the determination to continue driving despite being worn out from the long journey.

At about the time I phoned my wife, two of the hitchhikers I had picked up were seated in a cafe 200 miles to the west, off Interstate 35 near Ames, Iowa, not far from where we had stopped for gas and a bite to eat the night before.

I was running late due to heavy traffic around Chicago, partly because of an accident on the freeway, so I decided to call my wife again around 10 P.M. from a phone booth near Kalamazoo, Michigan, to say I expected to arrive around midnight.

Tuesday, April 23

I finally arrived home about 1 A.M. I didn't realize just how much I had missed my wife until I saw her standing in the doorway. After making love, we discussed the events that had taken place in my absence and made final plans for moving the family to California. It would require making one more trip, to haul the balance of our possessions in a U-Haul trailer to our new home. From there I planned to fly back to Michigan and drive to the West Coast in our other vehicle with my family, taking in the sights along the way.

Chapter 2: The Hitchhiker Murders

About the time I arrived home in Michigan, a man was shot to death 700 miles away, in a farming area seven miles outside Mankato, Minnesota.[1]

The next morning at about 11:30, a Chicago & Northwestern train with a string of 58 freight cars bound for Waseca, Minnesota, made its first run of the day from Mankato. The head brakeman, peering from the engine compartment, spotted a man lying beneath railroad ties along the edge of the tracks. He radioed the caboose.

"It looks like there's a man covered up with a couple ties on the north side of the tracks. Look it over."

The conductor and another brakeman jumped from the train as it ground to a halt and ran to the site. The brakeman yelled to the conductor, some distance behind him, "Call a doctor and ambulance," but as he neared the body, the brakeman could see no movement. In a softer tone he yelled again, "You might as well call the sheriff. He's dead."

Sheriff LaRoy Wiebold, accompanied by his brother, Sgt. Loren Wiebold, arrived at the scene within 45 minutes. They were met by deputies who had been called to keep curious drivers moving along

Highway 14, which runs parallel to the railroad tracks. Also at the scene was Thomas Simonson, a field agent with the Minnesota Bureau of Criminal Apprehension (BCA), the state's crime and forensic lab. County Coroner Delvin Ohrt soon showed up.

Overall observation of the area suggested that the railroad ties had been carried from a stack 18 to 25 feet away. One of the ties weighed in later at 120 pounds. The ties, laid across the body in a perpendicular manner, formed an X.

The contents of the dead man's wallet identified him as Michael Steven Jiminez, age 23, residence on Main Street in Mankato. His watch had stopped at 11:00.

Upon questioning, members of the train crew said they had noticed nothing unusual on the ten o'clock run the night before. The farmer who used the access road said his dog had barked at about 11:00 the previous night, which coincided with the dead man's stopped watch. Although the tire-tread impressions clearly showed that a vehicle had traveled from the highway onto the access road leading across the tracks to a farmer's field, the investigators did not compare these for a match to the farmer's equipment despite their being clearly too narrow for a full-sized automobile. Agent Simonson took measurements of the tire tracks only, and photographs were taken. There was no effort to take a plaster cast of the tread impressions.

The victim had died instantly from a gunshot to the back of his head. The coroner found both entrance and exit wounds, but no one searched for a projectile. For future consideration as to the time of death, the coroner made a mental note that Highway 14 was heavily traveled and that the murder was unlikely to have occurred during daylight hours. The local newspaper, TV, and radio stations converged on the scene.

An autopsy was performed that afternoon. To validate his own estimate of the time of death, the coroner conferred with the state's chief medical examiner and forensic pathologist, John Coe, in Minneapolis. Dr. Coe agreed with the coroner's finding that death had occurred the night before, between 9 P.M. Monday and 3 A.M. Tuesday. Later, at the grand jury hearing, Dr. Ohrt, when asked for a more definite time of death, replied that he would place it around midnight.

Sergeant Wiebold and Captain Larson went to the address given in the wallet; it turned out to be an upper flat. Searching the premises, they found the names and addresses of relatives along with evidence that Michael Jiminez was unemployed and that his wife was a part time student at Mankato State College. Checking at the college, they learned that Barbara Jiminez had not attended her Monday Classes.

The next day, the *Mankato Free Press* published photos of the crime scene, including a photograph of the dead man and a snapshot of his missing wife. A separate article reported:

[The Blue Earth County sheriff said] evidence at the scene was virtually intact and that his department had a "good case up to the present time. The evidence we do have is good evidence. And it is developing as time progresses. He never knew he was going to be shot. Believe me, a second shot was unnecessary." Yet Blue Earth Sheriff's officials have turned up no witness accounts of the incident other than the report of a dog barking around 11 P.M. Monday night. That could coincide with the murder, which the authorities placed eight to ten hours before the discovery of the body at approximately 11:30 A.M. Tuesday.[2]

The authorities contacted Michael Jiminez's sister, Rebecca Niehus, in Emporia, Kansas. She stated that her brother and his wife had arrived unannounced the previous Friday evening, having hitchhiked 540 miles south to Emporia to purchase a car from her. As Niehus later testified, the original purpose for the Jiminezes' trip was to attend a wedding at Michael Jiminez's mother's home in Le Mars, Iowa, 240 miles from Mankato.

When asked whether the Jiminezes were carrying a large amount of money (in consideration of robbery as a motive for the attack on Michael Jiminez), Niehus stated that they had only about six dollars between them. This was not enough to pay for gas on their return. The Jiminezes, according to Niehus, decided to hitchhike back from Emporia to Mankato on Sunday rather than wait until Monday for a transfer of the car title.

This should have and did raise questions for the investigators as to the true purpose for the Jiminezes' hitchhiking to Kansas, especially given the suspicious among law enforcement and rumors in the community that drugs were behind the murder of Jiminez and the disappearance of his wife, but an investigator who checked police records to discover that Jiminez had been arrested twice on drug charges testified at a pretrial hearing that he was, without explanation, removed from the case.

As testimony at the trial would reveal, a return trip to the Jiminez apartment uncovered a jewelry box containing hashish pipes and marijuana, a checkbook, some mail, and, in a kitchen drawer, $150 in cash. The investigators removed these items from the apartment.

The sheriff provided the media with details of a conversation with Michael Jiminez's sister, as well as a description of his missing wife:

An attempt to locate Barbara is the top priority at this time. Leads have been checked as far down as Ames, Iowa. [She is] 5-foot-2 [inches], 120 pounds, [has] green eyes and long, dark hair. She was wearing a dark-blue bandana on her head, blue jeans, white long-sleeve turtleneck sweater, long-sleeve khaki shirt, red wool socks, and brown leather loafers. She was carrying an olive-drab canvas pack and wore a copper wedding ring in a rope design.[3]

Since the last known sighting of the Jiminez couple was in Emporia, Kansas, authorities in the surrounding states of Kansas, Iowa, North and South Dakota, and Wisconsin were put on alert for the missing Barbara Jiminez. An editorial in the *Mankato Free Press*, titled "Lost Innocence-Slain in Gangland Style," expressed community outrage at the "14 or 15 drug-related murders" in the Mankato area. The editorial began: "A young Mankato man is found slain in gangland style, and authorities fear that his still-missing wife is a similar victim of ruthless violence. 'My God,' we say privately. 'What next,' we ask ourselves."[4]

The authorities were under heavy public scrutiny and political pressure to come up with a perpetrator. So, pacifying the media and thriving on the publicity, Sheriff Wiebold kept reporters informed of every aspect of the case. His actions eventually lead the prosecution to withhold vital exculpatory evidence (that is, evidence favorable to my case) from the public and subsequently from the jury.

As was later determined, the Jiminezes were two of the hitchhikers I picked up about 30 hours before the murder of Michael, but the evidence developed by the investigators supported my innocence. This evidence included that on Monday at least one other person saw the Jiminez couple 30 miles north of Ames, Iowa, and 200 miles south of where Michael Jiminez's body was found the next day. The *Press* reported knowledge of the sighting of the Jiminez couple in Iowa: "We are making progress."[5]

The progress referred to positively placing the young Mankato couple in Blairsburg, Iowa, at 4:30 P.M. Monday. Wiebold said the identification was confirmed with photographs. The couple was placed in a cafe in Blairsburg, a short distance away from where Interstate 35 ends. It was that highway route the couple had intended to hitchhike on to Mankato from Emporia, Kansas, where they had been visiting the murdered man's sister until noon Sunday. Wiebold said the Jiminezes had stopped at the cafe to eat and that they were alone.

Evidence later withheld from the jury included a sighting of the missing Barbara Jiminez in Waseca, Minnesota, as reported in the *Waseca Journal*:

> At press time today (Friday) the Blue Earth County Sheriff was apparently working on a new lead to the Jiminez murder case.
>
> Michael Steve Jiminez was murdered sometime early Tuesday morning and since that time his wife, Barbara, has been missing.
>
> A six-state search has been in progress for three days now in search for the missing woman who law enforcement officials fear may be murdered or being kept hostage.
>
> The new lead to the case has come from the Waseca

area with the owner of the B & J Cafe, Bob Guthrie, getting involved. Guthrie told the *Journal* at press time today that Thursday afternoon he served a young couple in his cafe who left behind a picture that closely resembled the missing Barbara Jiminez. He said that the young couple who stopped by his restaurant about 2:30 P.M. appeared very nervous while waiting for their food.

"They told me they were from the Rochester area," Bob Guthrie said, "but at the same time asked me how far the city was from Waseca and asked how long it would take to get there." [Rochester is located on a direct route 40 miles from Waseca.]

Guthrie said he didn't pay much attention to the picture until last night when he was watching the news on TV. "I saw a picture of the missing woman on TV and thought it closely resembled the Jiminez woman."

Guthrie said he was questioned by the Blue Earth Sheriff's Department about midnight last night, but law enforcement officials declined to say whether the picture was the missing Jiminez or not. However, they asked to keep the picture to check the information out more carefully.[6]

No investigative report of the contact with Guthrie surfaced. Apparently, the prosecutor initially planned to call on Guthrie to testify if and when someone was charged with the murder(s)-the trial judge for the murder of Michael Jiminez announced to the jury that witnesses included "a person from Waseca."[7]

Four days after Barbara Jiminez was seen in the cafe in Waseca, Sheriff Wiebold contacted the neighboring Le Sueur County Sheriff's Department to report that a shoe had been seen along a highway in that county.[8]

No shoe was found, but a search of the area resulted in the discovery of a coat a short distance from that sighting, under a bridge, partly in the

Cannon River. The highway over the river ran south to Waseca, where Barbara Jiminez had been observed in the company of a man at the cafe. The coat had the initial "B" on the collar. In the pockets were two packs of cigarettes of the brand Barbara Jiminez smoked, along with an elastic hair tie. The coat was found about 18 miles northeast of where the body of Michael Jiminez was discovered.

An article in the *Mankato Free Press* quoted Sheriff Wiebold: "The search for Barbara will continue on the speculation she is being held a hostage . . . The sheriff is encouraging farmers now working in the fields to be alert to any freshly dug holes or any articles of clothing." The article also stated that deputies stationed along the highway in Blue Earth County near where the body of Michael Jiminez was discovered had questioned drivers about seeing anything at the time of the murder with no results.[9]

After the discovery of Barbara Jiminez's coat in Le Sueur County, 50 deputies plus volunteers combed the countryside near the highway on horseback, looking for her. The search was futile.

Detective Dragnet magazine, which covered the trial for the murder of Michael Jiminez, featured a photo of Le Sueur County Sheriff Pat Smith mounted on his horse in a white western hat and cowboy boots with the caption "Tall in the Saddle".[10]

Two days later, the Le Sueur County Sheriff's Office received a complaint from a farmer McCabe. He had called about the presence of a vehicle late at night at Scotch Lake, a small, remote lake in the county. No one looked into the complaint. If someone had done so, he might have been able to save the life of Barbara Jiminez-or at least catch those responsible for her death.

The next day, the *Mankato Free Press* quoted Sheriff Wiebold on the murder of Michael Jiminez: "His department and the Bureau of Criminal Apprehension were concentrating on *'three separate persons that may have been in the area* or known to frequent the area.' He declined to elaborate on the subjects."[11]

Ten days after the discovery of Michael Jiminez's body, the trash box

I had discarded was turned over to the police in Waterville, Minnesota, who contacted the Le Sueur County sheriff's office. Inside the box were the "olive drab canvas pack," neatly folded clothing, unopened packs of cigarettes of the brand Barbara Jiminez smoked, and a shopping bag with a handwritten note-"35N" (the direct route from Emporia, Kansas, north to Minnesota). Another note-"MINNESOTA"-apparently had been added later. Niehus testified at the trial that she did not know when it was added or by whom. The box also contained a receipt showing my name and the name of the company (and its address) from which I had rented a typewriter in California.[12]

The *Press* reported comments of the two sheriffs. The Blue Earth County sheriff said: "Until her body is found, we can only presume she is alive." The sheriff of Le Sueur County, a man of 25 years more experience, did not share this optimism: "I'm reasonably sure Mrs. Jiminez is dead." And he voiced his fear that her body might be in a lake: "We will continue to search because I'm sure this body is in the area someplace."

Body Discovered in Le Sueur County

Twelve days after the search for Barbara Jiminez had begun, Roger Schmidt tried out his new boat on Scotch Lake near Cleveland in Le Sueur County. Schmidt made several trips around the lake and was heading back to the boat landing when he noticed what looked like a body in the water along the shoreline not far from the landing. He loaded his boat onto its trailer and walked over to the spot in question. Lying face down in the water was the nude body of what appeared to be a woman.

He ran back to his car, drove into the town of Cleveland, and called the sheriff's office. Someone there instructed him to go back to the lake and wait for the arrival of a patrol car. Deputies cruising close to the area were ordered to secure the site until Sheriff Smith's arrival. Sheriff Smith drove to the scene. BCA Field Agent Simonson and Sheriff Wiebold arrived shortly afterward.

A farm-implement end gate rod, used on wagon boxes by farmers, lay across the body. A piece of cloth with hair entwined in a knot lay nearby. Scanning the area, Sheriff Smith glanced up at a tree. There, six to seven feet above the ground, was a shoe, later identified as belonging to Barbara Jiminez-its toe pointing to the body.

There were several sets of tire tracks in the area of the boat landing but only one set led towards the body, and Sheriff Smith studied the set leading in that direction. He could see that the vehicle had driven through a mud hole, leaving deep-tread impressions on the far side, where the ground had since hardened. The vehicle's driver apparently had attempted to go up a small incline, and then spun the wheels. The foliage was disturbed from the tracks to the water's edge, indicating that the body had been dragged to the lake.

Agent Simonson measured all the tire tracks and had a photographer take pictures of those nearest the boat landing. Sheriff Smith reminded Simonson to have the tracks leading to the crime scene photographed and to make a cast of the tire-tread impressions. Instead, since Simonson had already measured them and determined that the measurements were different from those at the other crime scene, he ordered the photographs but did not make a cast.

Sheriff Smith, later recalling the complaint from McCabe about a vehicle in that exact spot in the middle of the night, seemed disappointed that no cast was made.

During a thorough search of the area along the lake, a torn blouse, two scarves, and torn panties were found in an abandoned farmhouse. These items were turned over to the Sheriff's Department of Blue Earth County. It has never been revealed whether the clothing, ultimately discarded, belonged to Barbara Jiminez.

Jo E. Anderson, a family physician and Le Sueur County's deputy coroner, arrived at the scene to view the body. He attended the autopsy as an observer and announced the cause of death as "apparent strangulation". He based this conclusion on a strand of hair around the front of the neck, which could have been embedded in the swollen skin during decomposition. As evidence in the *Free Press*, the authorities capitalized on his conclusion: Sheriff Wiebold stated the death of Mrs. Jiminez was "apparent strangulation".

As to the time of death, it was "just a guess that no more than 24 hours had elapsed between the death of Mrs. Jiminez and that of her husband. She had been dead almost as long as he had." and the sheriff's department was "very heavily pursuing one suspect . . . there are three suspects involved in the investigation of Michael's death [their identity was never revealed] . . . There are still reasons to believe that Jiminez was shot to death gangland style and his wife used for games before she was disposed of."[13]

Coroner R. H. Sanford, who performed the autopsy of the body of Barbara Jiminez, found no physical evidence supporting strangulation. Instead, he found an accumulation of water in the lungs consistent with drowning. Sanford contacted forensic pathologist Coe in Minneapolis, who directed him to "authorities" who also determined that the evidence supported death by drowning. As to the time of death, Sanford determined, according to his testimony at the trial, that she had been dead "at least three days". This contradicted Sheriff Wiebold's unqualified "guess".

Scotch Lake is 15 miles west of the bridge where Barbara Jiminez's coat was discovered partially in the Cannon River. The lake is about 17 miles northeast of where her husband's body was discovered in Blue Earth County.

The two crime scenes suggest the murders of the Jiminezes were drug-related. On the one hand, the body of Michael Jiminez carried identification. It was found in an open area along a busy highway, and railroad ties were placed across the body in a manner to draw attention to it. On the other hand, Barbara Jiminez's body was discovered in an isolated area. The inexpensive copper wedding ring, two signet rings, and the earrings she had worn were missing, as Rebecca Niehus later testified, but Barbara's shoe was wedged in the crotch of the tree with the toe pointing towards the body! Perhaps that and the X of the railroad ties were meant to point out what might happen to those who crossed the drug dealers, who had permeated the town.

Mankato's Drug Scene

New exposés on events taking place before, during, and after the death of the Jiminez couple outlined Mankato's drug problem:

> Since neither the police department nor the sheriff's office has a narcotics squad or officer, local drug dealings had gone largely unchecked . . . Mankato is a wide-open town. It's still a center for drugs. That was also Mankato's reputation in the early 1970s.[14]
>
> Some local legitimate businessmen have entered the drug business. Mankato has about five or six "top-notch" dealers, and several others who are doing well . . . Wholesalers are what the BCA's Gunderson calls those that bring quantities of drugs into the community. And he said Mankato could probably support about 20.
>
> Some high-level dealers in town claim to have ties with the Mafia . . . we're getting more reports on straight-looking, older, legitimate business interests becoming involved. Another narcotics agent contended that some families in Mankato "didn't get all their money honestly. Several sources claimed to have heard about the involvement of various moneyed or prominent people in Mankato but could not substantiate it . . . [A former drug dealer] was advanced eight pounds of cocaine for regional distribution on one occasion . . . At the time . . . a street value of about $400,000 [in 1970s dollars]."[15]

In the Mankato area, drug-related violence had included:

- Dec 8, 1973 - Michael Hinkel, 21, died and Teddy Oftedahl, 22, was paralyzed from a heroin overdose.

Sources claim the Mankato men were intentionally sold heroin that was unusually potent.[16]

- Aug 8, 1974 - Scott Lester, 23, was run down by an automobile after word got out that he was an informant.

- Sept 1974 - Mark Guentzel, 23 . . . given a new identity and transported to another state . . . identified as the informant in a major drug bust. [A local district court judged identified Guentzel as the informant.]

- April 11, 1976 - Robert McCumber, 28 . . . found floating in the Minnesota River . . . He too, was suspected of being an informant. Sheriff LaRoy Wiebold and his men are proceeding with the investigation . . . Wiebold is declining to release any details surrounding the matter. [McCumber's murder went unsolved.]

- July 3, 1979 - An Amboy woman, 19 . . . beaten and forced to shove gravel up her anus and vagina . . . She was going to be an example for "people like her . . . There's a lot of profit to protect."

- Carl Thompson, charged in Blue Earth County's largest drug bust . . . Authorities seized $32,000 in cash and about two pounds of uncut cocaine valued at nearly $1 million . . . Thompson ran the food service for the Minnesota Vikings training camp in Mankato.[17] [Thompson did not receive a prison sentence until later, in an unrelated case in federal court.]

- Just the news that the Vikings are in Mankato keeps our name before the public in the Midwest. For many players, however, Mankato and training camp are just dirty words. "I see Mankato as a black hole," said Dennis Swilley, who is in his ninth Vikings camp . . . "I hate it. I guess I shouldn't badmouth it too bad because at least I don't have to live here. I feel like I drop off the edge of the world every time I come here."[18]

- [Federal] Judge Edward Devitt on Monday sentenced Georges Fayez Ghassan 20, of Mankato, Minn., and his brother Ibrahim Fayas Ghassan, 23, of Bloomington, each to eight years in prison . . . Voussef Georges Issa, 32, of Bloomington, was sentenced to six years . . . The three, who pleaded guilty . . . [to] importing 15 pounds of heroin worth $75 million to $80 million on the street, were linked to a large international drug ring . . . Ibrahim Ghassan had received an undergraduate degree in physics and had first come to [Mankato State] university in 1978. He enrolled last fall to study for a master's degree in physics . . . the mayor of Mankato, said that he knows the Ghassan brothers.[19]

- [Federal] indictments were issued against Duane W. Carson 34, Kasota, Minn., And Sheila J. Burgess 28, Lake Crystal, Minn. Burnsville police found slightly more than three pounds of nearly pure cocaine and 64 grams of cocaine in Burgess's car.[20]

- On April 23, 1973, Tyler was charged with kidnapping and raping a 17-year-old Minneapolis girl and robbing her fiancé . . . sentenced to up to 20 years in prison. Corrections officials concluded that "Tyler was a rather dangerous individual who showed no remorse or guilt." They quoted [Tyler]: "I'll meet up with her again some day."

Eleven months later, Tyler was paroled . . . with a football scholarship to Mankato State University. Four Months after his release from prison, Tyler was shot and his companion killed in a fracas with a Des Moines heroin dealer . . . months after that, Tyler . . . sold a pound of marijuana to an undercover agent . . . Three months later, Judge Mason agreed to reduce Tyler's sentence. [Judge Mason, later presiding over my trial, made statements in open court revealing concern about what the public thought of him granting a continuance requested by the defense.]

Tyler has recruited "a lot of heavyweight support" for his earlier release from prison. Because of the Tyler case, other incidents, and what narcotics agents described as a lack of cooperation from Mankato police and other Blue Earth County agencies, the Bureau of Criminal Apprehension withdrew its resident agent in early 1976 . . . A *Minneapolis Tribune* survey of drug cases indicates that nobody has been imprisoned from Blue Earth County on drug charges alone during the past three years. Three-fourths of the drug defendants-including one arrested in possession of 32 plastic bags of heroin-have been given probation. Agents now describe Mankato as a "doper's haven".[21]

As these excerpts show, the community had good reason to question the predominance of drug-related violence, including the deaths of the Jiminezes, in the vicinity, but citizen outcry also put pressure on the authorities for quick closure to the Jiminez case.

After it was completed, however, the prosecutor, who also had a private law practice, tried to maintain the status quo. The newspaper noted "public outcry over the resignation of County Attorney John Corbey shortly after he was reelected to another four-year term, and over Corbey's suggestion that his law partner be appointed to the position for the full term."[22]

Chapter 3: The Arrest

Based solely on evidence that at some point I may have come in contact with the Jiminezes, Blue Earth County Sheriff Wiebold met with County Attorney John Corbey about obtaining an arrest warrant. The prosecutor felt a typewriter rental receipt alone wasn't probable cause for arrest. He wanted me to be questioned first as to whether I had contact with the Jiminezes.[23]

Learning I had since returned to the Sacramento area, the Minnesota authorities contacted the Sacramento Sheriff's Department for assistance in locating the Edward Clark whose name appeared on the typewriter rental receipt. Detectives went to the California Business Machines location and told the owner to contact them should I return to rent another machine. They said, "We have a warrant for his arrest." They did not have one. Upon arriving in Sacramento, I did return to rent a typewriter, and the owner notified the detectives.

The California and Minnesota authorities, in a rush to make judgment and without grounds for arrest, so conspired to make an illegal arrest, and after the fact of the arrest, they made a ploy to justify it. The conspiracy is revealed in the transcripts of phone calls between Sheriff Wiebold and the Sacramento detectives, included in the argument for appeal:

Sheriff:

> Now that the car should have somewhere around 5,000 miles on it, fresh miles. Let's hope he hasn't vacuumed the thing. If you can get him and get it impounded-now we don't have a warrant out yet.

Detective:

> How soon will you have it?

Sheriff:

> God, the county attorney up here is the analogue to your DA [district attorney] down there. He kind of has cold feet, and he wants us to find the truck and find anything that could connect him to her then all the better and arrest him on probable cause and then get-I hate doing it that way myself, as a law enforcement officer, but you know . . .[24]

Since the arrest couldn't take place until about 12 hours after the California authorities knew I was back in the area, they had plenty of time to seek an arrest warrant from a judge, but they did not seek one. Instead, at 10:40 A.M., the detectives directed the deputies at roll call there: "If the subject is apprehended, do not question the subject or do not question nor advise of his rights [to have an attorney present during questioning]."[25]

It had been a hot day in Sacramento, and I stopped at a bar/restaurant for a wine cooler on my way to retiring for the day. As I sat at the bar, someone behind me asked, "Are you Edward Clark?" I responded that I was. Before I could turn around, a detective threw me against the bar and cuffed my hands tight behind my back.

Assuming this had something to do with the lawsuit of my former business partners, I said, "This isn't necessary to serve me papers." I received no response but was hustled out, placed in the back seat of a patrol car, and transported to the sheriff's office for interrogation.

Sitting opposite me in an interrogation room, the detective shoved a form across the table for me to sign. It was a waiver of my right to have an attorney present during questioning. I refused to sign it. Then he ordered me to turn over my wallet. Rummaging through it he found and removed a receipt for the storage locker in which I was keeping furniture and personal items brought on my two trips west.

Finally, he told me I was under arrest as a suspect in two killings in Minnesota. I immediately thought of the three hitchhikers I had picked up near Des Moines on my trip back to Michigan, who were nowhere in sight when I awoke to discover I was in Minnesota. I assumed that, if the hitchhikers were the victims, they had been killed the same night I picked them up.

Defensively, I responded: "I haven't been in Minnesota for three years," referring to a time when my wife and I traveled through Wisconsin to Duluth, Minnesota, for a scenic drive along Lake Superior's north shore, up into Canada, then back down to Michigan.

The California authorities then transported me to the county jail, just a few blocks away. The desk sergeant informed the detectives that they had four hours to get something to hold me, otherwise I would have to be released.

According to the California Penal Code, anyone arrested without a warrant must be taken before a magistrate for a determination as to the existence of probable cause for arrest.[26] That did not occur in my case. Without that I could be released within a few hours, so the detectives placed a second phone call to Sheriff Wiebold:

Detective:

> We have got him and we have got the car, and if we do not get some type of warrant or something within three hours, they will release him from the jail. They have nothing to hold him on except the information that you gave us, and he said that within four hours he has to be out, and one hour has already passed. Nothing says we can hold the car either, so that's our problem. And if he gets released, the judge is going to say if you don't have probable cause to hold him, what makes you think you

have probable cause to hold the car? Is there some reason why your county attorney is so hinkey?

Sheriff:

> Yes, he wants, well, up here we can proceed on probable cause before the warrant.

Detective:

> Well, we can't. They feel if there isn't probable cause for the search warrant, there isn't probable cause for arrest.

Sheriff:

> Let me get a hold of my county attorney, and if that's the case I'll call you back.

Detective:

> Yes, we have got to have something because otherwise we will have to turn him and everything loose and then he's gone.

Sheriff:

> I'm going to let him make that decision. Sarge, I'm going to get a hold of him right now.

Detective:

> We are monitoring his phone calls right now so we will have to see what he says here.[27]

After conferring with the Blue Earth County attorney, Sheriff Wiebold returned the call. The dialogue indicated an after-the-fact effort to justify an illegal arrest:

Detective:

> Is he going to issue an arrest warrant or what is he going to do?

Sheriff:

>He's going to issue.

Detective:

>Okay, good, terrific, that's beautiful.

Sheriff:

>Any information that you can give us that will hold him? Now, what I would like to do, Sarge, is just hang on while I dictate this, and we'll make any additions or corrections you want. Send a Teletype message, Jack.

Detective:

>Send a Teletype message saying that you have a warrant and so on and so forth. Any information that you can give us that will hold him.

Sheriff:

>We are in the process of issuance of a complaint and murder warrant for Edward Richard Clark-

Detective:

>Yes.

Sheriff:

>Request your jurisdiction to apprehend . . . and execute search warrant based on previously supplied probable cause statement. Will that do?

Detective:

>Yes, just give some indication when the warrant will be forthcoming.

Sheriff:

>Well, Sarge, up here on a first-degree-murder warrant,

just so you understand, a first-degree-murder warrant has to be issued by a grand jury.

Though I was already under arrest (without a warrant) and though he had already stated that Minnesota law requires a grand jury to indict on a first-degree murder charge, the sheriff instructed the detective to Teletype: "To apprehend..." me. He also stated there that I was charged with "Murder in the First Degree".

A couple of days later, during which I was held at the jail in California, I was again taken to an interrogation room. Two men entered.

The older one said, "I'm Sheriff Pat Smith of Le Sueur County."

The other man, about my age-in his mid-thirties-proclaimed, "I'm Sheriff LaRoy Wiebold of Blue Earth County, and I assure you I know how to do my job."

I thought to myself, "This man has an identity problem, and questions his own competence."

Then, having never heard of it, I asked, "Blue Earth County?"

"Yeah," he responded, "in Minnesota."

Under any other circumstances, I would have found his demeanor and announcement comical. I stated that I had nothing to say until I could talk to an attorney. An attorney friend had inadvertently provided that course when he remarked, years earlier in a casual conversation, that when their sole interest is to find something incriminating, the police put the burden of proof on the individual, and that when they don't have another suspect, they may concentrate on building a case against an individual who may be innocent.

Ignoring my response, the two sheriffs unlawfully continued their interrogation. Four times more I said that I had nothing to say until I could talk with an attorney.

Finally, Sheriff Smith responded, "Well, we do want to protect your rights. We've come a long ways to talk to you and want to know if you want to sign a waiver and come back to Minnesota with us and get this matter straightened out?"

I said I wouldn't sign anything until I talked to an attorney. Sheriff Smith's pleasant manner turned to anger: "We'll be back tomorrow, and you are in damn serious trouble" But they did not return.

The detectives and the two sheriffs from Minnesota conducted a search of my storage locker and of the Ford Bronco. The search warrant listed still-missing items that belonged to the Jiminez couple, but none were found. Curiously, even though Michael Jiminez had been shot, there was no firearm mentioned in the search warrant. Nevertheless, my rifle, its carrying case, and a box of cartridges were removed from the storage locker.

The copy of the search warrant I was handed did not carry a judge's signature. The line for the judge's signature showed only a typed-in name. The search warrant contained two different typefaces, indicating the addition of items to the list after its first typing.

The Bronco received a thorough going-over: It was dusted for the fingerprints of the Jiminez couple, but none was found. Tire-tread impressions were made on paper. The vehicle and its contents were vacuumed. Insects from the radiator and soil samples from the undercarriage were forwarded to Minnesota for comparison to evidence found there. A crime-lab technician in Minnesota later testified that no comparison tests were done. I suspect there may have been tests showing results in my favor. The search of the Bronco turned up nothing to incriminate me in the murder of the Jiminez couple.

The detectives handed me a list of items removed from my storage unit and observed my reaction for signs of guilt. I asked that they retrieve my reading glasses from the Bronco. When they returned with the glasses, they took more photos (with me wearing the glasses) for the purpose of finding witnesses in Minnesota and Iowa who could identify me.

Newspapers in the Mankato area reported on the events in California in articles headed: "Arrest Made in Jiminez Murders" (describing me as "unemployed", as if I were a drifter) and "Clark Arraigned in Sacramento".[28]

The Extradition

Upon advice from a public defender who subsequently became a prosecuting attorney in California, I made the mistake of signing a waiver that allowed my extradition to Minnesota. Newspaper reports in Mankato on this development included "Clark to Court for Extradition" and "Clark Waives Extradition".[29]

While the authorities had informed reporters of each step of the investigation to this point, they took every precaution to isolate me from the media. Instead of traveling on a direct flight to Minnesota, they took me first to Los Angeles for a connecting flight. When the plane landed in Minneapolis, I was taken off the back of the plane to a waiting patrol car instead of through the terminal.

The Search for Witnesses Continues

With photographs of me and the Bronco-of an uncommon two-tone color and sporting a car-top carrier-the authorities searched for anyone who might have seen me or my vehicle. Capt. Larson and Deputy Ross Wilder of the Blue Earth County Sheriff's Department traveled south from Mankato, armed with those photos and others, including some of the Jiminez couple. They met with no success until reaching Alden, Minnesota, near the Minnesota/Iowa border. Glen Bjorklund, owner of a Standard Oil station, recognized both me and the Bronco that he had serviced in April. He stated, "The driver was alone in the vehicle."

From Alden, the investigators headed 125 miles south to Blairsburg Corners, near Ames, Iowa. Relying on a previous investigative report, they showed the photos to the waitress Helen Troxel at the M & M Cafe. She had waited on the Jiminez couple on Monday, April 22, at approximately the time I called my wife from Belvidere, Illinois (it was the day before

Michael Jiminez was found murdered in Minnesota at approximately the time I arrived home in Michigan).

Troxel stated that the couple "entered alone" and "left alone," walking towards the highway. Shown the photographs of the Bronco and me, she said I was not at the cafe. She then signed a statement to that effect.

Thinking that perhaps I had dropped off the Jiminezes and gone to the service station next to the cafe, the investigators interviewed station attendant Ernest Ties. On seeing the photographs, Ties also stated that he did not see the Bronco or me. He did, however, positively identify the Jiminez couple. He stated that it was easy to remember them because while the man went into the restroom, the "attractive" woman had waited outside for him.

The investigative report revealing the existence of Ernest Ties and Glen Bjorklund was kept secret until files were subpoenaed during appellate proceedings after the trials. If the report on Ernest Ties had been revealed earlier, the prosecutor would not have been able to tell the jury that Helen Troxel was "obviously mistaken" about seeing the Jiminez couple in the cafe.

While investigators from the Blue Earth County Sheriff's Department had prepared this supplemental report, it was discovered later only in the files of the Le Sueur County prosecutor. Apparently both the Blue Earth County attorney and the sheriff's department removed this evidence supporting my innocence from their files, before being subpoenaed for the appellate hearings, and apparently they also withheld it from the attorney who represented me in the second trial, as he stated at the appellate hearing that he had had an investigator looking for exactly that kind of evidence.

On learning I was from Michigan, BCA Field Agent Thomas Simonson, along with a Le Sueur County deputy sheriff, traveled to Michigan to look for evidence against me. What they expected was not the case: I was not involved in drugs. I had a family, and I had a beautiful wife, who told them of my arrival home at 1 A.M. on Tuesday, April 23, confirming that I was not in Minnesota when Michael Jiminez was killed.

She said she was positive of the date because she had canceled a dental appointment as well as a date to take the children to a ballgame on that day. After all the hype over my arrest and extradition to Minnesota, I had an alibi.

The investigators then interviewed my former employee Edward Newberg, who stated he had seen me during the time in question. Later, when a transcript was discovered in the subpoenaed files of the Blue Earth County attorney and the sheriff, we learned that this interview had been recorded on tape and withheld.

Again, the investigators visited my wife. This time they wanted her to talk to them in their car. Since Simonson had tape-recorded the interview with my former employee, he probably recorded this interview with her as well. In the car the acoustics would be better, and the tape recorder could be concealed.

The investigator repeated the questions, and my wife repeated her answers. In desperation, Agent Simonson asked whether she was willing to take a lie-detector test. She stated that she was, and this frustrated Simonson all the more. He threatened, "If you insist on sticking to that story, you will be charged with perjury." Later, when Agent Simonson testified at the trial, he made erroneous claims about what she said, as the prosecution attempted to discredit her. If she *had* made the statements Simonson claimed, the prosecutor would have introduced a recording or transcript into the evidence.

The investigators then interviewed my mother. She confirmed that she had received a phone call on Monday, April 22, from my wife, who told her when I would be home. My mother also said that later that morning of my arrival, I came to her home, was perfectly normal, and took the time to do some house painting for her that day.

After obtaining a list of customers from my auto-repair business records, the investigators questioned several of the women who had taken my Powder Puff Mechanics course to educate women on vehicle maintenance and emergency repairs, including changing a flat tire without assistance and protecting themselves against unscrupulous repair shops.

More than 200 women had taken the course over a two-year period, some accompanied by their teenage daughters.

Since there was no drug connection, Agent Simonson pursued another line of questioning in an attempt to establish a motive-that Michael Jiminez was murdered so the perpetrator could sexually attack Mrs. Jiminez. Simonson contrived this motive on the basis of the discovery of her nude body.

My wife told me she received phone calls from some of the women students, complaining about the agent's unethical behavior. In the presence of their families, friends, and coworkers, he announced: "I'm from the Bureau of Criminal Apprehension," leaving out "of Minnesota." He asked these women whether I had ever made sexual advances towards them. When they denied that I had done so, Simonson suggested that they had been intimately involved with me.

Because my family learned of this agent's unprofessional behavior, including his threats to my wife, my sister's husband remained home during the questioning of his wife. My sister had nothing negative to say about me, and as Simonson was unaware her husband was in law enforcement, his inquiry turned into an interrogation. My brother-in-law interrupted Agent Simonson.

"How dare you talk to my wife or any member of this family like that! For your information, I'm a detective with the police department, and I don't talk to people that way. From now on, mister, when you leave your motel to interview people around here, you will be escorted by local authorities. Now get the hell out of here!"

The Public Defenders

With my assets tied up, I had to continue representation through a court-appointed attorney. Because of that, I came to know why some people refer to public defenders as "public offenders". The media raised a question of conflict-of-interest for the public defender appointed to represent me-he had also represented the murdered Michael Jiminez on drug charges. One *Mankato Free Press* article included the attorney's response: "Att. Charles 'Chuck' Adamson has said he will accept the appointment as public defender for Edward Clark . . . 'We feel we owe him the service.' Adamson's statement refuted rumors that the Mankato public defender would not accept the Clark case."[30]

With the rumor mill suggesting the murders were drug-related, this article might have led the community to believe Adamson was reluctant to take the case. Actually, as a public defender, he was required to defend me. The article was introduced into evidence during appellate proceedings, as one of many arguments that Adamson denied me effective assistance of counsel because his statement might have a negative impact on the community.[31]

Adding further to the negative publicity, the jailer, assuming I was asleep, brought visitors on tour late one night, pointing me out through the bars. He indicated I was the infamous killer from Detroit! And my name was kept continually in the public eye. Over the next eight weeks, a minimum of eight articles reported the case, with captions including:

- "Suspect" (This was a mug shot taken in Sacramento, when I was booked into the county jail, during the early morning hours. It had been sent out over the old wire service, so it projected me as a hardened criminal.)[32]

- "Clark Hearing May Be Held Today"[33]

- "Clark Pleads Innocent; May Request Venue Change"[34]

- "Bail Set for Clark; Judge Morse Studies Case"[35]

- "Two Grand Juries Called" (There were two grand juries because the bodies of the Jiminezes were discovered in counties located in separate judicial districts. The article also alluded to the grand jury in Mankato hearing evidence in an unrelated murder.)[36]

- "Grand Jury Meets Again"[37]

- "Jiminez Testimony Finished"[38]
- "Clark's Wife Here" (This caption appeared over a photo of my wife and my sister, who was married to a police detective, at the jail with a local minister. Someone must have tipped off the newspaper as to the time my relatives would be leaving the building.)[39]

I discovered how cold it can get in Minnesota, even in the month of May. To save on costs when the facility was built, the builders provided no heat to the jail cells. Keeping warm required wearing a blanket over my shoulders and pacing. There was no ventilation, and during the summer months the heat was stifling, as the jail was on the top floor and the roof absorbed the rays of the sun. Weight loss was inevitable because the county had a contract with the sheriff's wife, who prepared the meals. They were neither nutritious nor of sufficient quantity. Rarely warm, the meals usually consisted of just a piece of lunch meat or a slice of cheese between two slices of bread. As a supplement, I purchased overpriced candy bars from the commissary, also operated by the sheriff's wife. In contrast, when I was transported to Le Sueur County for hearings, Sheriff Smith's wife prepared me a hearty, hot lunch.

Knowing I was an auto technician by trade, the Le Sueur County sheriff asked me about why he had had to replace the batteries in the county's new patrol cars after only a few months. He asked whether I'd mind taking a look at a patrol car that had just driven up behind the building. I said I'd do it. The deputy shut off the engine but left the keys in the ignition. Once I looked at the car, I said that with some tools I could easily correct the problem. The deputy brought out a toolbox and walked back into the building, leaving me unescorted.

With the keys in the ignition, I could have taken off in the patrol car, but I was no fool. Doing that would make me look guilty in the eyes of the public, and I had a family. Besides, how far would I get? Were the keys in the ignition an accident? After tightening the fan belt on the alternator that charged the battery, I carried the tools back inside and told the sheriff it was only a loose fan belt, that the fan belts on all the patrol cars should be checked before replacing any batteries.

Sheriff Smith responded, "That's all it needed? You mean we've been ripped off into buying new batteries? We'll just have to deal with that guy." He was probably referring to the local gas station that serviced the patrol cars. I thought to myself, "This is one sheriff I wouldn't want to cross."

After lunch, I was taken to the second floor of a hardware store opposite the county courthouse, which was then under renovation. A man, indifferent to his tie hanging to one side over a shirt with the top button undone, approached and introduced himself as Richard Genty, the public defender for Le Sueur County. We went into a small room containing a table and two chairs. Genty asked me basic questions-my age, marital status, address, and place of birth.

Without asking my side of the story, and with a foregone conclusion as to the outcome of the trial, Genty recommended I plead guilty. This seemed to be (and was, as I learned later in meeting other of his incarcerated clients) routine advice to those for whom the county picked up the tab. In a cavalier manner, he said that if I didn't plead guilty, the sentences would run consecutively and I wouldn't be eligible for parole "for 35 years, when you're 70 years old."

I thought, "Why, you incompetent moron. I'd be better off representing myself than having you in the same courtroom." I refused to plead guilty. I pleaded not guilty and was bound over for trial.

Years later, when Genty retired, a Twin Cities newspaper revealed the pressure of judges and prosecutors on Genty to avoid the time and expense of trials: The judges were determined to pick Genty's replacement, regardless of the responsibility of the State Board of Public Defense in the matter. The board took the matter before the State Supreme Court, which ruled that judges do not have the authority to choose a public defender's successor. A newspaper article revealed that of 1,500 felony cases in that judicial district, only eight had jury trials in which the defendant had to rely on a public defender. The chief public defender in Minneapolis said of the judge's intent: "A direct slap at the concept of justice . . . kind of makes one wonder how the Bill of Rights would fare down there."[40]

For the first five weeks of confinement, I was kept in isolation in the jail in Mankato in a unit designed to hold four prisoners. I was denied the right to attend religious services conducted by local churches during this period. The purpose for this isolation was twofold:

> 1. As documented after my trial, a tape recorder was hooked up to the audio-monitoring system in the jail, so as to (surreptitiously and illegally) eavesdrop on attorney/client conferences in my cell, as argued on appeal. The conference rooms designed for attorney/client conferences, where we also met, were bugged.[41] (Thus, the authorities knew which evidence, supporting my innocence, to suppress.)
>
> 2. The authorities also wished to wear me down, with the prospect that I would plead guilty since the case against me was circumstantial and there were no eyewitnesses to the murders. A finding of "not guilty" would raise more fears in the community about drug-related violence and more criticism of the local authorities.

The Indictments

When the indictments were handed down by the grand juries, the authorities put in motion a ploy to get me to say something incriminating. When I didn't say anything incriminating, they claimed that I did anyway:

As I was writing my daily letter to my wife, the steel door to my cell opened, and Sheriff Wiebold walked over to sit down across from me. He had never done this before, so I knew something was up.

He said, "There's something I want to tell you, man to man."

The Le Sueur County Grand Jury had just brought in its indictment, charging me with the murder of Barbara Jiminez. With an additional charge of rape!

Holding my composure, I did not respond.

Wiebold then asked whether I wanted to talk about it. I answered that I had nothing to say, as it was obvious in the way I had been treated that they weren't interested in the truth. The sheriff walked out.

A day earlier, I had been informed that the Blue Earth County Grand Jury indicted me for "First Degree Murder" in the death of Michael Jiminez. Now I faced not only two first-degree-murder trials, but also charges for a crime I couldn't understand being committed under any circumstances. It was the one crime I deeply resented; I treated women with respect and never forced myself on anyone.

Now feeling the full weight of what I had to look forward to, I began to lose my composure. I thought of the Reverend Lundeen, who had said during a visit that if I felt the need to talk to him, I could ask the jailer to give him a call. I scribbled Lundeen's name and phone number on a piece of paper and handed it to the jailer. Stunned that all this was happening, I sat down and waited.

Instead of making the phone call, the deputy handed Sheriff Wiebold my note. The sheriff instructed another deputy to record on tape what was about to be elicited from me. For about 45 minutes I just sat and waited, burying my head in my arms. I heard the door open, and thinking it was the Reverend, I said, without looking up: "Reverent, the girl was raped."

"Let's talk about it," said the person who had entered.

Recognizing the voice of the sheriff, I responded, "I've got nothing to say."

The strategy continued. About half an hour later, the chief deputy sheriff, who headed the investigation out of Le Sueur County, entered my cell. Acting as if he were not aware of what was going on, he repeated the indictment in the death of Barbara Jiminez. I reiterated that I did not kill the Jiminezes.

Storming out of the cell in disgust, he yelled back, "Well, we have all kinds of witnesses," But, of course, they didn't.

When Reverent Lundeen did come in, he indicated that he had been notified that I wanted to see him only shortly before his arrival.

The next day, May 31, 1974, I was transported to the courthouse for a pretrial hearing. Attorney Adamson advised me that the sheriff would be taking the stand to testify regarding the statement I had made the previous day in my cell. I was puzzled.

Sheriff Wiebold took the stand:

Prosecutor:

>Yesterday, in the jail, did you have occasion to go up and visit the defendant?

Sheriff:

>I did.

Prosecutor:

>What was the purpose in your going there?

Sheriff:

>To assure his well-being, I received a radio communication that he was quite upset, distraught, and behaving in an other-than-normal manner.

Prosecutor:

>Did you state anything to him?

Sheriff:

>I believe my entering comment was something to the effect of "What's the matter, Ed? [From the outset he was lying, including his projection of our being on a first-name basis. In fact there was animosity between us. He couldn't have cared less about my "well-being"]

Prosecutor:

What was said?

Sheriff:

> Ed at this time had his head on his hands, pillowing his head, and he made a statement to the effect that "that girl wasn't raped." Then he looked up and recognized me and said no more."[42]

At this point, I informed my attorney, Adamson, of the sequence of entries into my cell and what had actually been said. On cross:

Adamson:

> Then, did you indicate to him, well, let's talk about it? Why don't you get it off your chest?

Sheriff:

> I indicated to Ed that if he wanted to talk to me, he should feel free to contact me at any time, and I left.

The only sense I could make of this was that the sheriff was attempting to build a case against me, to prove that I was present when the Jiminezes were murdered and that I knew the circumstances surrounding their deaths. I subsequently learned that the indictment actually read: "Attempted rape".

The sheriff, when asked whether the incident had been monitored, responded that he "didn't know" but that if it was monitored, the jail log would indicate so. Indeed, the jail log carried this entry-"1250 Recording, Max South" (where I was confined). This showed that the taping began at 12:50, when the sheriff entered the cell to inform me of the indictment. Not until two hours later, after the attempt to elicit incriminating statements, was Reverent Lundeen notified of my request-"1450 Rev. Lundeen on Floor".[43]

Unfortunately for me, my attorney, Adamson, did not take the time to check the jail log, even though he was in the building on many occasions during the five months before the trial. If he had checked it, he could have subpoenaed the recording and impeached Sheriff Wiebold. The issue was raised on appeal-in failing to check the jail log, Adamson denied me effective assistance of counsel.[44]

Adamson did move to suppress the allegations about my statement from the prosecution's case. He argued that even if I *had* said those words, the communication was privileged-because I had thought I was talking to the minister. Nevertheless, the judge ruled the sheriff's allegation admissible.

The jail log contained another entry reflecting on my public defender's loyalty (or disloyalty), which I also discovered after the trials. Adamson told me that a man who was vice president of a local bank wanted to visit me. At the time I thought to myself that maybe someone in the community with status was beginning to question the whole situation and wanted to hear my version of coming into contact with the Jiminez couple. So I readily agreed to meet with him.

But the man's interest was in hearing about my movements from the time of my waking the morning after I had picked up the hitchhikers until the time I arrived home. The visit was short, and he never returned. I wondered why Adamson was not present and why the visit took place in a private room, with just the two of us, behind a closed door. Obviously the man had influence.

I also wondered why, if I was considered dangerous, they would put me in a room alone with one of Mankato's leading citizens. I made note of this event, including the time it occurred-the same date and time of this entry in the jail log: "Someone from Att. Gen. Office to see Clark".[45]

The man had not introduced himself as being from the state's Office of the Attorney General, whose duty it is to represent the state or assist in prosecution. His misrepresentation, plus his talking to me outside the presence of my attorney, was in violation of my constitutional rights, and my public defender had arranged it!

Subsequently, as he escorted me to a hearing, the Le Sueur County deputy sheriff in charge of the investigation for that county-who also went to Michigan to question my wife-orchestrated a discussion with another deputy on the subject of light aircraft.

The chief deputy turned to me and asked, "Ed, you're a pilot. Which aircraft do you think is better-a Cessna or an Apache?"

I responded that I wasn't a pilot and didn't know anything about aircraft. Sitting next to me in the back seat was a man wearing coveralls, who was not a prisoner. He apparently was a local farmer. If I had knowledge of light aircraft or had known how to fly, he might have been an unbiased, independent witness against me. Apparently, this subject had something to do with the time of Michael Jiminez's death. Because I was unable to see any of the newspaper articles, I was completely in the dark about the circumstances or time of his death.

An investigator from the State Public Defenders Office, a retired FBI agent from Minneapolis, arrived to investigate the case. I found communication with him difficult because his 25 years in law enforcement had hardened him against the accused. He was naturally skeptical of my claim that I was innocent. After he visited the two crime scenes, however, he concluded in his investigation report that the person responsible for the murders must have been familiar with the area.

The events following make it obvious my attorney was keeping me in the dark:

- I was flown to Minnesota on a connecting flight out of Los Angeles instead of on a direct flight from Sacramento, and then taken off the back of the plane to avoid the media when it landed in Minneapolis.

- My wife was asked whether she would take a polygraph test, and she was threatened with charges of perjury should she testify as to when I arrived home in Michigan.

- The authorities questioned me about whether I was a pilot.

- The authorities kept me in isolation for more than a month; I was not allowed even to attend religious services.

- The sheriff lied about my response to hearing the indictment against me in the death of Barbara Jiminez.

- My public defender refused to divulge the case that the state claimed to have against me.

I wanted to see the autopsy reports on the Jiminezes, particularly the times of death, but for me to obtain this information, my wife had to make another trip to Minnesota. She looked pale and had lost considerable weight over this ordeal, and it made me ashamed that she was being put through all this, but, as always, she continued to be optimistic about our future and the fact that friends in Michigan were willing to testify on my behalf should the case go so far as a trial. Despite her traveling all the way from Michigan to see me, the sheriff reduced our visit from an hour to ten minutes.

The day after our ten-minute visit, my wife returned and said that Adamson claimed to be too busy to see her. She waited until he left, went back into his office, and cornered his associate, who was cooperative. He laid out the facts of the case and gave my wife a copy of the autopsy reports.

The autopsy reports revealed the reason for the actions by the authorities: Michael Jiminez's death occurred more than 24 hours after I picked up the hitchhikers-not on the night I picked them up. The estimated time of death was supported by the fact that his stomach contained no food. If he had died the night I picked them up, his stomach would have contained the food he ate when we stopped at the service station and restaurant.

The autopsy report on Barbara Jiminez, however, revealed that her stomach did contain food. This indicates that she ate again, sometime after her husband's death. Her eating in the cafe in Waseca, two days after the discovery of her husband's body, further supported this fact.

The autopsy on Barbara Jiminez also revealed that her blood contained ethyl alcohol and isopropyl alcohol. I mentioned this to a law student working as an intern in Adamson's office. The student said he minored in chemistry in college and that isopropyl is an ingredient in alcoholic beverages, while ethyl alcohol is a rubbing alcohol that is tasteless and odorless. These chemicals can cause nausea, unconsciousness, even death, if consumed in large quantities. I thought to myself that perhaps Barbara Jiminez was incapacitated in this manner during the time her husband was murdered and/or shortly before her death.

I also thought back to my feeling nausea after drinking from the thermos when I returned to the Bronco at the truck stop. The third hitchhiker had returned directly to the vehicle instead of joining us in the restaurant. This might lead to additional evidence supporting my innocence. The thermos had not been used since then, so I wrote my wife, asking her to have her parents go to the storage unit in California and retrieve the thermos for testing. They reported back that they could not find it, even though I had placed the thermos where it would be visible. Since I had to give all my letters to the jailer unsealed, I suspect that the county sheriff's office notified the Sacramento Sheriff's Department detectives and that they removed the thermos.

Now that I knew Michael Jiminez wasn't murdered on the night I picked up the hitchhikers, I thought back to my movements after waking to find them gone and resuming my drive to Michigan. I had no idea where I had stopped for gas after waking up that morning, but apparently the authorities knew-it was Glen Bjorklund's Standard Oil service station in Alden, Minnesota, about ten miles from the Iowa border. As I have previously stated, the prosecutors withheld this evidence.

I recalled stopping at the first service island on the interstate running south from Wisconsin towards Chicago, from which I phoned to tell my wife when I'd be home. I placed the second phone call from along the expressway near Kalamazoo, Michigan.

I informed Adamson of the importance of the phone records. He dismissed the idea, claiming the phone company did not keep records beyond 30 days. I knew this wasn't the case. He then angrily stated, "The public defender's office does not have the funds to go running around the country-only the state does, and they have already spent over $18,000 investing in this case."

So again, my brother-in-law, the police detective, became involved. He contacted the Illinois State Police, who went to the phone booth I had called from first. Along with obtaining that phone number, they found out whom to contact about researching the records of the phone company.

William Martin, security director for the General Telephone Company of Illinois, researched the company's records before my first trial, providing evidence that supported my presence in Illinois and Michigan at the time of Michael Jiminez's murder in Minnesota. On Monday, April 22, at 5:03 P.M., a collect call was placed from that phone booth to my home phone number. The call from the Kalamazoo, Michigan, area could not be documented as it was prepaid. Nevertheless, the evidence of my travels in relation to the movement of the Jiminez couple shows clearly that I could not have killed them:

1. On Monday, April 22, around 4:30 P.M., the Jiminezes were seen in a cafe at Blairsburg Corners, Iowa.

2. At 5:03 P.M. the same day, I placed a phone call to my wife from Belvidere, Illinois, about 200 miles east of Blairsburg Corners.

3. On Tuesday, April 23, around midnight (CST), Michael Jiminez was murdered near Mankato, Minnesota.

4. Around that time (1:00 A.M. EST), I arrived at my home near Detroit, Michigan, 700 miles from Mankato.

5. On Thursday, April 25, Barbara Jiminez was seen in the company of another man in a cafe in Waseca, Minnesota.

6. On Saturday, May 4, the body of Barbara Jiminez was discovered in Scotch Lake, Le Sueur County, Minnesota.

This exculpatory evidence meant nothing to the authorities. The prosecutors in both counties were determined to go ahead with the trials. After all, there was enormous publicity, and cases with a magnitude of publicity are a prosecutor's dream. Judge Noah Rosenbloom, who conducted the appellate hearing regarding the conviction in the Michael Jiminez case, described the publicity of my case as the most ever experienced in Southern Minnesota: it "was given wide publicity and was a topic of conversation in the court's own observation."[46]

Every part of it had been exploited by the media-my arrest and extradition to Minnesota, the public outcry about drug-related violence in Mankato, and the failure of authorities to find, at least with the evidence to charge, those responsible for the killings. I was to be their scapegoat.

I told Adamson I wanted the phone records introduced as part of my defense and that my wife would testify as to the phone calls and the time I arrived home. Disgruntled about her obtaining the autopsy reports and about the evidence of my phone call from Illinois (which he had said didn't exist), Adamson said that he would not call her to testify: "She's a liar."

I wrote to the judge, asking that Adamson be replaced as my defense counsel, and the judge scheduled a hearing. Previously when I had been brought to the courthouse for a hearing, the transport parked conspicuously near the front entrance to accommodate the media. In this case, I was delivered to the back entrance and hustled into a service elevator, because Adamson did not want the hearing publicly known.

Adamson was waiting outside the courtroom. He meekly asked whether I would talk to him in private before going before the judge. Nervously, he apologized about his past attitude and said he had been busy on other cases. Now, he said, he would devote his full attention to representing me, and he would introduce the phone records as well as call my wife to testify.

Because of my lack of experience dealing with the justice system, I thought that part of my distrust of this public defender had been rooted in a paranoia brought on by the charges of murder and by my confinement in a jail in a strange town. Also, it was by now close to the start of the trial; a change of defense attorney at this late date might do more harm than good.

We went into the courtroom, which was empty except for the judge. Making the biggest mistake of my life, as the trial would reveal, I withdrew my request for the replacement of Adamson.

The Mankato community's animosity towards me is exemplified in another prisoner, a 19-year-old man who was moved in with me because prisoners in another unit were harassing him. He had killed his younger sister, and then turned the gun on himself. He nevertheless survived. His parents, studying to be missionaries, came to visit-the visitors had to stand in the corridor outside the cell while conversing through a window. Seeing me in the background, his mother asked her son who I was. He said I was charged with killing the Jiminez couple.

His mother, horrified, shouted, "What?! They put you in with that murderer?"

Part II

The Michael Jiminez Case

CHAPTER 4: PRETRIAL EVENTS

Public defender Adamson failed again to represent me adequately at a pretrial hearing: I had been arrested without a warrant, and one of the arresting detectives from Sacramento testified that probable cause was based on the phone call I made from Belvidere.[47] Adamson should have challenged the detective-the authorities could not have known of the call until weeks after my arrest and extradition to Minnesota. I did not know the time of Michael Jiminez's death until I saw the autopsy report, and my brother-in-law did not contact the security director of the phone company until after I knew the time of death.

Furthermore, the phone call was not probable cause- it was the key to my alibi! I had made the call from Illinois, approximately seven hours before the death of Michael Jiminez in Minnesota. If my defense counsel had challenged the legality of the arrest, he could have moved to dismiss the charges as well as any evidence obtained after the arrest. Such a motion, however, would not have sat well with the community upon which his law practice relied.

Adamson said it was in my best interest to ask the judge for a continuance because he wanted to attend a "lawyer's conference" scheduled in the state. He claimed it would assist him in preparing my defense. I agreed to a motion for continuance. In granting the motion, the judge revealed his concern about public opinion: "I am granting this motion, but I'm concerned what the newspapers will think of me for allowing it."

Looking back, I believe the wish to delay the trial until fall laid with Prosecutor Corbey rather than with my defense counsel. With the Jiminezes falsely portrayed as college students, the community likely would be more outraged (and eager for a scapegoat) if the trial took place during the college semester.

Public defender Adamson went through the motions of seeking to have the trial moved to another part of the state, at the same time implying I was guilty.[48] He included numerous newspaper articles in his motion. One was the editorial describing the murder of Michael Jiminez in "gangland style."[49] Adamson addressed the court:

> Reports received in our law office have been that the opinion of the public is that law enforcement has arrested and the grand jury had indicted a person who, in fact, is guilty of these crimes and that the feedback to his office has been that opinions have been formed by the general public regarding the guilt or innocence of the above named accused.
>
> The feedback that we get back in our law office is that people have simply convicted the defendant in their own minds- it would be unlikely, if not impossible, for Mr. Clark to obtain a fair trial here.[50]

Making sure the trial would take place in Mankato, public defender Adamson guided the judge into denying the motion, stating further: "I have indicated to the defendant, Your Honor, that changes of venue are hard to accomplish."

Adamson never indicated to me that a change of venue would be difficult to obtain. And, in denying the motion, the judge cited a case that wasn't applicable: The defendant, an attorney charged and subsequently convicted of hiring someone to kill his wife, had already been granted one change of venue.[51] If Adamson had looked up the case, he could have argued further for the motion.

The judge did leave open the option for my attorney to renew the motion if circumstances warranted. Such circumstances, including the harassment of jurors, did come to warrant a change of venue. When the harassment was discovered, however, Adamson did not renew the motion. During my appeal, later, that failure was included as an argument as to the denial of effective assistance of counsel.[52]

When the hearing ended, Adamson turned and noticed a man in an expensive suit observing the proceedings. Adamson asked nervously whether I knew who the man was; I did not. This further convinces me that Adamson was subject to outside pressure.

Selecting the Jurors

The public defender's failure to provide me with competent representation was especially evident in the jury selection process (voir dire). He literally left it to me to pick my jury, a task, as argued on appeal, that required the expertise of an experienced trial lawyer.

At the appellate hearing, Adamson matter-of-factly admitted under questioning by the appellate attorney, "I didn't want to be the one that's telling him who should be on and who should be off the jury."

The brief (written argument) submitted by the appellant attorney to the appellate court underscores the seriousness of Adamson's indifference and provides one more reason he should have renewed the motion for a change of venue:

Failure to Aid in the Jury Selection

Appellant submits that failure to aid in the selection of the jury deprived appellant of the assistance of counsel during the most crucial proceeding in the trial. Selection of a fair jury is difficult in even the simplest of cases. In a murder trial that process becomes even more difficult. In the instant case, where the pretrial publicity permeated the entire community and reached virtually every prospective juror, selection of a fair and impartial jury demanded the services of a highly trained criminal lawyer. Whether Mr. Adamson could have filled that role is academic, for by his own admission he chose not to do so.[53]

The appellate attorney outlined the difficulty I experienced in picking the jury:

> 0. Nearly all prospective jurors acknowledged they had read newspaper accounts of the death of the Jiminezes, and several had heard radio or seen television accounts of the case as it progressed.
>
> a. Several prospective jurors stated they had already made up their minds that appellant was guilty because of previous news coverage.
>
> b. One woman stated she was "too nervous," and that she could not consider the appellant innocent.
>
> c. Another woman, almost in tears, indicated she was afraid to sit on the case and that she had concluded the defendant was guilty based on what she read in the newspapers.
>
> d. Two prospective jurors discussed the case in the jury room in the presence of a third prospective juror and reached a conclusion as to what the outcome of the trial should be.
>
> e. Rumors circulated among the prospective jurors that drugs may have been the motive for the

murders.

    f.   Six of the jurors who were accepted knew witnesses for the state, generally Sheriff Wiebold.[54]

The prospective juror who revealed that the two others had discussed the case and reached a conclusion as to its outcome-that I should be found guilty-could not recall who the two jurors were. So it is possible one or both of them subsequently determined my fate.

The *Mankato Free Press* gave as much attention to the jury selection process as to the trial, in articles including: "Jury Selection Begins Tuesday in Clark Case" and "Clark Trial Jury Selection Begins."[55]

When I accepted a prospective juror who I hoped would not be biased, the prosecutor (in a "peremptory strike" or "challenge") summarily disqualified that person without having to provide a reason.

Another article, "Jury Selection Toughens Overnight," was the result of the judge's announcement in open court: "Ladies and gentlemen, you will notice a new court reporter at the desk . . . the reporter who we engaged to take this case lives at Windom [Minnesota], and he was killed in an accident on his way here last night."[56]

This announcement served to enhance rumors including that I was connected with the death of the court reporter. I learned of the public impact of this action only after I was sent to prison. Another inmate, who resided in Denver at the time of the trial, told me he had read in a city newspaper of the death of the court reporter and assumed the defendant had something to do with it.

Adding to the stress of my effort to pick a fair jury, Adamson misinformed me that I was running out of prospective jurors and would have to choose from the few remaining on the list. Because of this, I accepted two that I might not otherwise have considered-one was the owner of a pizza parlor catering to college students, the other a dean at Mankato State College, where Barbara Jiminez had enrolled part-time.

Other *Mankato Free Press* articles included "Selection of Clark Jury Nears Finish" and "Jury Selection Ends in Murder Trial of Clark."[57]

The latter article included the juror's names, addresses, and occupations. Revealing the identity of the jurors was one of the most damaging events denying me a fair trial. It exposed the jury to outside pressures, as evidenced in an announcement to the jury about an incident I was unaware of at the time. Before the testimony began, the judge stated:

> I'm sure, ladies and gentlemen, you realize that this case is an important one, both to the defendant and to the State of Minnesota. You remember, of course, the Court's admonition not to discuss the case even among yourselves or with anyone. Since the case is of such importance, it might be that you receive a telephone call anonymously or otherwise. If you do, I trust you will inform the Court immediately. That you are to make a decision in this case based on the evidence which you will hear and not on any extraneous circumstances.[58]

Before the next day's proceedings, at a conference in the judge's chambers, he clarified his earlier statement:

> I think this is a good time to state for the record that counsel was informed of yesterday morning by the Court before the case started. All that occurred prompted the court . . . to caution the jury they might receive telephone calls from pranks or otherwise about the case due to the importance of it. One of the jurors, Mr. Graham, came to the Court yesterday morning and said that on Friday of last week he was not home but his wife received a telephone call from a lady who said, "Is this Mrs. Graham?" I'm saying as much of what I remember of what Mr. Graham reported:
>
> "Yes, this is Mrs. Graham."
>
> "Is your husband there?"
>
> "No, he's not."
>
> "Well, I'm one of the jurors," this lady said to Mrs.

Graham.

Mrs. Graham said she didn't think it was a juror because the jury had been instructed not to discuss the case among themselves or with others.

She [the caller] said, "You know, this is a very important case and the defense has a lot of friends around here."

Mrs. Graham replied to the caller, "Yes, I'm sure my husband knows the importance and will so consider it."

When Mr. Graham came home at 10:30 . . . he got a phone call, very noncommittal and I don't recall the words reported to me. He said it was a man.

"Is this Mr. Graham?" he said.

"Yes."

Then he [the caller] hung up.

On Saturday night, Mr. Graham told me he was to go out, he and his wife, but decided not to go because he was afraid that his children . . . might be subjected to telephone calls. So he stayed home.

That's the state of the record at the present time. I advised counsel yesterday morning and I think no further action will be taken at this time. I told Mr. Graham not to discuss it with the other jurors, but if anybody mentioned anything to him to have them be sure to talk to the Court.[59]

In the subsequent appeal, my appellant attorney quoted the above in arguing that the court should have granted a change in venue and that it was Adamson's duty to reopen the voir dire-to call to the stand and question the jurors as to whether they had received intimidating phone calls or been approached in any other way-and to renew the motion for a change of venue from Mankato.[60]

In addition to the Grahams' fears about leaving their children home alone, to which they testified at the appellate hearing, Graham also may have considered that if the verdict were "not guilty," he might suffer financially because as a salesman at a local retail store he had direct contact with the public.

And if I had been aware of the intimidation of jurors and Adamson's subsequent inaction, I would have renewed my request to the court to replace my public defender.

An editorial, years later, in the *Minneapolis Tribune* underscored how public release of the names of jurors can compromise the fairness of a trial:

> There's no compelling reason to identify jurors by name... Federal Judge James Rosenbaum said he worried about the harassment of jurors. "My concern is for the private individuals who didn't volunteer for the job. They are subpoenaed to serve."
>
> Ramsey County District Judge David Marsden agreed in principle with Rosenbaum..."They are ordinary citizens called to serve the public, and in many cases using their names would put them in jeopardy."[61]

The judge in the first murder trial also informed the jury that one witness was to be a "person from Waseca."[62] This was Bob Guthrie, who had seen Barbara Jiminez in his cafe in Waseca two days after the discovery of her husband's body near Mankato. The prosecution, however, did not call Guthrie to the witness stand because Guthrie would have supported my defense. Adamson should have called Guthrie to testify as a witness for the defense, but he did not.

Commercial enterprises capitalized on the trial as well: A local theater reran a two-year-old movie, *The Mechanic*, the story of a hit man for the Mob. Sold out for every showing, the film was held over an extra week. Even the prosecutor in my second trial referred to me as a "mechanic" from Detroit, implying to the jury, "Don't let his looks, manners, and education deceive you."[63]

The pretrial hearings and jury selection had taken place in the county courthouse, which had ample parking and an entrance for the defendant separate from that used by the jury and the public. But the trial was scheduled for a small courtroom on the second floor of the Post Office, in the center of the business district, across from the *Mankato Free Press*. I came to see this location as a distinct advantage for the prosecution.

The evening before the trial began, I asked defense attorney Adamson what effort had been made to locate the third hitchhiker. If Adamson was good at anything, it was avoidance-he ignored my question. As to bringing character witnesses in from Michigan (my wife had provided their names) to undo the character assassination perpetrated by the media, Adamson said he had no intention of doing so. During the heated exchange, I told him in no uncertain terms that, as with the issue of my wife testifying, he better give it a second and more serious thought, or I would stand up in court and fire him in front of everyone.

"Oh Christ, what theatrics!" one of the deputies exclaimed on the first day of trial testimony, when he saw the Blue Earth County sheriff standing in the street with his radio pressed against his ear, as though directing my officer escorts. The officers were receiving nothing over their radios. The parking lot was some distance from the entrance of the building, which allowed for parading me, the defendant, down the busy sidewalk. The audience, including employees of the newspaper, crowded against the bay windows of both floors of the building to catch a glimpse of the alleged murderer.

The only access to the courtroom was up a flight of stairs. Four uniformed deputies were stationed at the foot of the stairs, waiting to escort me to the second floor. The jurists, climbing the staircase as well, observed me daily in shackles and under heavy guard, which projected me as a dangerous man. My appeal raised this tactic as highly prejudicial.[64]

This kind of concern for security was contrary to my treatment on the second floor: I was left alone in a room behind a closed door with an open window to wait for the proceedings. I could easily have dropped to the sidewalk and, because I was wearing a suit, could have lost myself in the crowd. The thought was only fleeting. I had a family, and I was determined to have my day in court.

My wife had waited in the corridor, and she winked at me in support. She had been in Mankato through the jury selection process and would remain there through the trial, while my mother (and, when she testified, others) took care of our children. Staying with a minister's family in Mankato, my wife spent some time with his wife, who was well known in the court system for her involvement in foster-home care and for seeking probation for juveniles who needed a second chance. As my wife and I were talking in the hallway, a janitor approached the minister's wife nearby. Sipping a cup of coffee, he commented on her befriending "that murderer's wife."

She responded, "Oh, and would you like to meet her?" He wasted no time in making an exit, claiming he had to get back to work.

Spectators packed the courtroom and hallway. One row of seats in the courtroom was reserved for part of the day for a class of middle-school or junior-high students. The judge welcomed them to experience first-hand how "justice works".

The reporter covering the trial for the *Mankato Free Press*, whose article had named the jurors and thus subjected them to harassment, sat down next to the writer for *Detective Dragnet* magazine, attempting to open a dialogue with him. Agitated, the writer moved to another seat. In his subsequent coverage of the trial, the magazine writer concluded that there were "a lot of unanswered questions." This is significant considering that murder trials were his regular gig for a magazine working to get the cooperation of law enforcement agencies in obtaining stories.

The Le Sueur County Attorney, prosecutor at the subsequent trial regarding the death of Barbara Jiminez, sat in the front row with pad and pencil in hand. When he crossed his legs, I noticed holes in the bottom of his shoes and mentioned this to some other prisoners at jail during the lunch break. When I returned to court, the prosecutor gave me a dirty look, but he had on a new pair of shoes. Apparently I was monitored in the jail, and he was informed of my comment.

Chapter 5: The Case for the Prosecution

The last thing the powers of the community wanted was for the deaths of the Jiminezes to be associated with drugs. So in his opening statement, prosecutor Corbey told the jury that the motive behind Michael Jiminez's death was "the defendant's desire to have sex with Jiminez's wife." He emphasized the attractiveness of Mrs. Jiminez."[65]

He had no evidence of this motive, and the judge conducting the second trial, regarding the death of Barbara Jiminez, dismissed that charge in the indictment[66], but his dismissal was meaningless because the theory already had been impressed upon the juries at both trials.

The prosecutor also told members of the jury they would hear a recording of statements I had made in California. This was news to me since I hadn't made a confession and it hadn't been brought up at the pretrial evidentiary hearing for determination as to admissibility.

Sheriff Wiebold of Blue Earth County took the stand.[67] He testified about being summoned to the crime scene, approximately seven miles south of Mankato along the main highway leading to the city. He stated there were tire tracks where a vehicle had turned off the highway onto the access way leading to the railroad tracks. At the crime scene, he said, he found a skull fragment 35 to 45 feet from the body, indicating the victim had been carried from where he was shot. Two railroad ties lay across the body; one later weighed in at 120 pounds. The sheriff also said that two ballpoint pens and a matchbook, all with distinctive advertising, and a cartridge casing from a fired bullet were found at the scene.

I recognized the pens and the matchbook as having been in the Bronco when I picked up the hitchhikers. And if the empty cartridge casing was of the same caliber as my rifle, it could have been among others resulting from my target practice from the Bronco in the mountains at Lake Tahoe. I had fired from inside the vehicle because of the cold and snow.

The sheriff stated that, with the exception of the cartridge casing, the items had been turned over to the crime bureau's field agent as evidence. He said he had placed the cartridge casing in his pocket and turned it over later in the day. The prosecutor asked the sheriff to testify on the subject of ballistics, but the defense raised an objection in regard to his competency in this field.

That the sheriff would keep the cartridge casing apart from other items allegedly found at the scene seemed strange to me. In legal terms, this was "breaking the chain of evidence." His action raises the question of defense attorney Adamson's failure to challenge the introduction of the casing as evidence. Later testimony, by a firearms examiner for the state, brought into question whether the cartridge casing could have come from the crime scene at all.

I asked myself, "Why would one of my spent cartridges, the pens, and the matchbook have been removed from the Bronco and left behind at the crime scene, if indeed they were found there?" These things seemed like a lot of evidence to have been left by accident at the scene of an apparently premeditated murder. The question was introduced, not in this trial, but in the trial for the murder of Barbara Jiminez, along with all the other evidence from the first trial.

There also was no mention of these items, nor even intent to search for firearms, in the application for a warrant to search the Bronco and the storage unit I had rented in California. As would be discovered after the trials, the authorities were not above withholding evidence supporting my innocence. Moreover, the *Mankato Free Press* quoted the sheriff as saying that the investigation was concentrating on "three separate persons that may have been in the area or known to frequent the area."[68]

If the items, identified as originating from the West Coast, were found at the crime scene, why would the authorities have been looking to local people as suspects? The sheriff never revealed who they were, even when the defense attorney asked him as much on cross examination. And, apparently, the investigative reports revealing their identity were not turned over to the attorney representing me in the second trial. Otherwise, he would have used them during his diligent representation of me in that trial.

Touring the Crime Scenes

The public defender advised me that the prosecutor was moving for the court's tour of the two crime scenes. He wanted to know whether I objected. I did not object; I wanted to see them myself. But I did not want to be in shackles during a tour, as that might further prejudice the jury. The Judge agreed and instructed that I not appear in shackles. But the four uniformed deputies at the sites-where there was nowhere to run to anyway-had the same prejudicial effect.

A caravan of vehicles, waiting outside the front entrance of the Post Office Building for the beginning of the tour, ensured a plethora of media reps. A *Mankato Free Press* article subsequent to the tour included a photo, obviously taken from the second floor of its building, of the judge, court reporter, and jury boarding a bus.[69] I rode in the backseat of a patrol car, another car of deputies followed, and the media behind them.

Seven miles outside Mankato, more deputies waved on curious motorists along the heavily traveled two-lane highway. There were no signs or landmarks identifying the area, called Smith's Mill. It was flat farmland with no trees. There was nothing but an obscure access way leading from the highway, across the railroad tracks, and into a farmer's field. So unnoticed would this access way be at night that the driver would have to have known it was there.

I noticed that the traffic consisted mostly of trucks; their drivers had a good view of the surrounding area. As the medical examiner later testified, he took this into consideration in determining the time of death. Perpendicular railroad ties lying across a body wouldn't have gone unnoticed on the day before discovery, as the prosecution claimed upon hearing of my arrival home in Michigan about the time Michael Jiminez was murdered in Minnesota.

The sheriff walked across the crime scene, pointing to:

- The place where the body was discovered

- The stack of railroad ties from where the two ties lying across the body had been carried

- The place the skull fragment was discovered

- The place the spent cartridge casing allegedly was discovered

- The place tire tracks had been visible on the access way

- The place on the access way where the two ballpoint pens and matchbook allegedly were found.

Given his location of the ballpoint pens and matchbook, I thought, "It would be sheer luck for a vehicle driving back out to the highway not to run over some of the items."

After our return to the vehicles, the procession headed towards the place in Le Sueur County where the body of Barbara Jiminez had been found. The caravan traveled on a narrow road, winding around lakes and slowing nearly to a stop at some of the sharp turns.

Public defender Adamson, sitting next to me in the back seat, carried on a conversation with the sheriff, indicating they knew each other well. Their discussion was mostly about real estate-one might have thought they were out looking for property rather than in the midst of a murder trial. The sheriff pointed to a huge home across a lake, saying it was where his "campaign manager" lived.

I thought, "What the hell does a local sheriff need with a campaign manager in a county that is for the most part an unpopulated agricultural area?"

After about an hour, the caravan came to the town of Cleveland (Minnesota), the length of a city block. After passing through town, the vehicles made a sharp turn onto a narrow gravel road. About two miles farther, we made another turn to where some Le Sueur County deputy sheriffs were waiting. Below the road was the obscure and isolated Scotch Lake.

I could see why the investigator from the State Public Defender's Office had determined that whoever was responsible for the murders must have been familiar with the area. Especially with no direct route between the two murder sites, it seemed virtually impossible that a stranger could have stumbled across this small, unpopulated lake on the same night he murdered Michael Jiminez in another county.

On another front, if the intent was to dispose of Barbara Jiminez's body in a lake, why would the murderer bypass other lakes, most with few cottages or homes, along the route we had traveled? Was she held nearby and taken to the lake from another direction? Even if Barbara Jiminez hadn't been seen in Waseca two days after her husband's death, the route and distance should have raised doubts that Barbara Jiminez was killed the same night as her husband.

Le Sueur County Sheriff Pat Smith waited by the lake to indicate points of interest in the area where Barbara Jiminez's body was discovered. He noted:

- The shoreline along which the body was discovered in the water

- The farm-implement end gate rod across the body

- The place where pressed-down foliage indicated the body was dragged from a vehicle

- The place where the cloth with hair entwined in the knot was discovered

- The small tree in which one of Barbara Jiminez's shoe was wedged, with the toe pointing to her body.

The sheriff then guided everyone to a mud hole that had dried over the summer months. Tire impressions were still visible in the caked mud. I understood why Sheriff Smith had wanted castings made of the tire impressions-comparing the treads to a suspect tire would have been more conclusive than simple photos and measurements. Obviously the vehicle involved wasn't of the four-wheel-drive type, like a Ford Bronco. The tracks led to an incline where the vehicle apparently had spun its wheels in an attempt to return to the road in another direction, a faster and easier course than a tight turnaround.

We returned to Mankato late in the afternoon. News reports of the day's events included a photo showing the Blue Earth County sheriff climbing the front steps of the Post Office Building with charts and graphs, under the heading "Bringing Evidence". Apparently the *Mankato Free Press* prearranged this photo op. Also there was a sketch of the two crime scenes labeled "At the Scene."[70]

The Prosecution Continues

The trial continued the next day with the testimony of Delvin Ohrt, the pathologist who performed the Michael Jiminez autopsy.[71] Dr. Ohrt testified that Jiminez's death was caused by a gunshot to the head, that the bullet had entered behind the right ear and exited slightly behind the left. To determine the time of death (in addition to that indicated by the extent of rigor mortis) Ohrt removed and analyzed fluid from the vitreous humor of the eye. He determined that death had occurred the night previous to the autopsy, sometime between dark on Monday, April 22, and as late as 2:00 or 3:00 A.M. on Tuesday, April 23.

To validate his findings, Dr. Ohrt consulted with the leading forensic pathologist in the state, John Cole, who agreed with him. Ohrt testified that he also took into consideration the area in which the body was discovered. Such a shooting probably would not have taken place along a well-traveled highway during daylight hours. He said his best estimate was that the death had taken place around midnight on the night preceding the discovery of the body.

(Dr. Ohrt's findings as to the time of death of Michael Jiminez supported my alibi defense, and thus contradicted the prosecution's case. So he was not called as a state's witness in the subsequent trial, regarding the death of Barbara Jiminez. Instead, he was a witness for the defense.)[72]

During this first trial, Raymond Sanford, the coroner who performed the autopsy on Barbara Jiminez, gave extensive testimony in the trial regarding her death. He stated that the death was caused by strangulation with Barbara Jiminez's hair, referring to it as "braided". The autopsy photos however, showed only a strand of hair embedded in her swollen neck. He admitted it could have been there due to bloating of the body during decomposition. As to the time of death, he stated that based on decomposition, death had occurred at least three days before discovery.[73]

Prosecutor Corbey then pursued a line of questioning regarding the "vaginal area" of Barbara Jiminez so as to imply that the motive for killing Michael Jiminez was the (alleged) rape of his wife. Since I was on trial for the murder of Michael Jiminez, not his wife, Adamson finally objected to the detailed testimony on the body of Barbara Jiminez. This resulted in the judge inviting the attorneys to his chambers.

With the break for discussion in the judge's chambers, I had the opportunity to view the autopsy photos, including those of Barbara Jiminez's bloated and discolored body. Describing the colored photos as "gruesome and inflammatory," which we did in the later appeal, was an understatement.[74] They were so grotesque as to arouse anyone not involved in pathology as a career. When the judge returned to the courtroom, he noticed that I was looking at the photos and the effect they had on me. He announced a recess.

I went into a room with my attorney, my voice raised in anger. Being charged with these murders infuriated me. Adamson told me to calm down, as the jury was in the next room and could hear me. I couldn't have cared less. If *I* found the photos that upsetting, what effect would they have on the women jurors? After viewing those photos, they would find it difficult if not impossible to be objective.

Upon cross-examination, Dr. Sanford admitted that he had found none of the trauma to the throat normally associated with strangulation. He did, however, find an accumulation of water in the lungs consistent with drowning.

The *Mankato Free Press* shouted, "Colored photos of Victims among Evidence in Trial," above an article including a sketch that showed Dr. Ohrt displaying autopsy photos of Michael Jiminez's body to the jury. The sketch also showed, and its caption named, the juror closest to him. Another report gave the gruesome details of Barbara Jiminez's body, under the heading "Jury Hears of 2nd death." With the prosecution relying heavily on her death to build its case, another story announced, "Prosecution Attempting Tie-in of Jiminez Cases."[75]

Rebecca Stovall, formerly Rebecca Niehus, sister of Michael Jiminez, testified that the Jiminezes had arrived at her apartment in Emporia, Kansas, on Friday, April 19, at about 9:15 P.M. She said her brother's visit was unexpected as the Jiminezes were supposed to attend a wedding at his mother's home in Le Mars, Iowa. (Emporia is 300 miles south of Le Mars.)[76]

She said that her brother and his wife hitchhiked to Emporia to purchase a car from her but also that the Jiminezes had only about six dollars between them. She said that because the title couldn't be transferred on a weekend, the Jiminezes decided to hitchhike back to Minnesota. They left around noon on Sunday.

This did not add up. If all they had was six dollars, how could the Jiminezes expect to pay for the vehicle, much less title transfer and the gas to return to Minnesota? With so little money, why would they have hitchhiked all the way to Emporia? And since, as she testified, Rebecca Niehus was at the time a divorced woman whose ex-husband had custody of their child, the Jiminezes could not count on her being home on the Friday evening, or even during the weekend, of this unexpected visit. Further, I wondered, why hitchhike all the way back to Minnesota on Sunday instead of waiting just one more day to transfer the title of a car they could drive back?

These inconsistencies raised questions as to the real purpose for the Jiminezes' being in Emporia and the motive for their slaying. My attorney should have drawn attention to them, at least in his closing statement to the jury. From the time of the discovery of Michael Jiminez's body, rumors in the community, as reiterated by some jurors from the outset of the trial, suggested that the slayings were drug-related.

Stovall testified that her brother was unemployed because of seizures caused by a head injury, for which he carried medication. The medication was neither found on him nor introduced into evidence. She also said she helped her sister-in-law pack their duffel bag and that she made a sign from a shopping bag. It read "35N". She said the Jiminezes picked up a road map of Iowa on their way to be dropped off on the highway.

Stovall identified a photo of the Jiminezes, which she had taken as they stood by the road, hoping to hitchhike back to Minnesota. This photograph had appeared in newspapers and on TV during the search for Barbara Jiminez. Shown the duffel bag and some folded clothing discovered in the trash box, Stovall stated that it was the clothing she helped Barbara Jiminez pack into the bag. She identified the coat found in the Cannon River with the initial "B" on the collar, and the shoe found at Scotch Lake, as belonging to Barbara Jiminez.

Curiously, the brown suede jacket that had covered the box I discarded was neither shown to Stovall nor entered into evidence. As the trial in the death of Barbara Jiminez later revealed, the Blue Earth County Sheriff's Department had discarded an "old brown jacket," perhaps because it supported my attesting to a third hitchhiker.

The prosecution recalled Sheriff Wiebold to the stand. Through him, the prosecution introduced weather charts for the Mankato area for April 21-24 into evidence. The only purpose they served, along with most of the other 200 exhibits, including one on my employment in California, was to overwhelm the jury-to suggest a strong case against me by the sheer volume of exhibits. Actually, the prosecution based its case on circumstantial evidence.[77]

The sheriff stated that no money was found on the body of Michael Jiminez and that the purpose of removing $150 in cash from the apartment was "safekeeping". He made no mention of removing the drug paraphernalia during direct examination. Neither did Adamson ask about it during cross-examination.

The prosecution set up a chart; the sheriff marked on it where at the Smith Mill crime scene each piece of evidence allegedly was found. He said he kept the cartridge to have it photographed and have it on hand for the autopsy. But it was the duty of the state crime lab's agent-who was in charge of the investigation-to handle the evidence.

Then the prosecutor turned to the matter of the sheriff's claim about what I had said upon notice of the indictments.

Wiebold:

> I entered Mr. Clark's cell and observed him to be in a distraught state…He had his head pillowed in his arms. When I was in his cell, he made the statement, "That girl wasn't raped." He looked up and said, "Oh, I thought you were the minister."

I immediately caught the discrepancy between what the sheriff was now stating and what he had alleged at the pretrial hearing the day after the incident occurred. With the transcript of that hearing on the table, I looked up his testimony and pointed out the discrepancy to public defender Adamson. He used the transcript in his challenge:

Defense:

> In referring, Sheriff, to page 68 of the transcript, do you recall saying, "Then he looked up and recognized me and said no more." Was your recollection as to what he said better then or is it better now?

Wiebold:

> It should have been better then, but I distinctly remember his saying, "Oh, I thought you were the minister."

Defense:

> So, I take it your recollection is better now than May 31st, the day following what you testified to what you heard? Is that your testimony here?

Wiebold:

> It is.

Defense:

> Can you tell the jury why it was that you didn't recall that on the day after you heard this statement?

Wiebold:

> I don't know why I didn't. I should have.

Defense:

> Well, let me refresh your recollection.

The prosecutor objected, stating the question was repetitious. The judge sustained the objection. Defense counsel then raised the question as to whether the incident had been monitored. Sheriff Wiebold admitted it was "by sight and sound". Then:

Defense:

> And was it also monitored, for example, when he had visits with Reverend Lundeen?

Wiebold:

> I would presume it was from time to time.

Defense:

> I take it you didn't listen in on that conversation, but someone else may have? Was that the idea?

Wiebold:

> I didn't listen in on any conversations up there.

Defense:

> Did someone else, as far as you know?

Wiebold:

> I don't know

While the *Mankato Free Press* did not print anything about the sheriff's false testimony, the local television station (KEYC-TV) criticized him during its evening newscast for changing his testimony. (By this time, an anonymous donor had provided me with a television set, and I watched the newscast myself, though I don't remember the date.) Evidence developed after this trial and during the appellate hearings revealed that the sheriff instructed the deputies to record all my conversations and turn them over to him.

As mentioned in chapter 3, public defender Adamson denied me effective assistance of counsel by failing to check the jail log and review the tape recordings. If he had, he could have impeached the sheriff.

The prosecution flew in witnesses from Iowa and California, their testimony for the prosecution to reinforce the nearly 200 exhibits piled on a table close to the jury. Some witnesses for the prosecution, however, testified to my benefit-by supporting my defense or describing me in a manner more favorable than that of the prosecutor.

Mark Hart, owner of California Business Machines, and one of his employees identified the typewriter-rental receipt found in the trash box

I discarded. The prosecutor asked Hart to identify me as the person who rented the machine. When asked on cross-examination to describe my demeanor upon returning to rent another typewriter, Hart looked at me with a smile, said that I was friendly and "very nice and polite . . . Mr. Clark conducted himself very well in my presence."[78]

Mr. and Mrs. Eugene Ward, from whom I rented a room during my stay in the Sacramento area, testified regarding the dates I was there and when I left to return to Michigan. On cross-examination, the Wards said that when I left before the end of the month, I insisted they keep the full month's rent because of the inconvenience and cost of running another newspaper ad. The Wards said they considered me a good roomer. And Mr. Ward said that I offered my assistance when Mrs. Ward was rushed to a hospital.[79] The Wards looked over to smile at me several times during their testimony.

On redirect questioning, the prosecutor implied that I had been carrying on a relationship outside my marriage. He asked about phone calls I received from a woman named Mildred. (My wife revealed in later testimony that Mildred was her mother). As Eugene Ward left the witness stand, he walked over to the defense table and shook hands with me.

Walter Martin, service manager for Burke Chevrolet of Folsom, California, where I was employed as an auto technician, testified to the dates I worked for the dealership. Martin identified the two ball-point pens allegedly discovered at the Blue Earth County crime scene as being available at the dealership. Introduced as evidence and added to the table full of exhibits were my employment application and several time cards that were immaterial to the case.[80]

On cross-examination, Martin said I had received quite a few phone calls from my wife in Michigan and that I had informed him of the trouble I was having with my former business partners. He stated further that I had helped with public relations by volunteering to assist, without compensation, in judging students enrolled in an auto-technician course at a local college. Martin, also smiling at me in a friendly way, stated that the quality of my work was excellent and that, if given the opportunity, he would certainly hire me again.

Since Martin was the last witness of the day, he and the Wards chatted with me and my wife in the courtroom after the court recessed. The *Mankato Free Press* revealed the contradiction between how the media had projected me and the friendly manner of the "California people" towards me in "Landlord, Employer Praise Clark".[81]

The testimony continued the next day with Richard Picard, a cashier manager for Harrah's Casino Hotel at Lake Tahoe, Nevada, acknowledging that he cashed $60 of my traveler's checks. He further testified that the book of matches allegedly discovered at the Blue Earth County crime scene came from Harrah's.[82]

Aaron Bell, a special investigator for Bank of America in California testified to the procedure for purchasing traveler's checks. He also listed the places where I had cashed checks during my return trip to Michigan: Lake Tahoe (California/Nevada), Wyoming, Nebraska, Iowa, and Michigan, where I rented another U-Haul trailer for my second trip to the West Coast.[83]

A representative of the American Automobile Association (AAA) gave the distance between points from California to Iowa, where I cashed the traveler's checks. If public defender Adamson had elicited from her, in support of my alibi, the distance from Mankato to Belvidere, where I called my wife, and from there to Detroit, her testimony could have served the defense. My defense attorney did elicit these distances in the second trial, to show that I couldn't have been in Minnesota when Michael Jiminez was murdered.[84]

Detective Richard Kelley, one of the arresting officers with the Sacramento Sheriff's Department, testified to my arrest in a distortion of the truth. He claimed the officers had told me who they were and stated that I was under arrest. The prosecutor then asked Kelley a question that was inadmissible: Had I been advised of my rights? Again, Kelley distorted the facts, claiming that I had been read my rights and that I had received a form to acknowledge that I had been read my rights and understood them. In fact, the form I received was a waiver of my right to have an attorney present during questioning, which I refused to sign.[85]

Public defender Adamson finally objected to this line of questioning, and the judge ordered it stricken from the record. Nonetheless the jury heard it. The prosecutor then asked Sergeant Kelley about statements I made while being interrogated. Adamson again objected. The judge ordered the jury to leave the courtroom, stating that he would have to review the tape recording of the interrogation in California.

The prosecutor then told the judge he wanted the tape recording, but only portions of it, played to the jury. Played in entirety it would show that I asked to talk to an attorney five times during the interrogation. Just one such request requires that all interrogation cease.

I asked the judge for permission to speak.

"You may," the judge said. "This statement is being taken on the record. You understand that?"

I responded:

> Yes. Your Honor, I feel it should be considered that I did not see an attorney prior to these gentlemen coming in to interview me . . . Here I am in this kind of situation, that if somebody asks questions without an attorney standing right there and saying "Don't answer that" . . . he's bound to answer them, if for no other reason than he is a human being. That he is not going to be defensive as an attorney would be who looks at it from the law's point of view. . .It's, in effect, like somebody walking in off the street and asking a question. He would impulsively answer.
>
> So that is my personal objection as to why it shouldn't be entered. If this recording is played to the jury, then the entire recording should be heard rather than excerpts which take my statements out of context.

The judge asked the prosecutor about the purpose of playing the tape to the jury.

"To hear the inflections in his voice and showing the answers to these questions," responded the prosecutor.

The judge ruled the tape recording was inadmissible.

The prosecutor complained, "I have already told the jury in my opening statement what we intended to prove through that tape."

Again the judge ruled it inadmissible.[86]

"One thing more, Your Honor, for the record," defense attorney Adamson said. "That is that at this point in the trial it is my intention to advise Mr. Clark to testify in his own behalf," but as he had never discussed with me whether or not I should testify, this was news to me. Adamson further stated that he would examine me about the recording, even though the judge had just ruled it inadmissible. Was this an alliance between my defense attorney and the prosecutor? A case of the prosecutor not being able to introduce the tape, so the public defender offered to do it for him?

The jury retired to the courtroom, and the judge announced: "The Court listened to a tape recording, which has been referred to by Mr. Corbey in his opening statements. Ladies and gentlemen, after deliberations, the Court decided that tape will not be allowed to be heard by you, and no reference will be made to it at this point."[87]

As argued in the appeal, this announcement and any other references to statements I made under interrogation were more prejudicial to my defense than had the jury heard the tape recording, which wasn't incriminating. The announcement by the judge implied I had made a confession, but that due to a legal technicality the jury would not be allowed to hear it.[88]

The jury, at no time during the prosecutor's opening statement or at any time during the trial, should have been made aware of the statements I made to the authorities during interrogation, as Corbey was attempting to do in this case. Part of the reason the U.S. Supreme Court has ruled so is that prosecutors could take out of context what a defendant has said. In its ruling in *Miranda v. Arizona*, and as quoted in the appeal of my conviction, the U.S. Supreme Court noted:

> The defendant may waive effectuation of these rights, provided the waiver is made *voluntarily, knowingly, and intelligently*. If, however, he indicates *in any manner and at any stage of the process* that he wishes to consult with an attorney before speaking, there can be no questioning. Likewise, if the individual is *alone and indicates in any manner* that he does not wish to be interrogated, the police may not question him.[89]

Although the judge in my second trial also ruled my statements inadmissible, the appellate courts turned a deaf ear to this violation of my constitutional rights.

Sergeant Kelley again took the stand and, in regard to the California investigation, stated that the tires on the Bronco were measured at "65 ½ inches" wide from outside to outside.[90] That measurement was half an inch greater than the tracks found at the two crime scenes. The prosecution later claimed the widths were "similar" (but not identical). In spite of this difference, the prosecutor introduced numerous photographs of the tire tracks found at both crime scenes to imply the Bronco was at both sites.

Douglas Palmer of Ames, Iowa, testified that he was employed in April of that year as an attendant at a truck stop outside of Ames, which is off Interstate 35, north of Des Moines. He said that sometime between 3:00 and 11:00 P.M. on Sunday, April 21, he accepted a $20 traveler's check that I cashed there. He said he was able to identify neither the person cashing it nor the vehicle the person was driving.[91]

Upon cross-examination, Palmer said there were no signs anywhere on or near the truck stop to indicate its location. There was only a sign announcing "Skelly Truck Stop". His testimony supported my claim that there was no way of knowing the location of the truck stop where the hitchhikers and I had stopped for gas and a meal. Perhaps that is why the third hitchhiker, the one who drove the Bronco, kept to himself and didn't come into the restaurant to eat. Perhaps he feared that in conversation I might ask how far we had come on Interstate 80, heading east. We were *not* going east on 80, but instead heading north on Interstate 35.

Helen Troxel, waitress at the cafe at a truck stop at Blairsburg Corners, Iowa, about 30 miles north Ames, testified that she waited on the Jiminez couple on Monday, April 22, between 11:00 A.M. and 1:00 P.M.[92] (The media reported earlier that the Blue Earth County sheriff said she waited on the couple about 4:30 P.M.) No matter which time, I was at least 200 miles farther east (in the Belvidere, Illinois, area, or beyond). Troxel stated that the couple was alone and that, after their meal, the Jiminezes walked to the edge of the highway and without carrying anything like a duffel bag.

In cross-examination defense counsel Adamson asked Troxel whether she knew the identity of the investigators who had her sign a statement about seeing the Jiminez couple in the cafe. Her response indicated that at some later date, probably when she came to testify, she was told by the prosecutor that her testimony would help the defense: "They didn't tell me who they were when they came in. They just told me they were from Mankato. I mean, they did not tell me-they didn't give me a card or they didn't tell me they were for the defense for that man!"[93]

In other words, Troxel would not have cooperated by signing a statement in the first place (regardless of whether it was a search for the truth) if she had known it might help prove a person's innocence. Troxel's position exemplifies the overwhelming prejudice of the average citizen against the accused.

Even though Helen Troxel was a witness for the prosecution, the prosecutor downplayed her testimony in his closing statement to the jury, claiming she was "mistaken" on seeing the Jiminez couple at the cafe. In essence he was admitting that he couldn't "fit her story into the State's case".[94] He would not have been able to do this had the jury been aware that station attendant Ernest Ties also saw the Jiminez couple there alone, and that he did not see me or the Bronco.

Le Sueur County Sheriff Pat Smith Sr. took the stand to describe the Scotch Lake scene where Barbara Jiminez's body was discovered. Through him the prosecution introduced the photos of the crime scene. On cross-examination the defense counsel asked Sheriff Smith about a specific set of clear tread impressions in which the sheriff had shown interest. A vehicle that had driven through a mud hole had left the impressions. Asked whether castings were made of the tracks, Smith said that a call was made to the state crime bureau to ask that they be done. Asked whether the casting were made, he responded, "No".[95]

Smith also revealed that his office had received a complaint on or about April 30 by a local farmer about a vehicle observed in the exact same area late at night, when Barbara Jiminez was missing and where her body was later discovered. That complaint was not investigated.

The prosecution called Thomas Simonson, the state crime bureau's field agent in Mankato, to the stand. I could see why my brother-in-law, a police detective, had chewed him out. The agent's appearance reflected his unprofessional manner. He wore a wrinkled shirt, with the top button undone because his neck was too large. His tie was skewed to one side. He stated that his employment before becoming a field agent with the BCA was with the Mankato Police Department.[96]

Simonson displayed 28 photos of tire tracks taken at the two crime scenes. He claimed there were no identifiable characteristics in "any" of the tire tracks, in spite of their being clearly visible in the dried mud at the Scotch Lake scene. He further stated that there was a "similarity in the width, although the measurements were different," of the tracks at the two crime scenes.

On cross-examination Simonson had difficulty testifying without looking at his notes. When public defender Adamson asked when he had prepared the notes, Simonson hesitated, seemingly unable to comprehend the question. His answer reflected the content of his notes rather than when they were prepared. When Adamson repeated the question, Simonson responded, "I don't understand."

Since public defender Adamson had access to the investigative and crime lab reports, just as did my attorney in the second trial, he could have revealed that the crime lab had eliminated the Bronco as having made any of the tire tracks-especially those that went through the mud, up the incline, and away from where Barbara Jiminez's body apparently was dragged to the water's edge. (Water was found in her lungs, so she may have been alive at the time.)

Richard Fowler, sales manager with the Ford dealership in Mankato, testified that the track measurements found at both crime scenes were "similar" in width to those of a Ford Bronco. On cross-examination, however, he admitted he was not familiar with the measurements of named vehicles made by other automobile manufacturers. The prosecution did not call him to testify at the second trial.[97]

Pat Smith Jr., chief deputy and son of Le Sueur County Sheriff Pat Smith, took the stand. In describing Scotch Lake, he said, "There are some farmhouses adjacent to the lake, quite a distance, and on the northeast corner, there is a cottage that is probably occupied two weeks out of the year."[98]

In cross-examination, public defender Adamson asked Deputy Smith about his conversation with me, while transporting me to Le Sueur County, about the civil suit filed with Michigan by my former business partners. He admitted knowledge of the pending lawsuit and the problems it was causing. He also admitted he said it would have been better to sell our house before the lawsuit was instigated. Smith had also been involved in escorting me to Minnesota from California:

Defense:

> I take it then that Mr. Clark came back with you voluntarily without having to go through the extradition proceedings, true?

Dep. Smith:

> That is true.

Defense:

> And as you indicated, this was because he wanted to come back here and get this cleared up?

Dep. Smith:

> This is what he stated to me.

The prosecution called Walter Rhodes, an assistant identification officer with the state crime lab, to the stand. He stated he had been in law enforcement for 26 years, 16 in which he had worked on the identification of fingerprints. He testified that in this case he had examined more than a hundred miscellaneous items for fingerprints. Rhodes found no fingerprints, not even mine, on items I had contact with-not on the matchbook, ballpoint pens, or the spent cartridge casing allegedly found at the crime scene, not on my rifle, rifle case, or box of ammunition. This made no sense to me.

The exceptions were the cardboard trash box I had discarded and a crumpled piece of paper (from the box) with undisclosed writing. Each had a fingerprint, but Rhodes did not lift them for comparison.[99]

According to Rhodes, even the Iowa road map picked up by the Jiminezes in Emporia and the sign made from a shopping bag to indicate their destination did not have fingerprints.

Rhodes stated that eight prints were lifted from unspecified items, however. Five of these could be used for comparison. Fingerprints were also removed from the Bronco where it was impounded in California. For some undisclosed reason, Rhodes did not forward any fingerprints to the Sacramento Sheriff's Department for comparison.

Rhodes further testified that he never ran a comparison check with the crime bureau's master fingerprint list, even though the sheriff had claimed during the investigation that there were "three suspects" in the murder of Michael Jiminez "known to frequent the area". Rhodes claimed that in order to run a comparison check, he would have to have a name to run with the prints (even though the FBI had been cataloging and cross-checking fingerprints for 50 years.)

After a recess, while waiting for the judge to return from chambers, the prosecutor raised, with his back to the jury so that it could also see, an enlarged 8.5 x 11 inch photograph of a fingerprint. He studied it for a considerable time. He used this strategy to give the appearance of fingerprint evidence for the state, of which there was none. The recess also gave the prosecutor an opportunity to consult with Walter Rhodes.

When Rhodes again took the stand-to discount my anticipated testimony as to a third hitchhiker-prosecutor Corbey asked a question meant to lead the jury to conclude that the discovered fingerprints could be those of Barbara Jiminez.

Prosecutor:

> Just one point I would like to clear up on your report. You have one sentence that, of the latent prints developed, none belong to the two victims or to the suspect. I wonder if you could clarify that?

Rhodes:

> That is wrong because we never had any fingerprints of Mrs. Jiminez to compare. It should be just the victim, the male victim, and not both victims. Just the male.

The prosecution would not have been able to mislead the jury this way had defense attorney Adamson introduced Rhodes's report, which did list Barbara Jiminez's print classification, into evidence.[100] Why defense attorney Adamson, who had access to this report, neither challenged Rhodes nor used the report to impeach him is a mystery.[101]

The prosecution knew that Rhode's report supported my defense, as it was withheld from my attorney in the second trial. Not until the prosecutor's files were subpoenaed during appellate hearings did the report surface. Only after both trials were complete was it introduced as an exhibit.

On cross-examination, defense attorney Adamson served the prosecution well by projecting Rhodes as an expert, asking him to describe to the jury how fingerprints are classified through "arches, whirls" and "loops". Adamson even reinforces Rhodes's claim of being unable to make a comparison check with prints on file:

Defense:

> Do you know, Mr. Rhodes, if any effort was made to identify the latent prints which were developed by you in

this case? Were prints sent to the FBI?

Rhodes:

No, sir.

Rhodes again insisted he had to have the name of a suspect to compare prints. And he reiterated that the only prints he had run a check against were those of "Michael Jiminez and Edward Clark."

As Adamson had represented defendants, including Michael Jiminez, in other cases, he must have known better, and he should have continued his cross-examination. Or he might have brought in someone knowledgeable about fingerprint identification for rebuttal. If the expense of providing this testimony was a concern-one he had expressed about obtaining phone records-he might have called the retired FBI agent who by this time was working as an investigator for the State Public Defender's Office. Since the investigator had visited both crime scenes, he may also have been able to express his expert opinion that the murderers had to have known the area well.

The next witness from the crime lab was firearms examiner Janis Seestrom. She said she was employed by "The State of Minnesota, Department of Public Safety, Bureau of Criminal Apprehension Laboratory". She said her experience consisted in working on microscopic examination of vital organs and blood tests and then firearms: "Two years training and now working on cases". She said there were no powder burns or residues to indicate Michael Jiminez had been shot at close range. And there was no foreign matter in the head wound.[102]

She also said that when a gun is manufactured it leaves burrs and that a file is then used to file away the burrs. This, she said, leaves distinguishable file marks in the breech that holds the cartridge. "Breech face impressions" occur when the shell slams against the rear of the breech when the gun is fired. She said such markings in my rifle were identical to those found on the spent cartridge allegedly discovered at the crime scene and that with this finding she was "100 percent sure" the cartridge was ejected from my rifle.

Since the guns are precision-manufactured out of hardened steel, the "burrs" she described are highly unlikely. Even so:

Prosecutor:

> In attempting to make an identification of the cartridge such as you have done here, is there any need to test-fire any other weapons?

Seestrom:

> No

Seestrom again said she removed two bullets from the box of shells taken from my storage unit for test-firing to compare with the cartridge casing allegedly found at the crime scene. She claimed she "lost" one of those two cartridges. First of all, it is unlikely she could lose a cartridge in a controlled testing environment. More significant, however, is that my cartridges were a different brand from that of the label on the box, as I found the smaller box more convenient. The cartridge allegedly found at the crime scene was the same brand as that of the cartridge box but not of the brand of cartridge I was using.

This raises the question of whether the cartridge casing allegedly found at the crime scene actually was that of the second cartridge she claimed to have test-fired but said was lost. In the second trial, defense counsel challenged whether she made such tests at all (the rifle barrel was clean, though she said she had not cleaned it after the test-firing).

During Seestrom's direct testimony, public defender Adamson's dislike for her arrogance and evident love of attention seemed to motivate his aggressiveness in questioning her experience and credibility in the field of ballistics:

Defense:

> Did you test any other .44 cartridge from any other weapon to check any comparisons between any other weapon other than the weapon is now being sought to be introduced into evidence here?

Seestrom:

> Not in this particular case.

Defense:

> And I take it you did not use another Rugar in connection with any of the tests you performed here?

Seestrom:

> No, we did not.

Defense:

> I take it that when we use the term ballistics, it would not actually apply to the type of job that you do in the firearms identification?

Seestrom:

> We do get into it a little bit but, basically, no. We don't monkey with ballistics. I'm what you would call a firearms identification person rather than a ballistics expert.

. . .

Defense:

> Did you make examinations regarding ejector marks, extractor marks, anything like that?

Seestrom:

> No, I did not.

Defense:

> Did you make a microscopic examination of ejector marks?

Seestrom:

> I made the examination under the microscope.

Defense:

>Did you make any conclusions? Isn't it true that ejector marks can also form a foundation for conclusions that two cartridges have been fired from the same weapon?

Seestrom:

>Yes, they can.

. . .

Defense:

>Can you tell the jury why you made no further tests?

Seestrom:

>Because the breech face impressions was such a good example of the match that I didn't feel I needed it.

Defense:

>Could you state for the record, Miss Seestrom, the number of .44 magnums that you have test-fired in your experience with the Bureau?

Seestrom:

>Two.

Defense:

>Did you . . . recall a similarity between the breech face impressions on the other .44 Rugar magnum . . . and the one here in question?

Seestrom:

>I don't remember any similarity.

Seestrom's responses to the following questions reflected the crime lab's objective of obtaining a conviction for the state and its tactic of avoiding technology that might contradict what it chose to testify about:

Defense:

> Miss Seestrom, in my own understanding in the area of firearms identification, I take it that the observations that you have here and that you shared with the jury would have been photographed in some way so that you could have exhibited to the jury the comparisons that you made. Am I completely wrong on that, or what?

Seestrom:

> We do not photograph in our laboratory.

Defense:

> Do some laboratories do so?

Seestrom:

> I guess I am under the impression that some laboratories do photograph some matches, yes.

Defense:

> Do you have the equipment to photograph the matches, as you refer to them?

Seestrom:

> No.

In other words, Seestrom had no evidence to support her claim.

Other elements of Seestrom's testimony raise questions as well. When asked about a search for the fired bullet, she admitted that though means were available, there was no search. But if the fired bullet had been found and wasn't damaged, its caliber might have been identified, and its lack of damage might have proved whether or not it was fired from my rifle.

As in his questioning of the BCA's assistant identification officer Walther Rhodes, public defender Adamson did not seek independent expert testimony to challenge Seestrom's claims. Again, evidence of their false testimony was yet to be revealed-by the private attorney representing me in the trial in the death of Barbara Jiminez. He had the fingerprint classification for Barbara Jiminez and the crime lab's elimination of the Bronco in making the tire tracks that Adamson had access to in the earlier trial. Unfortunately for me, the continual reminding of the jury in the second trial of the outcome of the first case overshadowed the fact of the states' expert witnesses giving false testimony.

If Adamson had called a ballistics expert to testify, he or she could have revealed that my bullets were soft-tipped hollow points that exploded on impact and would have left foreign debris in whatever was left of the man's head. Seestrom testified that no such debris was discovered in the wound. And as argued on the appeal, Seestrom couldn't have been "100 percent sure", based on the breech face markings, that the cartridge case came from my rifle. This I also confirmed after the trials, through an independent forensics firearms laboratory that reviewed the transcript of Seestrom's testimony, as well as through other sources, including the U.S. Bureau of Alcohol, Tobacco, and Firearms, expert as to determining whether a spent cartridge is from a particular firearm through comparison of firing-pin impressions and ejector marks.

As stated in the appeal of the conviction:

> The BCA expert testified that she matched the cartridge found at the scene (. . . Exhibit 27) with a cartridge test-fired from a rifle found in the storage shelter in California (. . . Exhibit 138). Although she concluded that the cartridge found at the scene was fired in the weapon found in the shelter . . . she admitted she had not test-fired from any other weapon . . . nor had she attempted any further tests . . . Nor was she provided with the fired bullet which could have been used for identifying the firearm from which it was propelled . . . Ms. Seestrom should not have been allowed to testify that the single test she performed established conclusively that the cartridge was fired from appellant's rifle . . . In any event, her testimony does not establish that the bullet was fired from that gun.[103]

Wallace Sorum, a micro analyst who routinely made physical comparisons of blood, hair, fibers, glass, and paint, was the state's final witness for the prosecution. Employed by the state's crime lab at the time of its examination of evidence in the Jiminez case, he had since transferred to the Washington State Patrol Laboratory.[104]

(Over the years it has been shown by the media that those giving expert testimonies who work for state crime labs often transfer to crime labs in other states when their findings continue to be questioned or proven false. This occurs most often where they have testified in high-profile cases catching the attention of the appellate courts and the media. Whether or not that is the case with Wallace Sorum remains to be seen.)

Asked about tests he had conducted on the hair discovered in the knot of the cloth found at Scotch Lake for comparison to Barbara Jiminez's hair, Sorum replied:

> First of all, you look at the girls' length of hair, does the hair have roughly the same length. You look at them under a stereo microscope. That is magnifying them maybe 30 to 60 times to see if they have the same color and hue. If these all compare-I guess spread known hairs alongside of the question hairs and observe the two side by side in kind of a comparison type situation under the microscope where you are looking at them under 500 times magnification.

Asked whether he was able to make a comparison, Sorum responded, "No, sir." When asked why not, he said, "Well, I feel that the hairs are a very poor type of evidence. It's very difficult to take-it would be hard for us to take hairs off my head and say the two came from the same head. The hairs are so tremendously variable that it's rather an inconclusive type of evidence."

Sorum also testified that he had microscopically checked the hairs from the knot and those found on the items from the Bronco, including the sleeping bag, against hairs from Barbara Jiminez. Again he said he was unable to make a comparison. While there would not have been any foreign hair in my sleeping bag, it is puzzling that there would not have been similarities (even though DNA sampling technology had not yet been developed for this use) enough to conclude that the hair in the knot came from Barbara Jiminez. This assumes, of course, that she had used the cloth in place of the elastic hair-tie later found in the pocket of her coat.

Wallace Sorum testified that the cloth discovered at the Scotch Lake scene (which the prosecutor referred to as a "gag" because of the hair entwined in the knot) was torn from the sheet I had used as a dust cover in the Bronco. If public defender Adamson had measured the cloth (as did the attorney representing me in the second trial), he could have told the jury that it was too short to be used as a gag.

In cross-examination, Adamson asked Sorum whether the cloth had been tested for foreign matter such as blood or saliva.

"It was not," he responded.

Sorum stated in the second trial that he "did not" perform a microscopic analysis of the hair, contradicting his statement in the first trial that he did. Because of this, the attorney in the second trial impeached him.[105] Sorum was impeached again in a murder trial (in which he claimed to have "positively" identified hair at a crime scene as coming from a defendant) after transferring back to Minnesota.

This is just one example of a state's crime lab's allegiance to winning the case for the prosecution rather than to objectivity in its findings. Because of their misplaced loyalty, some witnesses, such as Wallace Sorum, contradicted themselves in subsequent testimony in the second trial.

In 1993, the U.S. Supreme Court gave federal judges the authority to scrutinize expert testimony based solely on the experience of an expert without scientific evidence to support his conclusions.[106] This authority has not been awarded to judges in state courts.

During representation of the state's case, I observed a strategy that I assume most prosecutors attempt to apply-that is, whenever possible, to schedule the testimony of expert witnesses for the prosecution to end the day. This way the members of the jury will have only what the prosecution wishes them to hear until the following day or even the following week. An unsequestered jury, as in my case, might then be exposed to newspaper and television reports about that testimony or come under additional pressure from persons known or unknown, as experienced by juror Graham. This end-of-the-day prosecution strategy can be insurmountable for the defense, even when its later cross-examination reveals countering evidence.

Upon the prosecution's calling of the last of its witnesses, the *Mankato Free Press* published a list of all who had testified for the state.[107]

Chapter 6: The Case for the Defense

Public defender Adamson opened the defense by calling to the stand William Martin, the security director for the General Telephone Company of Illinois. Adamson, who had belittled my request to obtain the record of my phone call from Belvidere, Illinois, before the murder of Michael Jiminez in Minnesota, now took credit for it.

Defense:

> At my request, Mr. Martin, did you make a search of your records to determine whether or not a telephone call had been made to a certain number at Royal Oak [Ferndale], Michigan, on April 22, 1974?

Martin:

> Yes.[108]

Martin, reading from phone company records, told the court that a call was placed on Monday, April 22, to my home number from a telephone inside a Standard Oil Station at a toll way oasis on Interstate 90 in Illinois. He said the call was placed at 5:03 P.M., and lasted two minutes and 50 seconds. This phone call, placed within a couple of hours of the time the

Jiminezes were in a cafe along Interstate 35 in Iowa, made it impossible for me to have been in Minnesota, 300 miles to the northwest, about seven hours later when Michael Jiminez was murdered.

With no way to disprove the telephone records in cross-examination, the prosecutor asked ridiculous questions of Martin to suggest that anyone could have made the call. In addition, the prosecutor in this trial, as well as the one in the second trial, would conspire to discredit Martin through an altered transcript of the testimony.

Public defender Adamson called my wife to the stand. Her demeanor and physical attractiveness obviously impressed those in the room. After the preliminary questioning:

Defense:

> Now, Mrs. Clark, calling your attention to April 22nd of 1974, do you recall having any telephone calls from your husband on that day?

Wife:

> Yes.

Defense:

> Do you recall when the first telephone call came to your home from him?

Wife:

> Around dinnertime, between 5:00 and 6:00.

Defense:

> And how is it that you can fix April 22nd as the day on which you received that call?

Wife:

> Because I had previous plans. I was taking the kids to a baseball game.

Defense:

> Did you also have an appointment with a dentist on the following day?

Wife:

> Yes, at noon.

Defense:

> And that would have been on the 23rd, correct?

Wife:

> Yes.

Defense:

> ... Your husband indicated to you where the call was being placed from? What did he indicate in that regard?

Wife:

> He said outside of Chicago.[109]

On the thruway entrance was a sign with the word *Chicago* and an arrow pointing in the direction. Nothing told the distance.

Defense:

> Did you receive a later telephone call from him?

Wife:

> Yes ... that was around 10:00 in the evening.

Defense:

> And did he indicate to you where that call had been made from?

Wife:

> Yes, Kalamazoo, Michigan.

Adamson again made it appear he assisted in finding the origin of the phone calls:

Defense:

> Now, as regards to the last telephone call, do you know from the assistance that you have given us here in this case that we made an attempt to find the record of that phone call, too, but no records were kept? Is this correct?

Wife:

Yes.

Defense:

> And as far as the first telephone call was concerned, did you at the request of your husband and our office make an effort to find the place from which the call had been made?

Wife:

> Yes, I did.
>
> . . .

Defense:

> Can you state for the record where it was that you discovered that first telephone call to have been made from?

Wife:

> It was on an oasis on the toll way, the first one south of the Illinois-Wisconsin border.

Defense:

> Now, do you recall, Mrs. Clark, about what time it was that your husband arrived at your home after having received the phone calls that you have alluded to in your

testimony?

Wife:

Yes, about 1:00 in the morning on the 23rd.

Defense:

At that time, did you make observations regarding your husband, look at him?

Wife:

I gave him a big hug. [She glanced at me and smiled.]

Defense:

Was there anything about his manner or demeanor or appearance that in any way struck you as being unusual?

Wife:

No, not at all.

Defense:

And after having stayed with you a length of time, do you know where he went from there?

Wife:

Yes, his mother's.

Defense:

Could you tell the jury the circumstances around him not staying with you that evening, going to his mother's?

Wife:

Well, by the time he left our house, it was about 4:00 in the morning and the kids get up between 6:30 and 7:00. He was tired and wanted to sleep, plus the fact that he did not want the Bronco parked in front of our home for any length of time.

Defense:

    Was that in connection with his civil suit?

Wife:

    Yes.

Defense:

    Where did he stay the following evening?

Wife:

    Well, he came over and spent some time with the kids and me and then in the late evening he went back over there again.

    . . .

Defense:

    Before this time, had there been efforts made to serve civil papers on your husband, Mrs. Clark?

Wife:

    Yes.

Defense:

    Had there been efforts made at your home?

Wife:

    No, they knew that he wasn't there.

Defense:

    Can you state for the record and for the jury what plans you and your husband had regarding the home and the move to California?

Wife:

> We had attempted to sell the home and move to California, but through the civil suit that was filed, the house was tied up. So, at this point, our plans were for him to take a trailer load of furniture out there, fly back, pick up the second car, the kids, myself and the dog and the rest of the miscellaneous household things and we were going to rent out the house in Michigan until the suit was settled.

Defense:

> Could you state for the record what your home phone number is in Michigan . . .

Because the prosecutor, in cross-examining the Wards, had implied I was having an affair with a woman in California named Mildred, Adamson asked my wife her mother's name. Having heard the earlier testimony, my wife smiled and answered, "Mildred."

In cross-examining my wife, prosecutor Corbey attempted to mislead the jury through fabrication, implication, and outright distortion of the truth:

Prosecutor:

> When he called you on the telephone the night of the 22nd, he told you that he was in Chicago, did he not?

Wife:

> I don't recall whether he said in or around. He mentioned Chicago.

Prosecutor:

> But in your checking as to where that call came from, I understand that you found the place where it had originated, and that was up near Rockford, Illinois?

Wife:

It is Belvidere, if I remember right.

Prosecutor:

Did he say anything about picking up any hitchhikers?

Wife:

He mentioned it when he was home that week about picking up hitchhikers.

Prosecutor:

When was the first time he told you about the hitchhikers?

Wife:

Well, when he was home for that week, he told me that he did pick up hitchhikers. I remember it very vividly because at the time I was busy in the kitchen with the kids and he said something about picking up hitchhikers and I said, "Well, I don't think that was a great idea." He said, "Well, it helps pass the time and I was tired."

Prosecutor:

Do you remember anything else that he told you about a hitchhiker?

Wife:

No.

Prosecutor:

Did he tell you anything about putting a hitchhiker out of the vehicle?

Wife:

No

Prosecutor:

Were you having marital problems?

Wife:

Well, we were having ups and downs, yeah.

Prosecutor:

Did you tell anybody that you were on the verge of seeing a lawyer?

Wife:

No.

Prosecutor:

Mrs. Clark, did your husband leave for California because of those marital problems?

Wife:

No.

. . .

Prosecutor:

Did you tell anybody that the Bronco was so full he could not have picked up any hitchhikers?

Wife:

No, I never saw it.

Prosecutor:

You never told that to Agent Simonson or Pat Smith, Jr.?

Wife:

No.

. . .

Prosecutor:

    So, I take it that when he arrived home and during this period that you described, there was nothing unusual about him at all? He never made a mention about being in Minnesota?

Wife:

    No.

Prosecutor:

    Did he tell you how he drove from Lake Tahoe to Michigan?

Wife:

    Yes, he told me he drove in the Bronco on Interstate 80.

Prosecutor:

    So, I take it at that time you didn't pay any attention to the fact that 80 does not go through Minnesota?

Wife:

    I had no reason to even look on the map.

The only way the prosecutor could ask my wife about our privileged communications and so distort the truth was in response to public defender Adamson's opening that line of questioning. Because of this, the prosecutor badgered my wife unmercifully in the second trial, taking out of context what she had testified to in the first.

The prosecutor asked questions but ignored the answers to those questions for the sole purpose of misleading the jury, a perfect example of the tactics of some lawyers and law enforcement agencies determined to win rather than to search for the truth. In his effort to win the case by any means, prosecutor Corbey recalled Agent Simonson as a rebuttal witness against my wife after the defense rested:

Prosecutor:

>Did you have a discussion with Mrs. Jere Clark . . . referring to the Bronco, did she make any statement to you as to her observation of the Bronco? . . . What did she say?

Simonson:

>Oh, the question was directed by Deputy Smith. She was asked if Mr. Clark had mentioned picking up hitchhikers. She stated, yes, that he had picked up one hitchhiker. He mentioned picking up one hitchhiker and that the hitchhiker had apparently taken off his shoes and they were rather bad smelling and when Mr. Clark filled with gas he drove off. The next stop he just filled with gas and he just drove off and left the hitchhiker behind.

Prosecutor:

>Did she say anything as to her observations of the Bronco?

Simonson:

>Oh, another question directed by Deputy Smith. She was asked if she had, if he had mentioned picking up two hitchhikers. She stated no, she didn't know how he could possibly. The way the Bronco was so full, she didn't know how there could possibly have been room for two separate people in the Bronco.[110]

Public defender Adamson cross-examined Simonson:

Defense:

>Did she indicate to you when Mr. Clark arrived home?

Simonson:

>On the second time we interviewed Mrs. Clark, she stated that he arrived home at approximately 1:00 A.M.

on the 21st.

Defense:

    Did she also indicate to you that she had received a telephone call from Mr. Clark later than 4:00 or 5:00 or 6:00 o'clock on the 22nd from Kalamazoo, Michigan?

Simonson:

    No, sir, she did not.

Defense:

    Was there any effort made by your office to check out the telephone call that had been received by her in the late afternoon or early morning hours of the 22nd?

Simonson:

    My knowledge is the records of the phone call, the phone records were subpoenaed through the Blue Earth County Sheriff's Office.

Defense:

    Where are they?

Simonson:

    I have no idea, sir.

Defense:

    Now, you kept the notes, Agent, of all your connections with this case, have you not?

Simonson:

    Yes, rough notes.

Adamson asked Simonson whether there was any evidence found at the crime scene in Blue Earth County that had not been introduced in court:

Simonson:

    I'm not aware of anything, sir.

Defense:

    How about a sales slip from Sherwood Auto, Mankato, Minnesota?

Simonson:

    Oh, yes, sir. I have that in my possession.

Defense:

    Was that ever turned over to the crime lab?

Simonson:

    No, sir.

Agent Simonson's testimony didn't make sense. He first alleged that my wife said I mentioned picking up "one" hitchhiker, but that his feet smelled so bad I drove off and left him after stopping for gas. Then Simonson claimed my wife "didn't know how there could possibly have been room for two separate people in the Bronco." This flew in the face of my picking up any hitchhikers and was detrimental to the prosecution's case.

As to the second phone call placed to my wife from the Kalamazoo, Michigan, area, why wouldn't she refer to it if it weren't true? The first call I made, from the Belvidere/Rockford, Illinois, area, established my alibi. The second phone call was simply consistent with the direction I was driving and the distance covered in that amount of time.

Simonson indicated that the Blue Earth County Sheriff's Office had subpoenaed the phone records. In reality, my brother-in-law, who was in law enforcement, was responsible. The sheriff's office would not have assisted in obtaining evidence supporting my innocence.

As outlined earlier, the first interview of my wife took place in our home, the second in the investigators' vehicle, where the acoustics were better for recording purposes. Escorted by Deputy Smith during one of the appellate hearings after the trials, I casually asked what had happened to the taped conversation they had with my wife. He responded, "Simonson had it"-thereby validating my suspicion that it had been recorded. Also, a transcript of a recording made of an interview with my former employee, Edward Newberg, was found in the subpoenaed files of the prosecutor at the time of the appellate hearing. While the prosecutor claimed he "did not recall" when he received it, Corbey admitted the underlinings in the transcript were his.[111]

That the prosecutor asked Agent Simonson rather than Deputy Smith, who had asked the questions of my wife, to testify, was significant. I was getting to know Deputy Smith; he appeared to be a man of integrity, one who would not conspire to give false testimony.

Also as revealed earlier, Agent Simonson engaged in unprofessional conduct when interviewing my wife, other members of my family, and women either who had been customers of the automotive repair business or who had taken the Powder Puff Mechanics course. He had threatened my wife with charges of perjury even though she was willing to take a polygraph test.

Adamson would better have served the defense had he subsequently recalled my wife to the witness stand to reveal Simonson's threat. He chose neither to recall her nor to argue the point in his closing statement to the jury.

The Defense Continues

The defense called my mother to the stand:

Defense:

> You are the mother of Mr. Clark, the man who is sitting right here with me?

Mother:

Yes, I am.

Defense:

Calling your attention, Mrs. Clark, to around the 22nd and 23rd of April this year . . . Were you advised sometime on April 22nd that your son, Edward Clark, was on his way home to Michigan?

Mother:

Yes, I was.

Defense:

And who did you receive that information from?

Mother:

His wife.

Defense:

Do you recall what time of the day it was that she so advised you?

Mother:

Yes, it was around suppertime on Monday.

Defense:

Did you then expect Mr. Clark, your son, to come to your home later that night?

Mother:

Yes. She told me he would come.

Defense:

Do you recall the time it was that Mr. Clark came to your home after you were advised that he was on his way there?

Mother:

> It must have been 4:00, 5:00 o'clock. I can't tell you the correct time. It was dark.

Defense:

> If I understand your testimony, that would be the day or the morning following the time that you were advised he was on his way home?

Mother:

> Right, the 23rd.

Defense:

> The following day, did you notice anything unusual about his manner or his way of speaking?

Mother:

> No. In fact, he was just telling me how he likes California and when they get settled, he would like for me to come out and visit.

> . . .

Defense:

> Did you notice anything unusual about any of the clothing that you washed for him? Did you notice any blood or anything like that?

Mother:

> No, I did not. Only just the ordinary soil from wearing his clothes. That's all.[112]

The prosecutor's questioning of my 74-year-old mother was limited. He took care not to imply she was untruthful, as that would not have set well with the jury. Still, he managed to imply my wife and I were having marital problems.

The judge announced: "We are going to adjourn . . . On Thursday, there may or may not be any evidence taken. If there is any, it will only be from 9:00 o'clock until 12:00 o'clock because the Court will be detained for the rest of the day in other matters." The "other matters" pertained to the judge's attendance of inauguration ceremonies for the new president of Mankato State College.

In addition to my wife and mother, six character witnesses-two with their wives and from all walks of life-flew to Minnesota from Michigan to testify on my behalf. Public defender Adamson tried to convince me not to call them, saying that if they knew I had plead guilty ten years earlier to unauthorized use of a motor vehicle, their opinion of me would change. I knew better and demanded they be allowed to testify. One of the wives, whose family had known my family for many years, ran over and gave me a big hug while her husband and I shook hands. They mentioned a big party planned for me when the trial was done.

The character witnesses did an excellent job, as stated later by my attorney for the appeal: "The character evidence offered on appellant's behalf lends support to the alibi defense and refutes the circumstantial evidence relied upon by the State."[113]

Public defender Adamson asked generally the same questions of the character witnesses, for example:

Defense:

> Have you ever heard remarks that were derogatory or reflected upon Mr. Clark's honesty?

Prosecutor:

> I object to that, Your Honor, on the grounds of insufficient foundation.

Judge:

> Overruled.

Defense:

Will you tell the jury what the reputation is?

Witness:

Very good, excellent.

Defense:

Based on the general reputation of Mr. Clark for truth, veracity, would you believe him under oath?

Witness:

Yes.

Defense:

Now, in forming the opinion and drawing the conclusion that you have . . . are you now aware that Mr. Clark in 1965 had plead guilty to the unauthorized use of a motor vehicle and paid $100 in costs and was placed on probation for two years. Are you aware of this?

Witness:

Yes, I am.

Defense:

Does that in any way change the opinion that you have given to the jury?

Witness:

No.

Actually, there was no reason for my defense attorney to bring up the unauthorized use of a vehicle. It could only be introduced-by the state-if shown to be a pattern of behavior similar to what I was on trial for in Minnesota.

The character witnesses included an attorney who knew me on a business and social basis. His wife, Charlotte, testified that she had been a student in my Powder Puff Mechanics course. During her testimony, I thought back to the last day of the course, on which it was my practice to take the students to dinner and celebration of their "graduation". Charlotte stood out because of her wit, her off-the-cuff, hilarious remarks. It was a joy having her in the class. At the restaurant, I called Charlotte to the front of the group.

With the other restaurant's patrons and employees enjoying the scene, I asked, "Once in awhile, we have a student who had her heart set on an occupation as a mechanic; that is why she takes the course. Although Charlotte may feel somewhat disappointed with me telling her she will never make it as an auto mechanic, I have a gift for her that should be useful in the field she is best suited for." I reached beneath the table, then handed Charlotte a toilet plunger, painted gold, and decorated with a ribbon. (This was years before women were accepted as auto technicians.) When my wife and I attended our last New Year's Eve party together at their residence, we saw the plunger on their fireplace mantel-a memento and topic for conversation.

John, a certified public accountant, testified that he had handled the books for my business, Automotive Services, Inc. He said our relationship was basically business in nature; he consulted with me regarding the operation of the business. He further stated that I worked long hours and always on weekends. He characterized me as "very honest, very trustworthy, very conscientious and hardworking." The defense proceeded:

> As an incident to the business, do you know, for example, if he allowed discounts in certain areas to certain groups of citizens?
>
> Yes, he was very concerned about senior citizens, whether or not they were getting a fair shake in the automobile market. Then . . . he gave a discount to the powder puff people, women who had cars.[114]

Tom, a pension specialist with Prudential Insurance Company, testified that he knew me on both a business and social basis, and that our families had visited each other's homes. He stated that our business dealings started when I went into the auto-repair business and he wrote a group health program for my employees. Then:

Tom:

> We issued a $ . . . term life insurance policy from Prudential on Mr. Clark . . . I was monitoring his situation very closely. I wanted to see him do well in business. I had my car worked on there several times. He also did an excellent job and did what he asked. I referred him to people that had their car worked on because he just basically did a good, honest job. He was somebody you could trust.

Defense:

> Now, as far as the insurance coverage that your company provided Mr. Clark, particularly the $ . . . term policy, in connection with that, did your company cause to have Mr. Clark investigated?

Tom:

> Yes. A $ . . . term policy is not sold to anybody on the street. Especially by Prudential Insurance Company. He was investigated by the Retail Credit Company, which is a national credit investigation company. For this type of contract, it entails a written narrative that goes into his character, his stability, his honesty, his morals, pretty much done because, let's face it, it we are going to say we'll pay $ . . . if you should die in an accident or naturally . . . that's quite a substantial debt.

Defense:

> And as an incident of that, I take it, a thorough investigation was made on him in the background and stability you mentioned?

Tom:

> Yes, we go back four or six years where they have to, personally have to, talk to neighbors and associates of him.

Defense:

> I take it that the $ . . . policy was issued to Mr. Clark?

Tom:

> Yes, and the policy is still in force.[115]

At the conclusion of testimony by my character witnesses, Tom brought over and introduced to me the local agent for Prudential. Tom asked my permission to take my wife to dinner with the local agent and his wife. I expressed my appreciation and gave my approval. My uncomplaining wife needed some normalcy, even if just for a couple of hours, but nearby spectators were appalled at hearing about what they viewed as permissive behavior.

There was profound silence as I took the stand. Public defender Adamson's questioning began with my background: education, military record, working up to the position of office manager in a company, and subsequent self-employment.[116] Adamson asked about my snow removal business and my partnership in the automotive-repair business. I explained the reason for the falling out with my partners. They had wanted me to put my signature on altered stock certificates, which I knew was illegal. (Before I testified, my former business partners were flown in as rebuttal witnesses, but after I testified about their attempt to get me to sign new company stock certificates on which they would profit, the prosecutor refrained from putting them on the stand.)

I continued to describe my closing of the business, leaving instructions to my partners about liquidating the assets and paying off the creditors, and I told of my wife's yearning to move back to California, her home state, and our preparations for moving to the West Coast. I said that the falling=out with my business partners led to the lawsuit that tied up our assets, which prevented us from selling our home. I said too that my former partners hired a private investigator to find me in California, which was what I had assumed my arrest there was about. I told the court that after remaining in California for an extended time, I contemplated returning to Michigan as it was hard to be away from my wife, even though returning at that time was against the advice of the attorney I had hired to prepare a counter lawsuit.

Public defender Adamson asked my reason for going into the mountains after leaving the Sacramento area for my return to Michigan. I responded, "I had a lot of things on my mind, and I had to get away from everything and everybody and make some decisions as to what to do."

I went on to say that I spent a couple of days in the mountains, doing some target practice, which resulted in the spent shells scattered in the vehicle, playing some blackjack, and taking in a couple of stage shows at Harrah's in Lake Tahoe, and I cashed in some traveler's checks at Harrah's before starting my drive back to Michigan.

He asked about my movements prior to picking up the hitchhikers on my return trip to Michigan. I said that I left Lake Tahoe on Saturday morning, April 20, and stopped at Salt Lake City, Cheyenne (Wyoming), and North Platte (Nebraska) for gas, meals, and a brief rest.

I told how I met the hitchhikers and what happened following: On driving more than 1,600 miles in approximately 34 hours, I reached the outskirts of Des Moines, Iowa, around 6:00 P.M. on Sunday, April 21. When I stopped for gas, three hitchhikers approached me looking for a ride. They asked whether I was heading east. Since I was very tired and saw it as an opportunity to get some sleep, I asked one of the hitchhikers to drive.

I awoke later that evening when the Bronco was pulling into a truck stop. Seeing no sign of its location, I assumed we were still heading east on Interstate 80. At the truck stop, two of the hitchhikers and I had a meal, which along with the gas, I paid for with another traveler's check. The third hitchhiker chose not to join us, instead returning to the Bronco after he went to the bathroom. On returning to the Bronco, I drank a cup of coffee from my thermos, falling back to sleep as the vehicle started moving. The next morning, Monday, April 22, I awoke with the hitchhikers nowhere in sight. I discovered I was somewhere in Minnesota, that a suitcase containing sports clothes was missing, and that in my trash box was a dirty, brown suede coat covering the rest of the contents. As I used the box only for trash, I subsequently threw it away.

About five o'clock in the evening of the same day, I phoned my wife at the first service island on the thruway to Chicago, near Belvidere, Illinois, telling her I expected to arrive home around 10:00 P.M. I made a second phone call to my wife around 10:00 P.M., near Kalamazoo, Michigan, to let her know I was running late and expected to arrive around midnight. I arrived home at about 1:00 A.M. and, later that morning, drove over to my mother's to get some sleep.

Ten days later I made another trip to California with a U-Haul trailer containing most of the remaining family possessions. I intended to fly back to Michigan for the final trip to California by car, taking in the sights along the way—a family vacation.

Adamson asked whether I had attempted to conceal the sheet apparently from which came the cloth found at the Scotch Lake site. I said I made no attempt to conceal it, and that it was clearly visible in the storage unit. I had noticed a piece torn from one end, but I used it only as a dust cover and wasn't concerned.

He then brought up the 1965 conviction for unauthorized use of a motor vehicle, which had occurred nine years before this trial, asking the disposition of the case. Again, this had nothing to do with the charges against me in Minnesota.

The name Mildred again came up, and as my wife had stated, that was her mother's name. I further stated that I had intended to put together a Powder Puff Mechanics course in California as I had in Michigan.

As I responded to the questions without hesitation, the jury listened intently and appeared satisfied with my explanation of coming into contact with the Jiminezes and satisfied that I wasn't in Minnesota when Michael Jiminez was murdered.

While testifying, I could see through the windows of the courtroom doors that Sheriff Wiebold was pacing up and down in the corridor, occasionally stopping to look in. Rumor had it that if there wasn't a conviction, the sheriff would be out of a job because of his revealing the details of the case (including that "three suspects" in the Michael Jiminez case knew the area) and his penchant for attention by the media. He had also revealed that the Jiminezes were identified in a cafe in Iowa on the day before Michael Jiminez's murder. These slips by the sheriff came back to haunt the prosecutor, forcing him to call waitress Helen Troxel as a witness, who ultimately supported the estimated time of death of Michael Jiminez and thus my alibi. A verdict of not guilty would confirm public suspicion that the Jiminez murders were drug-related. Like so many others, it might go unsolved and reflect badly on the community. The authorities needed a scapegoat.

Adamson Ended his direct examination with questions pertaining to the crimes I was charged with and for which I was now on trial:

Defense:

> Now, you understand, do you not, Mr. Clark, that you stand here charged with the murder of Michael Jiminez? You understand that that is the charge here?

Clark:

> Yes, I do.

Defense:

> Did you assault in any way any of the hitchhikers that you picked up west of Des Moines?

Clark:

> I did not.

Defense:

> Did you kill anybody?

Clark:

No.

Defense:

Did you molest in any way . . . Barbara Jiminez?

Clark:

No.

The prosecutor opened his two days of cross-examination with insignificant questions that I had already answered on direct examination. His purpose was to find inconsistencies with my previous answers, but he found none. His cross-examination in this manner was lengthy, so I have reduced it to the main points here, starting with the prosecutor's question following my statement that my immediate response to arrest in California was that it was related to the private investigator hired by my former business partners:

Prosecutor:

Mr. Clark, what private investigator?

Clark:

The private investigator, or whomever it was, that was hounding my in-laws in California.

Prosecutor:

Can you tell us how you know there was a private investigator that existed?

Clark:

I can only go by the complaints my mother in-law received from her neighbors.

Prosecutor:

So, based on hearsay, you are making the assumption that there was a private investigator?

Clark:

> Yes

This was the second reason that the prosecutor did not call my former business partners to testify-he would have been unable to imply that there was no private investigator.

The court should not have allowed the following line of questioning by the prosecution, and public defender Adamson should have objected to the line of questioning as well. I had exercised my constitutional right not to be questioned without an attorney, the judge had already ruled the material inadmissible, and the judge in my second trial barred it as well.

Prosecutor:

> When you were arrested, Mr. Clark, you told Sgts. Kelley and Cowan that you had not been in Minnesota in the last three years, did you not?

Clark:

> Yes, I did.

Prosecutor:

> That was a lie, was it not?

Clark:

> Yes, it was.

Prosecutor:

> And you also told Sheriff LeRoy Wiebold and Pat Smith, Sr., the same thing, did you not? . . . Can you tell us how you justified that?

Clark:

> I believe that anybody under those circumstances, their natural reaction would be to deny anything when arrested in the middle of the night and charged with

murder.

Prosecutor:

> Did you ever give a description of the third hitchhiker to anybody and whom did you give that?

Clark:

> To the investigator who came down on behalf of Mr. Adamson's office.

Prosecutor:

> Other than that, you didn't tell anybody else or give anybody a description of that person?

Clark:

> No, I didn't.

Public defender Adamson's failure to object on my behalf at the start of this line of questioning constituted "ineffective assistance of counsel". This provided a basis for appeal, as the prosecutor is not supposed to make any reference to a person exercising the constitutional right to remain silent.[117]

The prosecutor then turned to my marriage:

Prosecutor:

> Were you having marital problems back home?

Clark:

> There were problems.

Prosecutor:

> And weren't those bothering you at the time?

Clark:

> Oh, yes. [I was referring to our ups and downs, not to

any serious problems in our marriage.]

Prosecutor:

> At the time you left for Michigan, you hadn't told anybody, that is, your wife or anybody back in Michigan that you were going to go back?

Clark:

> May I explain?

Prosecutor:

> Well-

Clark:

> Or do you want a direct answer, yes or no?

Prosecutor:

> Did they know if you were going to come back?

Clark:

> Possibly.

The prosecutor then turned to whether the Jiminezes were actually the couple I had picked up:

Prosecutor:

> ... Are they the people that you picked up?

Clark:

> I can't answer one way or the other if they are.

Prosecutor:

> Any reason why you can't?

Clark:

> Yes, because in the past four years, I have dealt with

no less than 4,000 people and most of them strangers. I am not a man who just goes to work and sees the same faces every day. I meet new faces every day and unless I see a person three to four times, I wouldn't remember them.

Prosecutor:

As a matter of fact, you didn't think there was any typewriter receipt in that box when you dropped it, did you?

Clark:

I could have cared less if there was.

Prosecutor:

When you say you could care less about the typewriter receipt being in there, the fact of the matter is that you made no attempt to hide the sheet in your shelter, did you.

Clark:

Oh, no attempt whatsoever.

Prosecutor:

And I take it, Mr. Clark, that you were satisfied to sit there and tell this Court and jury that you did not shoot Michael Jiminez?

Clark:

Absolutely not.

Prosecutor:

And you didn't strangle Barbara Jiminez?

Clark:

I did not.

While the exchanges between the prosecutor and myself were heated, my responses were prompt and sincere. On redirect examination, Adamson asked:

Defense:

> Now, one thing that Mr. Corbey did not ask you is the response that you made to any of those questions to you regarding your guilt or innocence . . . Do you recall your talking to them about the civil action and Sheriff Smith's indicating to that? Do you recall saying, "I'm sure I have nothing to worry about because I'm sure I am innocent?"

Clark:

> Yes, I do.

Defense:

> Did you also in other conversations with him at that time indicate to him that you were innocent?

Clark:

> Yes, I did.

Defense:

> At the time you were in California and before your return here, did you require that the authorities here extradite you back to Minnesota or did you come back voluntarily?

Clark:

> I came back voluntarily.

The prosecutor objected, arguing that the questioning was repetitious of testimony I had given at the beginning of the direct examination, though he continually did the same. The judge overruled the prosecutor's objection, and I repeated, "I did not fight extradition. I volunteered to come back."

Adamson's questioning continued on the topics of my not resisting arrest, my waiving of extradition proceedings, and the sheriff lying about what I said when I was in the county jail. Adamson concluded:

Defense:

> You look at the jury and you tell them whether or not you did any harm to the people you picked up in Iowa.

Clark:

> I did not.

Chapter 7: Closing Arguments and Verdict

Because Helen Troxel's sightings of the Jiminezes at the cafe in Blairsburg Corners, Iowa, did not fit the state's theory of the case, prosecutor Corbey's closing statement to the jury concluded that she must have been mistaken, that she was called to testify only to show the jury that nothing was concealed.[118] He would not have been able to make such a statement had the jury been aware that another person-gas station attendant Ernest Ties-also saw the Jiminezes there.

The prosecutor made this claim even though the coroner determined that Michael Jiminez was murdered the night before his body had been discovered, not 24 hours earlier. The coroner's determination supported both my alibi and the known whereabouts of the Jiminez couple before the murder of Michael Jiminez.

In reference to my placing the call to my home phone from Belvidere, Illinois, the prosecutor told the jury, "Anyone could have made the call." In essence, he said a conspiracy of unknown parties made the phone call to establish my alibi. Then he contradicted himself, admitting that I made the phone call: "He gets to Belvidere and he calls his wife and says, 'I'm in Chicago.'" I never made such a statement, though I did say there was a road sign pointing the way to Chicago.

The prosecutor then challenged the existence of the third hitchhiker:

> Do you know why Edward Clark is a liar? Because there is no third hitchhiker . . . Do you know why the mysterious hitchhiker didn't throw out that jacket or take the same route? Because there is no third hitchhiker. Do you know why there isn't the slightest bit of evidence as to a third hitchhiker? Because there was no third hitchhiker . . . There was no other man. No other man but Edward R. Clark, beyond a reasonable doubt.

Those were the only references the prosecutor made to the case. Then, though we found later that he had concealed evidence supporting my innocence-in his file, in the file of the Le Sueur County prosecutor, and in the file in the Blue Earth County Sheriff's Department-the prosecutor stated:

> Well, I want to tell you that I will match the record of what the Sheriff's Office in Blue Earth County, Le Sueur County, Sacramento County, and in Detroit, Michigan, I'll match that record against any complaint of the defense that the police didn't work hard enough.

Of the prosecutor's entire statement to the jury, my appellate attorney said, in part:

> As these excerpts vividly demonstrate, the prosecution's closing argument was replete with insinuations, speculations, personal opinion, unproven assertions, and wildly inflammatory and prejudicial statements only remotely based on the evidence of the case . . .
>
> The prosecutor's final argument is blatantly prejudicial and inflammatory. He . . . asks the jury if they are "going to believe the lies that this man is telling you in this courtroom?" . . .
>
> The prosecutor's attempt to discredit appellant's alibi defense is based on speculation which is highly

prejudicial. There is no evidence on which to base his insinuations that appellant did in fact ask the hitchhikers their destination, or that he knowingly changed his route from Interstate 80 to Interstate 35, and did so with Barbara Jiminez as his "target".

The prosecutor's stress on Barbara Jiminez, and her "long black hair," and his invitation to the jury to view the pictures and "decide if she isn't a beautiful girl," with the strong implication that appellant raped and murdered her, was highly prejudicial.

Appellant submits that the prosecutor's closing argument was a blatant appeal to the emotions and sympathies of the jury, which diverted widely from the proven facts of the case and which served to portray appellant in the worst possible light, by way of innuendo, insinuation, and opinion.

It is an elementary rule of law that the prosecution's final argument must be based upon reference to the evidence. Matters which cannot be regarded as evidence and which serve to divert the minds of the jurors from the facts to which their consideration should be given in determining whether the accused is guilty or not may not be introduced into the closing argument.[119]

The public defender's closing argument made no mention of my alibi, that I was 700 miles away in Michigan when Michael Jiminez was murdered, nor did he challenge the prosecutor's contention that "anyone could have made the call" from Belvidere, Illinois, around the time the Jiminezes were seen at the cafe in Iowa. Rather, the thrust of his argument concentrated on the unusual number of exhibits piled on the table in front of the jury. Defense counsel Adamson's closing argument isn't worth quoting.

In appealing the conviction, Adamson's failure to provide me adequate representation rested on the following seven points:

1. Counsel's Prejudicial Comments to the Media . . .

2. Failure to Aid in the Jury Selection . . .

3. Failure to renew the Motion to Change Venue . . .

4. Failure to Interrogate Juror David Graham . . .

5. Failure to Argue that the Wiebold Statement was Obtained Involuntarily . . .

6. Failure to Determine Effects of Monitoring in Blue Earth County and Sacramento Jails . . .

7. Failure to Present Certain Favorable Evidence.[120]

That evening, approximately eight hours after the close of the trial, the jury brought in its verdict: "Guilty of murder in the first degree," and I was sentenced to life in prison.

I was told later that this verdict shocked many people in the courtroom and in the community. A *Mankato Free Press* editorial stated: "Clark is guilty, in the jury's considered judgment. This does not preclude the possibility that he isn't."[121]

Given time alone together before I was transported back to the jail, my wife and I just sat, holding hands and realizing our world, our future together, had come to an end.

But I wasn't giving up!

Part III

The Barbara Jiminez Case

Chapter 8: Imprisoned, Preparing for the Second Trial

Two days later, I transferred to the state prison. As the gate-rolls of iron bars-slammed behind me, the full reality of my situation fell to my shoulders. I was escorted down the main corridor, where more than 100 prisoners milled, their backs against the wall, some sitting on the floor with outstretched legs. Apparently, there was little, if any, control at the prison; even the guards were oblivious to a prisoner screaming into another guard's face that he was going to kill him.

Along with the violence in the prison were the drugs. Drug pushers made daily rounds in the cell blocks without fear of guards busting them; the guards would rather quit their jobs than run the risk of walking the upper galleries. The pushers were always on the lookout for new customers, and they approached me many times. The sales pitch was that the drugs would allow me to deal with the nightmare of serving a life sentence while facing yet another murder trial. I had never used drugs, and I was not about to start, but so many others obviously did so to escape the realities of prison life.

While in the Blue Earth County jail awaiting the first trial, I had become acquainted with a man (whose name I can't recall) who had been in and out of prison several times, and who was about to be sent back to prison again. He said he had "connections" and that since I had communication skills (because of my business experience), he would help me get a good job if I should lose my case and end up in the state prison. When I arrived at the prison, he kept his word. I was assigned to the New Admissions Department, where I interviewed new arrivals. This proved a blessing in terms of being able to obtain information, including some helpful to my case.

A guard in charge of the Identification Section, where the new prisoners were photographed, showed me an antique camera. He pointed to an autograph scratched on its varnished surface. The signature was that of Cole Younger of the infamous Younger Gang, who along with the Jesse James Gang failed an attempt to rob the Northfield Bank in the late 1800s. The Younger brothers saved themselves from the gallows by pleading guilty and received life sentences. Bob and James Younger died in prison, and Cole Younger died in 1916, about 15 years after his release. The guard also showed me an old roster that had Cole Younger's name on it. A couple of entries below Younger's name was that of another Ed Clark.

One of the newly admitted prisoners, who shall remain unidentified, knew of the goings-on in Mankato. He told me that certain persons with political connections who were living in the Mankato area wanted me found guilty because of the tremendous amount of publicity in Minnesota and the surrounding states, about the deaths of the Jiminezes. He said that the murder cases were putting the spotlight on Mankato, which could interfere with Mankato's illegal drug operations and fraudulent real-estate dealings in the Southwest. He said the operation was so big that certain people in the legal and law enforcement professions were on the payroll. His information is supported by the articles quoted in chapter 2 and in another article published later about a former Mankato high-school principal who pleaded guilty in Arizona to a million-dollar-plus land-fraud scheme. Considering the salary of a high-school principal in 1974, the reporter raised the question of how he would have the capital to pull off such a scheme, unless he was just a front man. I asked the man why he was volunteering this information. His response was that he was absolutely sure I was not guilty.

My notoriety continued in Mankato, even after I was sent to prison. One business capitalized on it in an advertisement appearing about December 1974 in the *Mankato Free Press*:

> ED ESCAPED from his old worn out office chair when he was given a comfortable new chair from Paul's enterprises on Hwy. 22. We have IN STOCK over 1,000 chairs for you to choose from. Extra hours 'til Christmas: MON. & THUR. 7-9 P.M., SAT 9-5.

My wife told me that neither she nor my mother had been reimbursed for their traveling expenses to Minnesota. Witnesses providing alibi evidence in cases where a public defender represents the defendant are entitled to reimbursement. The prosecuting attorney steadfastly refused to authorize payment-until the state agency that investigates prisoner complaints of a legal nature (Legal Assistance to Minnesota Prisoners, or LAMP) threatened to take him to court if he did not do so.

Public Defender Richard Genty, who had been assigned to represent me in the second trial and tried to convince me to plead guilty, had a reputation with those in the prison for doing so. Other prisoners who had the misfortune of his representation complained that he had convinced them to plead guilty on the premise of receiving a lighter sentence. Later, they discovered that their sentences were the same as if a jury had convicted them.

As I was still facing the murder trial in the death of Barbara Jiminez, Genty showed up at the person, again trying to get me to plead guilty. He claimed there was a way out of my dilemma, that the prosecuting attorney and the judge would show their appreciation for avoiding the expense of a trial. The "deal" was that if I pleaded guilty-under the guise of my having a "split personality" and thus not knowing what I was doing at the time of the murder-the authorities would send me to the state mental hospital, and I would get out in a couple of years.

Seeing through this, I calmly asked, "What about the life sentence I'm now serving?"

"Oh, that's another issue," Genty responded.

Shaking my head in disgust, I thought, "Why, you bastard."

I yelled at him, "Get the hell out of here!"

Most defendants, even when innocent, plead guilty under such circumstances rather than spend what could be the rest of their lives in prison, but even with the prospects of no better representation in the upcoming trial, and the jury knowing I had been convicted of the murder of Michael Jiminez, I was determined to have my day in court.

Seeking Competent Legal Representation

David A. Wood, a prominent San Francisco pathologist and lecturer whose son is married to my wife's (now ex-wife's) sister, showed an interest in my case. In an attempt to interest a private attorney in taking my case, Dr. Wood wrote to well-known criminal attorneys in the Twin Cities area. He forwarded to me a copy of his letter and the responses from the attorneys. Dr. Wood's letter concluded:

> Convictions on circumstantial evidence have been especially distressful to me since my experience with two cases while I was on the faculty at Stanford and responsible for several quarterly lectures to senior medical students on medical jurisprudence. The only thing in common with the Clark case is that of circumstantial evidence. In each the latter was "strong" and due process of law had taken place, *including autopsies by locally appointed coroner's physicians*. Special dispensation in each case was allowed, with repetition of the autopsies by me. *Not only had the former been mediocre and misleading but completely wrong. Each victim of the accused was shown conclusively to have died of natural causes.* For a number of years I cited these two cases in lectures to my students. [Emphasis added here and in subsequent quotes in this chapter.][122]

Supporting my experience with the representation I received in

Mankato and that facing me in the upcoming trial, one attorney's response included this opinion:

> Many times, circumstantial cases are the most difficult to defend against, because there is no one to cross-examine and there is no obvious motivation on the part of any witness which could cast doubts on their testimony; however, it's also very common that the *public defenders are not terribly experienced in small counties* [as] they may be the youngest men available who are willing to work for less than experienced lawyers, and because *they appear in court frequently and represent the least meritorious cases, they may lose some of their credibility to the juries and the court, and they may not be anxious to present as forceful a case against the district attorney, their usual opponent.*[123]

In each of their responses, the attorneys mentioned the requirement of a substantial retainer fee, which I didn't have. Considering the amount of time any of them might have to invest in my case, I understood their position.

I had only one chance. I notified the media in the Twin Cities metro area that I was willing to be interviewed. Here I was, serving a life sentence for first-degree murder and facing another murder trial. The newspapers and radio and television stations were interested! At the ensuing press conference at the state prison, I declared my innocence, saying that I had neither the opportunity nor the motive to commit the murders. To pay for the services of a private attorney, I was asking for private donations. "The public defender is nothing more than the right arm of the prosecution . . . the average citizen cannot afford the services of a good lawyer and for [a proper] investigation," I said.

Criticizing the judicial system, I would discover, is not a wise thing to do. This cost me dearly in the second trial, and likely affected my appeal process as well.

The press conference was big news on television, radio, and on the front page of the Twin Cities' newspapers.[124] The *Mankato Free Press*, however, wasn't satisfied with the content of the interview, and with an imaginary quote dramatized my imprisonment in an article titled: "I'm living with This Every Day."

Radio KTOB in Mankato erroneously reported: "Edward Clark held a news conference and stated to the press that he was in Mankato the day Michael Jiminez was killed, just as he stated during the trial."[125] The minister's wife (the one who had befriended my family and sat through the trial) complained to the station about this false reporting and the effect it could have on my family. The announcer responded, "He doesn't have a family." The station did, however, retract its earlier statement.

Prison officials had tried to cancel my press conference after the media arrived, as they thought I might have contacted the media to complain about prison conditions, but when the reporters told the prison administrators they would obtain a court order if necessary, the officials backed down. As the interview was conducted behind a closed door, members of the prison administration, including its high-ranking officers, occasionally peered in, apparently concerned about what I might be telling the media. The fact that reporters had come into the prison created a thick tension among prison officials, which made my life a bit more difficult in the days following. So I wrote to the administration, saying that the sole purpose of the press conference was resolution of my case. This relieved the tension.

I received some private donations to defend my case but not nearly enough to pay all the legal expenses involved. My interview with the media did, however, impress one private law firm. Attorney John Wylde took my case and told me not to be concerned about paying the balance. Over a period of time, however, I did pay my benefactors. I had initiated the press conference but probably would not have caught any media or public attention if this had not been the biggest murder case Minnesota had experience in many years.

"He's Going to Kill Me!"

I turned over to my attorney a letter from the minister's wife stating that a member of the church who was upset about my first conviction had approached her. The woman said that her sister and nephew, who owned a farm in Le Sueur County, were positive that Barbara Jiminez had run up to their farm one night before the discovery of her body, yelling, "He's going to kill me. He's going to kill me."

Barbara Jiminez asked to use their phone and call a number in the St. Peter area, a short distance from the farm. Both the woman and her son got a good look at the man who drove up to collect Jiminez. They said he "positively was not Edward Clark," as they had seen photos of me in the newspaper and on television. They also said that the man who picked her up was younger than I. Attorney Wylde and his investigator interviewed the woman and her son, but over time they became increasingly apprehensive about testifying at the trial. Were they pressured into keeping quiet?

My defense attorney also placed a notice in the *Mankato Free Press* listing an 800-number, asking for information regarding the Jiminez slayings. An anonymous caller said an informer named Robert McCumber knew the Jiminezes and the details surrounding their deaths.

Several fellow prisoners familiar with the Mankato drug scene had mentioned McCumber. The investigator for the defense, who traveled to Mankato to find him, said that McCumber was coincidentally under arrest, and he remained in jail until the investigator left town. About a year later, McCumber, 28, was murdered, "found floating in the Minnesota River . . . He too was suspected of being an informer. Sheriff LeRoy Wiebold and his and his men are proceeding with the investigation . . . Wiebold is declining to release any details surrounding the matter."[126]

The sheriff's "declining to release any details" about McCumber's death contrasted with his earlier position of keeping the media informed on all aspects of the case regarding the Jiminezes. McCumber's murder went unsolved, like so many others.

Hypnosis

Without notice, my defense attorney's investigator showed up at the prison with Robert Bailey, head of the Sociology Department of the University of Wisconsin-River Falls. As a Fulbright scholar, Bailey had studied hypnosis in pursuit of his doctoral dissertation at the University of Utrecht in The Netherlands. It was explained to me that Bailey wanted to hypnotize me in hopes that more information about the hitchhikers and the events subsequent to picking them up would surface from my subconscious.

Before the first trial, I didn't imagine I would need more evidence of my not being in Minnesota at the time of the murder of Michael Jiminez. My wife and mother had testified as to the time I arrived back in Michigan, and there were phone company records documenting the call I placed to my wife from Belvidere, Illinois, which occurred at the time of the sighting of the Jiminez couple at the café in Iowa. Through hypnotic suggestion, I was able to put everything out of my mind and concentrate on whatever was asked. This included a description of the third hitchhiker, which I had been unable to remember before, as well as specific details of my movements from the time I picked up the hitchhikers until I arrived home.

I recalled that as I neared Detroit, I gave assistance to the drivers of two cars parked on the shoulder of the expressway. One of the vehicles had run out of gas, and I supplied a couple of gallons so they could drive to a service station. I recalled that the cars had California license plates and that I mentioned to the young men that I also had driven from the West Coast. They said they made the trip for the purpose of trading their older model cars for new or later models. This was not surprising, as Detroit, the "Motor Capital", had an abundance of used-car lots and dealerships. The competition there resulted in lower purchase prices for new cars, and by driving the cars back to the West Coast, they could save transport charges as well.

Under hypnosis, I relived the feeling of exhaustion I had had after driving 1,600 miles in 34 hours, as well as my frustration with my former partners' lawsuit and my concern at being away from my family so long.

Still, after this hypnotic experience, I had the most restful sleep of my life. It couldn't have come at a better time, as I had felt little but anxiety since my arrest.

As I was also able to describe (under hypnosis) the vehicles of the men I had assisted, some inmates working in the prison print shop prepared a flyer for me to send to friends in Michigan-to distribute to dealerships and used-car lots in the Detroit metro area. The title on the flyer read: "An Innocent Man Serving Life in Prison Needs Information You May Have That Could Free Him."

But nearly a year had gone by since I encountered the stranded motorists, and it was impossible to contact every dealership. There was no response, so my attorney petitioned the court for funds to cover the expense of his investigator traveling to Lansing, Michigan, to search the records of the Department of Motor Vehicles. According to my defense attorney, the judge-John M. Fitzgerald, who would preside over my second trial-refused to authorize the funds.

Following the second trial, an interview with Bailey appeared in the (Stillwater, Minnesota) *Prison Mirror:*

Bailey a Hypnotic Personality

> Bailey hypnotized Clark at Stillwater State Prison before the second trial and was convinced that Clark was telling the truth when he told the jury at his first trial that he picked up three hitchhikers near Des Moines, Iowa . . . Although experts agree that it is possible to lie under hypnosis, Bailey said that due to Clark's behavior under hypnosis he thinks Clark was telling the truth.
>
> "Clark was so deeply under hypnosis that he was reliving the actual experience," Bailey said. "The thing that was so dramatic about it was his intense emotional reaction."

Bailey's belief in Clark's story was also supported by the fact that Clark spoke in the present tense throughout the session. Also, Clark showed little emotion when talking about the hitchhikers.[127]

My attorney wanted Bailey to testify at the upcoming trial, but the judge ruled his testimony was inadmissible. Other articles on the hypnosis session were: "Convicted Killer Denies Crimes under Hypnosis"[128] and, in Mankato, "Clark Denies Killing Couple in Hypnosis".[129]

Although I never had any direct communication with Bailey other than in my hypnosis session, eight years later he sent me a copy of a letter he mailed to the TV program *Lie Detector*, hosted by defense attorney F. Lee Bailey. The body of the letter reads, in entirety:

> I called on you Wednesday, March 30. Here is more information on the Edward R. Clark case. I am convinced of his innocence. Any consideration will be appreciated. Ed Clark would be agreeable to a lie detector test.[130]

But the program was canceled soon thereafter, even though it reportedly had a growing number of viewers. Perhaps the program was too successful in revealing that there are innocent people in prison!

Fingerprint Identification

One of my duties as prison admissions clerk was to file FBI criminal history or "rap" sheets, which confirmed my belief that unknown persons may be identified through fingerprints. In many cases, rap sheets on an individual show that a person, when arrested, has used another name or alias, sometimes many, sometimes across the country. So the assistant identification officer with the crime lab, who said he had to have a name to crosscheck prints (specifically the ones on the trash box I discarded) with those on file, must have been lying!

In an attempt to find a rebuttal witness to the prosecution's witness for the second trial, I called detective agencies in the Twin Cities (Minneapolis and St. Paul). One agency's investigator, previously a fingerprint identification expert with the Minneapolis Police Department, confirmed my belief that a name was not necessary to identify fingerprints, but he said he would not testify because he feared his license might be revoked or turned down for renewal by the state.

Chapter 9: Eavesdropping - Motion to Dismiss

In working on my case, I interviewed a new prisoner in Stillwater, who looked familiar. He had been a trustee (janitor) at the jail in Mankato, while I was imprisoned there. The prisoner, Richard Severson, asked me a question: "Mr. Clark, did you know they were tape-recording your conversation in the jail?"

Recording the conversations of a suspect with his attorney provides an unfair advantage to the police and the prosecution in allowing them knowledge of evidence that may prove the accused is innocent (and which they might then suppress). So, in 1968 Congress passed the Title III Omnibus Crime Control and Safe Streets Act.[131] In part this made it unconstitutional to eavesdrop on attorney/client communication without a court order. If the recordings were available, they would show that Sheriff Wiebold was lying when he testified that I said Barbara Jiminez "was not raped". (With this false statement, he implied that I knew the circumstances surrounding her death.)

What Severson told me is only hearsay evidence on its own. But after the initial interview, I recorded Severson in a question-and-answer interview. From that recording, I prepared the following statement, which he then signed:

I state that during my incarceration at the Blue Earth county jail in Mankato, and I served in the capacity of head trustee, that I observed the following:

That Edward R. Clark was incarcerated in the section known as "maximum-south" in isolation and that a tape recorder was hooked up to the P.A. system for the purpose of recording all conversations that Mr. Clark had with any visitors.

That Mr. Clark was visited by his attorney and members of his attorney's staff.

That the deputies were instructed to rewind the tape every eight hours during the shift-change if he had not had any visitors. And to replace the tape with a fresh one if conversations had been recorded.

That I observed the following deputies playing, rewinding, and changing the tapes: Deputies Bob Pulis, Joe Hauer, Pat Gimble, Pat McGinnis, and another deputy by the first name of Rick.

I further state that the tape recorder is located inside the control booth, just to the right of the door inside of a cabinet.

I swear that this statement is true and that I will testify to it in a court of law. I have signed this statement the 9th of April, 1975.

I transcribed the recordings, and along with Severson's signed statement, mailed it to my attorney. Attorney Wylde moved to dismiss the indictment to the Barbara Jiminez case based on illegal eavesdropping on attorney-client conferences. Severson, another prisoner who had information on the eavesdropping, and I were transported to the courthouse for a hearing on Wylde's motion.[132]

Le Sueur County Deputy Sheriff Pat Smith, escorting me, noticed Blue Earth County Sheriff Wiebold and BCA Agent Simonson entering the courthouse and commented to me that the sheriff looked worn out. Deputy Smith said the Blue Earth County sheriff took a vacation following my conviction in that county. It was obvious to me that if the judge ruled to dismiss the indictment because of the sheriff's illegal eavesdropping, the fallout would land on Sheriff Wiebold's shoulders.

The only person in the courtroom who wasn't connected with the proceedings was reporter Lynn Closway from the *Mankato Free Press*. The judge took her into his chambers. Twenty minutes later she reappeared. Walking past me, she said in a low tone, "He's kicking me out."

This wasn't a good sign. The judge apparently wanted to avoid public attention and controversy about whether he granted the motion to dismiss the indictment in this high-profile case. A conviction had already been obtained in the Michael Jiminez case; dismissing the indictment would bring that verdict into question.

Under the headline, "Clark's Pre-Trial Hearing Closed", the -reporter's article stated:

> The hearing was to consider a pre-trial motion on matters concerning Clark's confinement in the Blue Earth County Law Enforcement Center in Mankato. Judge Fitzgerald told the press that he may enforce the "gag rule" throughout the entire duration of the trial. He noted the amount of the pre-trial publicity would make jury selection difficult and there is the possibility he would have to consider sequestering not only the jurors, but the entire pool of some 60 prospective jurors.[133]

Actually, if any jury were sequestered, it should have been the one at the first trial in Mankato that was so exposed to outside pressure and harassment, but it wouldn't happen now, either, due to its potential cost to the county.

At the hearing on the motion to dismiss because of eavesdropping, Severson took the witness stand and defense attorney Wylde questioned him, in part:

Defense:

> While you were a prisoner or inmate in the Blue Earth jail, did you see any evidence of eavesdropping by the Sheriff's Department..?

Severson:

> Just tape recording.

Defense:

> Would you describe the circumstances under which you saw these tape recordings?

Severson:

> Well, one of the deputies-I was making too much noise or something in the hallway-and one of the deputies asked me if I would keep the noise down because they were recording into one of the cells at that time.

Defense:

> Now, at the time that this statement was made to you by the deputy, did you see a tape recording? A tape recorder, I should say.

Severson:

> Yes, I did.

Defense:

> And where was that?

Severson:

> It's contained in the cabinet. As you walk in the control booth, it is on the right-hand side.

Defense:

> And did this happen on more than one occasion?

Severson:

> Well, they were taping as far as I could make out for two or three days.

Defense:

> You saw them operating the tape recorder?

Severson:

> Right. Rewinding and opening the door and shutting it.

Defense:

> Now, at any time were you aware that any activity or conversation that Mr. Clark was having with someone was being taped?

Severson:

> Yes. I was told that that is what the tape recording was for. It was for Mr. Clark . . .

Defense:

> Did you hear someone listening to a conversation of Mr. Clark?

Severson:

> Yes, I did.

Defense:

> And how did you hear the sound, the conversation? How did that come into the control booth?

Severson:

> I came in to ask a question, and the deputy had the . . . system on from one of the conference rooms with Mr. Clark in with somebody else at that time, and told me not

to bother him at that time.

Defense:

Did you actually hear, then, a conversation coming from one of the conference rooms?

Severson:

Yes, I did.

. . .

Defense:

Did you know for a fact that one of the voices belonged to Edward Clark?

Severson:

Yes, I do.

. . .

Defense:

Now, were you told of any particular misconduct or misbehavior on your part that caused your status as a trustee to be terminated?

Severson:

I was told by one deputy it was because I knew too much that was going on out there and that I shouldn't have known.

Defense:

Did you have occasion to visit with lawyers and different people in the different rooms yourself?

Severson:

Yes, I have.

Defense:

>Are those rooms equipped with this speaking device that you are aware of?

Severson:

>Yes.

Defense:

>When Mr. Clark was in max south, were there any other prisoners there with him?

Severson:

>No.[134]

On cross-examination, the county attorney, Christian who would be the prosecutor in the upcoming trial, asked Severson:

Prosecutor:

>Who was the deputy that told you Mr. Clark's conversation was being taped?

Severson:

>Robert Pulis.

Prosecutor:

>And who was the deputy that told you the reason you are being transferred is because you knew too much?

Severson:

>Pat Gemlo.

Next to testify was Stanley Young, the other inmate from the state prison. Defense attorney Wylde, questioned him, in part:

Defense:

>Mr. Young, at sometime during 1974 were you an

inmate in the Blue Earth County jail? Or, I guess they call it the Law Enforcement Center.

Young:

    Yes.

    . . .

Defense:

    Now, while you were in the Blue Earth County jail, did you know Mr. Edward Clark?

Young:

    Yes, I had met him twice . . .

Defense:

    Now, Mr. Young, during the time that you were an inmate there, did you see any evidence in the control room of taping, tape recording?

Young:

    Well, there has been times that there has been comments come back.

Defense:

    Such as?

Young:

    Well, one incident, this one inmate had a remark that he was told and it comes back through a deputy-in fact, come through two of them-that his conversation with his lawyer was being taped about making a plea bargain.

Defense:

    Apparently the inmate was talking about plea bargain with his lawyer?

Young:

> Right.

Defense attorney Wylde then addressed the court, stating in part that the evidence he submitted was sufficient to require the prosecution to present evidence to the contrary.

Prosecutor Christian argued that any eavesdropping in the Blue Earth County jail had no bearing on the charges against me in Le Sueur County, but Wylde reminded the judge that the statement allegedly made by me in the presence of Sheriff Wiebold regarding circumstances surrounding the death of Barbara Jiminez was to be introduced in this trial too, and that if the incident was recorded, I was supposed to receive a copy for my review and signature.

Defense attorney Wylde further stated: "I have learned to become a little more paranoid about some of these matters, and I would submit, Your Honor, that if this court should see a basis for concluding that there may be a potential surreptitious eavesdropping going on in the law enforcement facility which could involve this defendant, that that is a matter worth exploring."

The judge asked prosecutor Christian whether he had anything to say on this matter.

With indifference, Christian said, "No."

The judge then said: "On the point before the court, all I have here is a statement as far as witnesses on behalf of the defense. Aren't there going to be any witnesses called on behalf of the state?"

Again, with indifference, the prosecutor responded: "I have no intention of calling anybody. We have no statement that we are relying upon."

Attempting to impress upon the prosecutor the consequences for not presenting evidence in rebuttal and the precarious position that put the judge in if he had to rule in favor of the defense motion, the judge said: "I am not talking about that. We are talking about the tape recordings. Is anybody going to be testifying as to whether or not there was any tape recording going on down there?"

The prosecutor, anticipating that the judge would deny the defense motion anyway, responded: "Well, apparently that is what he is asking, Your Honor, for you to order us to make some kind of a showing of proof. It's not my position that we have to make that."

The judge said: "Well, I am sitting here with evidence introduced on behalf of the defendant to the effect that there was a tape recording going on down there in the jail. That is all I have got, period. I have also got a motion to dismiss the indictment because inferentially the court is supposed to determine that tape recording was being done of conversations Mr. Clark was having with his lawyer. The evidence before the court doesn't show that, but it certainly does show and it is going unrebutted that there was tape recording going on down in that jail. This is the way the prosecutor wants to leave this record?"

Obstinately the prosecutor responded: "Well, I don't want to leave the record in any sense, Your Honor. It's my understanding that counsel for the defense has asked the court to make an order. I think the record should reflect that the sheriff of Blue Earth County is here and the defense can call him and ask him questions if they want. I'll be glad to call him for what it's worth."

The judge encouraged the prosecutor: "I think before you do that, I think the record should show that as far as the court is concerned, that is the position that I am taking. I don't see how I can possibly rule intelligently on this motion without having some testimony regarding what the position of the state is with regard to whether there was tape recording going on, so I am so ordering. Go ahead."

Sheriff Wiebold took the stand, and on the question of the recording equipment, he responded: "Yes, there is recording equipment in the jail . . . It would be located in the jailer's cubicle. We have video recording equipment which sits on the jailer's desk area . . . counter area, and then there are two tape recorders housed in the cabinet area . . . of the jailer's cubicle. One is capable of recording third-floor jail."

There was more:

Prosecutor:

> Now, concerning Mr. Clark, Edward Clark, do you have any tape recordings of conversations that he made while he was a prisoner in the jail?

Wiebold:

> I do not.

Prosecutor:

> Were there ever any tape recordings of Mr. Clark?

Wiebold:

> To my knowledge, I don't know. I am not on that floor all the time so I couldn't say. The men are required to be trained with the recording. I don't know what they record. It's not used.

Prosecutor:

> Were any tape recordings ever played to you of Mr. Clark?

Wiebold:

> No.

During defense attorney Wylde's cross-examination, Sheriff Wiebold continued to give false testimony:

Defense:

> Sheriff, I assume, then, your testimony would be that you personally have never heard any tape recordings of any conversations between Mr. Clark and anybody else, is this correct?

Wiebold:

That's correct.

Defense:

Now, it is true, is it not, Sheriff, that you, in cooperation with law enforcement agencies in the state, such as the Bureau of Criminal Apprehension and the Mankato Police Department, have used your taping equipment to record statements given by suspects to police officers, have you not?

Wiebold:

Not that equipment, no sir. It's too unreliable.

Defense:

Have any of your deputies told you they made tape recordings of Mr. Clark's conversations with anybody?

Wiebold:

No, they haven't.

Defense:

There are three rooms, A, B, and C rooms, which are used for visiting rooms, is that correct?

Wiebold:

Those are conference rooms, yes [for interrogation and client-attorney conferences].

Defense:

Are there monitoring devices in those rooms?

Wiebold:

There are. There is no place on third floor that cannot be monitored.

Defense:

Where are they located in A, B, and C rooms?

Wiebold:

> A, B, and C rooms are one-way monitors only, and they are located in the ceiling . . . it's not a big room, it's like a little broom closet . . . in the upper right-hand corner.

In other words, it was a one-way system (to avoid detection) in the conference rooms where communications between the attorney and the client were expected to be privileged. The rest of the jail had a two-way P.A. system, though attorneys also held conferences with clients in their cells.

Defense:

> Did you give any special instructions with regard to any special security precautions for maximum south when Mr. Clark…

Wiebold:

> Oh, yes.

Defense:

> Such as?

Wiebold:

> This is during the time when the grand jury was bringing their indictment. Mr. Clark became very distraught, and I feared that he might try and do something foolish.

Defense:

> Other than that period of time, did you have any special instructions with regard to Mr. Clark?

Wiebold:

> No, Mr. Clark never gave us any problems after that.

Defense:

> Mr. Clark was alone in maximum south most of the time, wasn't he?

Wiebold:

> Not all the time. I can't recall for sure, Counsel, how much of the time he was alone. It was his desire to be alone.

Defense:

> When he was alone in maximum south, would it be the policy of the jail to give him his attorney visits in maximum south?

Wiebold:

> That would depend, you know, upon circumstances.

Defense:

> There was no fixed policy?

Wiebold:

> No. A lot of it is left up to the attorney, where he wants to visit.

Then the judge asked questions of Sheriff Wiebold:

Judge:

> Sheriff, you say A, B, and C, they're visiting rooms?

Wiebold:

> Conference rooms.

Judge:

> Yes, conference rooms. You say from the P.A. system was a one-way system?

Wiebold:

> Yes.

Judge:

> From the room back to the control room?

Wiebold:

> Correct, sir.

Judge:

> All right. If somebody wants to talk to the control room from the visiting room, they talk to the system and it would go down to the control room?

Wiebold:

> Yes, sir.

Judge:

> All right. The record will show that the matter is under advisement at this time, a decision will be made at a later date.

But given the judge's "later" ruling-dated the day of the hearing-and the judge's prodding of the prosecutor to provide rebuttal testimony, his decision to deny the motion for dismissal was a foregone conclusion.

In a short memo attached to his ruling, the judge stated: "At the very most, the evidence indicates that sound-monitoring devices were used in the Blue Earth County Jail for security purposes in areas where defendant was incarcerated and in the area of conference rooms A, B, and C, where he on occasion did have discussions with his attorneys. There was no evidence to indicate that these conversations were taped by anyone in the sheriff's office or that any information acquired by the sound monitoring of these areas would be used in the trial of the defendant for the charges involved in this case."

Courts in other states have dismissed indictments and overturned convictions, not simply because evidence presented at trial was the result of eavesdropping into attorney-client conferences, but because it gave the prosecution an unfair advantage to learn the defense's strategy and thus withhold relevant evidence.

The judge did, however, order the sheriff to disconnect monitoring capabilities in conference rooms A, B, and C, and other areas of the jail where attorneys met with their clients, thus indicating he was concerned that the illegal eavesdropping, if continued, could jeopardize future cases.

Eavesdropping on attorney-client conversations is not commonly exposed. My case was the first, perhaps is still the only case, in Minnesota, in which this has been raised as an argument to appeal a conviction. So after the trials, I researched past cases as well and filed a civil lawsuit against the county and the sheriff (*Edward R. Clark vs. County of Blue Earth and LeRoy Wiebold, Sheriff of Blue Earth County*). Newspaper articles about the lawsuit included: "Clark Says Sheriff Listened In", "Police Eavesdropped on Talks, Convict Says", and "Convicted Slayer Claims His Talks with Lawyer Bugged".[135] The civil attorney representing me, however, filed the suit in the state district court in Mankato, rather than in federal court. So the lawsuit was eventually dismissed.

Filing a lawsuit did provide the means to obtain additional evidence of the eavesdropping, including photographs showing that microphones were concealed by recessing them in the ceilings in the conference rooms designated for attorney-client conferences. This sophisticated recording system was introduced as evidence at my appellate hearings.[136]

At the first appellate hearing following the second trial, because of the evidence I had obtained, as well as my firsthand experience of court procedures. I made a motion, and it was granted, that I function as co-counsel. I moved that the subpoenaed sheriff and his deputies be sequestered so that they could not hear each other's testimony. This resulted in the deputies contradicting one another as well as the sheriff, who claimed he wasn't aware of the eavesdropping or of the fact that the tapes were turned over to him. While one deputy claimed that the tape recorder didn't work, another said they were free to use the recorder as they chose.[137]

So at the pretrial hearing on the motion to dismiss the indictment, had my trial attorney (Wylde) subpoenaed the deputies and had them as well as the sheriff sequestered, their testimony would have shown that the sheriff had full knowledge of the tape recording, that it was conducted under his directive, and that the tapes were turned over to him, thus impeaching him. This came out only after my second trial for murder. Otherwise the judge would not have been able to rule that there was no evidence to show conversations were taped.

Public Defender Adamson, who represented me in the first trial, testified at the appellate hearings that our conferences took place in the monitored areas and that we discussed trial tactics, witnesses, and basic theories of the case. (He exaggerated by claiming he discussed trial tactics with me.) He further admitted that he knew our conversations could be monitored but that he didn't forewarn me. Adamson reluctantly gave up this information because his failure to provide competent representation could (and would) be used as an argument on appeal. His admission wasn't revealed in the *Mankato Free Press*. Instead, the *Press's* article regarding the hearing was titled "Attorney Says No Eavesdropping Occurred".[138]

Despite the trial judge's ruling at the pretrial hearing that attorneys were to meet with clients only in unmonitored areas, I learned that the eavesdropping continued. After the trial and before the appellate hearings, I made a formal complaint to the Minnesota Department of Corrections, which oversees the jails in the state. The department's director of inspection and enforcement testified during the appellate hearing that he still found monitoring capability in the rooms used for attorney-client contact. He told the sheriff that he objected to it and pointed out that jail standards clearly prohibited it.[139]

The Department of Corrections' written response to my complaint was also introduced into evidence. It acknowledged in part:

> We do concur it was inappropriate to have this device in the interview area where confidential business was held. . .As of January 5, 1977, the practice has been

discontinued and all attorney-client visits or conferences will be conducted in unmonitored conference rooms.[140]

Another letter I introduced was from the Office of the Attorney General (of Minnesota). It was a response to my sending a copy of the Department of Corrections letter to that agency:

> I certainly do concur with Commissioner Schoen's assessment that it was inappropriate to monitor confidential matters such as conversations between an attorney and his client. According to the commissioner's letter to you, steps have been taken to ensure that these practices have been properly discontinued.[141]

Despite the attorney general's acknowledgement that it was "inappropriate to monitor confidential matters such as conversations between an attorney and his client", the state law enforcement agency nevertheless opposed my effort to obtain relief through the courts.

Joseph Hauer, a deputy named by Richard Severson, did not testify. The Sheriff claimed he was sick. This made me suspicious, and the appellate attorney, Ronald Haskvitz, said he would obtain a deposition from Hauer. But he did not. A few years later, Hauer lost a Mankato mayor's election. Considering the politics of that situation, he may have found leaving the Sheriff's Department to be in his best interest.

I hired a private investigator to find Hauer, and the investigator obtained his signed statement, in part:

> When Ed Clark was transferred to cell 344 I was informed by Deputy Pat Gemlo that the recording of Ed Clark was to be continued . . . If Clark did say anything, the tape was to be saved and given to either Jerry Wersal or Sheriff Wiebold . . . When I first came to the Blue Earth County Sheriff's Office in September of 1973, I began working in the jail and was made aware of the taping devices as well as their specific use. This recording was also to be visual as well as audio to be used at the jailer's discretion.[142]

Now there was evidence (in addition to that introduced at the pretrial hearing for dismissal) that the conversations in my jail cell had been taped—and that the tapes should have been available to impeach the sheriff regarding his allegations about what I said upon indictment for the death of Barbara Jiminez. But absent this evidence for the second trial would Judge Fitzgerald conduct the proceedings from a neutral position? Or would he allow prosecutorial misconduct to deny me a fair trial?

Chapter 10: Pretrial Events

The trial in the death of Barbara Jiminez was moved from the remote farming area of Le Sueur County to Minneapolis-not to provide a fair trial in regard to publicity on the case but to accommodate the county by reducing transportation and lodging expenses for witnesses from afar.

I was housed in a unit of the jail having a flight of stairs leading to a loft. The jailer escorting me said the loft had been used to hang condemned prisoners when the state still had the death penalty. The last hanging was botched-the rope was too long, so the prisoner was able to stand on his tiptoes. Deputies were instructed to grab his legs and pull down on him until he finally strangled to death. A reporter covering the hanging described the horrific scene-it took 14 minutes to end the man's life. Minnesota then abolished the death penalty.

The prisoners in my unit of the jail included an elderly derelict who was pleasant when sober. He said that when he drank he became violent and that he had spent most of his life on skid row or in jail.

Another prisoner, the hard-core career type with a temper to match, awaited transfer to a federal prison. As hard as he was, he also showed a fatherly instinct, protecting an 18-year-old at the jail who had never been in trouble before. As the protector was transferred, he asked me to "keep an eye on the kid [who had boyish features] so he wouldn't be victimized by the deviates".

The young man said he had been sexually abused by his father through his adolescent life and that his mother had divorced his father when she discovered the abuse. The charge against the young man was molesting a girl he had been babysitting. Having been in prison for nearly a year on my first conviction, I was aware of the hatred exhibited by other prisoners towards sex offenders, especially child molesters. Most of this resentment is because the majority of sex offenders show no remorse about ruining the lives of their victims. This may seem hypocritical of those incarcerated for more serious crimes, including murder, but most prisoners also have loved ones, including children.

This kid was different-I could understand why the girl's mother was willing to drop the charges if he received therapy. The problem, though, was that he was represented by a public defender who apparently was interested only in quick closure of the case. The young man said his mother had heart problems, so he didn't want to let her know the trouble he was in. I suggested she would better hear it from him than from strangers, so he asked me to phone her. I broke the news to her gently and told her he needed a private attorney. I didn't tell her who I was. She might have gone into cardiac arrest knowing that her son was confined with someone convicted of one murder and about to go on trial for another.

The boy's grandmother knew about his arrest and wanted to visit her grandson, but he was too ashamed to see her. I talked him into letting her visit, explaining that she must love him very much and wanted to help- and that refusing to see her was selfish as there was no way of knowing how much longer his grandmother would be around.

I became aware that the cells were monitored for sound when I advised a foul-smelling prisoner to take a shower before he got some unwanted assistance. A deputy appeared, ordering him to gather his belongings for his removal to another area of the complex.

The trial took place in July, in a courtroom uncomfortable for the jury.

As reported in the *Mankato Free Press*: "The trial is in a relatively small, modest courtroom in the old Hennepin County Courthouse. There is no central air-conditioning, and during breaks the judge has ordered that both the portable air-conditioning and a fan be kept running."[143]

Among the spectators was the minister's wife from Mankato, along with the woman in their congregation who had been upset about my conviction in the first trial. Her sister and nephew owned the farm home in Le Sueur County that Barbara Jiminez had run to when she was missing after her husband's murder-from there she made a phone call, after which a man-obviously not I-picked her up.

Before the jury was brought in, defense attorney Wylde moved to have the witnesses sequestered before giving testimony, as my court appointed attorney should have done in the first trial. Judge Fitzgerald's instructions to the second jury concluded with what should also have been required in the Mankato trial:

> Now, there is another thing, and that is the matter of reading about the case during the trial . . . or listening on the radio or the television about the trial and what goes on. This trial is open . . . anyone who wishes can come in and sit in on the trial, see what's going on . . . You are getting firsthand what happens in the trial right here in the courtroom . . . There is no reason why you should read about it or you should listen to anybody talk about what happened in the courtroom . . .
>
> Maybe what you read, maybe what you hear, maybe what you see outside of the courtroom isn't a fact, isn't what happened, is something that somebody concluded happened in the courtroom. That is why I am . . . directing you not to listen to anybody talk about it, either on the radio, television or read about it in the paper, or listen to anybody talk about it to you or in your presence. If you folks were on trial, that is what you would be entitled to, and that is what you would want. Both the State and the defense are entitled to no less from you, so please keep

that in mind.

I am not going to go into this speech in its detail every time, but I am going to touch on the high points every time that we stand in recess, so keep it in mind.[144]

Chapter 11: The Case for the Prosecution

The judge noticed the prosecutor fumbling conspicuously with an assortment of colored photos of the dead bodies so that members of the jury could see them from where they sat. The judge announced, "The jury will stay in the box. I will see the counsel in chambers."

In chambers, defense attorney Wylde argued against introduction of the photos into evidence, that it showed "the body of Barbara Jiminez in rather bloated discolored grotesque form". Among the photos were autopsy shots of the body of Michael Jiminez, despite this being the trial in the death of Barbara Jiminez.

The prosecutor responded that the photos "are not inflammatory" while admitting, "They might be, I suppose, I would have to concede they are, somewhat distasteful, but I do not believe that they are grotesque or inflammatory in the sense that would arouse the passion and prejudice of the jury. Further, it is the State's position that it is necessary to use the old adage 'one picture is worth a million words'."

Judge Fitzgerald ruled the photos admissible. The prosecutor then pushed for the inclusion of the photos showing a piece of skull and brain matter from the Blue Earth County crime scene. The judge ruled against introducing the additional photos at that time. He added: "Whether they come in or not, you were out there shuffling pictures before we came in here in chambers. They [the members of the jury] know you have a whole bunch of pictures."

After the noon recess, another meeting took place in chambers. Judge Fitzgerald stated for the record:

> After we came back from lunch . . . counsel for the State informed the court that Dr. Sanford was prepared to give certain testimony regarding the condition of the body, which would require the admission of additional pictures that the State had in its possession of the body in the lake-close-up pictures and rather inflammatory pictures in the mind of the court, certainly pictures that would be prejudicial to the defendant and would arouse the passion and prejudice in the minds of the jury, or at least this is the court's view of it.

The judge also asked my attorney for his argument in opposing the introduction of the addition photographs. Wylde stated:

> To summarize . . . I feel that they are extremely inflammatory and prejudicial. I do not see, frankly, what evidentiary value the pictures have over and above what the testimony that could be elicited would be.
>
> For example, assuming the foundation and the opinion with regard to sexual intercourse at some time as a result of what the autopsy reveals is the presence of semen of some strength or some degree in the vaginal cavity, the State, of course, wishing to demonstrate that the water could wash or had washed the vaginal area, which is graphically depicted in one of the pictures, I fail to see where the testimony couldn't be elicited that the body was in such a position that the water had access to the vaginal opening, as opposed to the graphic illustration in

the picture.

The prosecutor argued:

> I do feel that the pictures do have great probative value, and I certainly can't argue that they aren't distasteful to look at. On the other hand, I do not feel that they are that inflammatory, and like it as we may or may not in this particular case, that is a fact of life. I think that . . . we could have a witness three days to testify on what he observed, but one picture is worth all of that or more.

So the judge ruled that the prosecutor could introduce the photos, even though he himself had stated that they were certainly "pictures that would be prejudicial to the defendant and would arouse passion and prejudice in the minds of the jury".[145]

With no certainty as to what caused the death of Barbara Jiminez, Judge Fitzgerald allowed the prosecutor free rein to do as he pleased through most of the trial, rarely ruling against him. This included bringing in all the exhibits and witnesses for the State from the Michael Jiminez murder trial (with the exception of an expert witness whose testimony supported the defense). Included were the autopsy photos of Michael Jiminez.

The result was underscored when the conviction was appealed. Quoting the appellate attorney:

> The obvious problem that the court's ruling raised for trial counsel was indicated by [defense] attorney Wylde during the post-conviction proceedings. He testified that there was so much testimony concerning the death of Michael Jiminez, relating to time of death, manner of death, etc., that he was in effect trying two cases instead of one. In his opinion, the fact that the jury knew his client had been convicted in the death of Michael Jiminez was "an insurmountable obstacle".[146]

Along with hearing Judge Fitzgerald turn a deaf ear to defense attorney Wylde's arguments, the jurors no doubt viewed me as the cause of their discomfort throughout the trial. They were obviously irritated, sweltering in the heat for hours without hearing testimony.

The prosecutor arranged for the grieving father of Barbara Jiminez, a local resident, to sit in the front row after giving his testimony. Seated close to the jury, his continuous presence played on the jury's emotions.

Testimony for the Prosecution

Roger Schmidt was called to the stand. Schmidt testified, as he had in the trial at Mankato, that he discovered the body of Barbara Jiminez along the shoreline of Scotch Lake in Le Sueur County while trying out his new boat, and that he immediately drove into town and phoned the sheriff. On the sheriff's instructions, he returned to the lake to await the arrival of officers from the department.

Sheriff Pat Smith Sr. of Le Sueur County took the stand. He described Scotch Lake as Shallow, possibly seven to eight feet deep; it wasn't good for fishing and seldom was used by boaters. On a map of the county placed on an easel, he showed where the body was discovered. Through Sheriff Smith, some of the photos taken of the area were then introduced, with the sheriff stating that he was most interested in a particular set of tire tracks:

Sheriff Smith:

> There was tire tracks that were photographed in the area . . . where a car had driven in a mud hole . . .

Prosecutor:

> Showing you what has been marked as State's Exhibit H and State's Exhibit I, can you identify those?

Sheriff Smith:

> Yes, I can. These were pictures of dry tire tracks at the

crime scene that were made by a vehicle that had mud and snow tires on all four wheels.

Prosecutor:

And the pictures contain a picture of a tape measure in addition to the tracks themselves. Will you explain that?

Sheriff Smith:

Yes. This is a tape measure laying right in the tire track of this one picture.

Prosecutor:

Do the pictures-or, rather, the Exhibits H and I-correctly and accurately portray the tracks and the original process you observed on May 4, 1974, at the Scotch Lake scene?

Sheriff Smith:

They do.

While the prosecutor had the sheriff point to the location on the map where the body of Barbara Jiminez was discovered in Scotch Lake, he avoided asking him to point out where Barbara Jiminez's coat was discovered in another part of the county, below the Cannon River Bridge. I suspect the prosecutor was not sure whether defense counsel knew that Barbara Jiminez was observed in a café in Waseca. Since there is a direct route between the Cannon River Bridge and Waseca, that information would have supported the sighting of Barbara Jiminez in Waseca a couple of days after her husband was murdered.

Although unaware that Barbara Jiminez was seen in Waseca, defense attorney Wylde asked Sheriff Smith in cross-examination to mark on the map where the coat had been discovered. Wylde showed further that the tire-tracks photos were important:

Defense:

Now, in addition to the tire tracks that are depicted

in Exhibits H and I, the ones we were just talking about, there were several other tire tracks around here, too, which you didn't photograph, correct?

Sheriff Smith:

There were several other tire tracks, yes, sir.

Defense:

Did you assume that there was evidentiary value to the tracks, set of tracks that you did photograph?

Sheriff Smith:

I did.

Defense:

And I am sure that in directing this investigation, as the Sheriff of Le Sueur County, you asked these people to take the pictures they could. You asked them to concentrate on this, right?

Sheriff Smith:

Yes, I did.

With a tone of disappointment, Sheriff Smith revealed that he wanted plaster castings made of the tire tracks he considered to be evidence, but that none were made. Then:

Defense:

Sheriff, in your search, you found a lot of other items that you considered of evidentiary value that you sent to the BCA, didn't you, other than what you mentioned here?

Sheriff Smith:

We did.

The sheriff admitted that once the body of Barbara Jiminez was discovered, further investigation was minimal.[147]

Jo E. Anderson, a family physician in Le Sueur County, took the stand. Included in his testimony was the following:

Prosecutor:

> Directing your attention to the day of May 4th, of 1974, which I believe was a Saturday, did you have an occasion to be called to the Scotch Lake area to view the scene and the body of a young lady?

Dr. Anderson:

> Yes, I did. I was at an auction sale and was asked to stand in place of the coroner . . . to go with the ambulance, so I went to the scene with the Le Sueur volunteer ambulance.

Prosecutor:

> Now, perhaps, could you describe or give us your description of your observation of the body as you saw it?

Dr. Anderson:

> The body was laying face down in the water's edge and was partially exposed. There was no clothing on the body. It was obviously that of a woman, or a female. The skin of the upper portion of the body exposed from the water was in the process of decomposition and was partially separated from the body. The hair was lying, floating loosely in the water. The buttocks were raised in a half-crouched type of position.

Through Dr. Anderson, colored photographs of the body, which my attorney had argued in chambers were "inflammatory, prejudicial," and "grotesque", were introduced to the jury:

Prosecutor:

> Directing your attention to the exhibits that are before you . . . they obviously are in color and I believe they do show a discoloration or difference from that of a normal color of a Caucasian person. Do they accurately reflect the color?

Dr. Anderson:

> Yes, they do.

Prosecutor:

> So the skin was discolored, is that correct, especially in certain areas?

Dr. Anderson:

> Very much so.
>
> . . .

Prosecutor:

> Were you present when the autopsy was performed?

Dr. Anderson:

> Yes, I was.

Prosecutor:

> And when was it performed and by whom?

Dr. Anderson:

> It was performed later that afternoon . . . by Dr. Sanford, the coroner of Blue Earth County.
>
> . . .

Prosecutor:

> You have told us that the body as it laid there in the

lake was unclothed . . . Could you tell us what if any other observation you made at the scene or at the time of autopsy concerning, well, jewelry or the lack of it?

Dr. Anderson:

> Initially, before the body was removed from the water, the area on the back of the shoulders appeared to be decomposing and was a markedly different color, and I estimated or I assumed at this point that this was decomposition, air decomposition and sun decomposition . . . There was evidence of puncture wounds in the ear lobes, such as is present with pierced ears, but no jewelry was present. There was no jewelry on the fingers.

The prosecutor's questions then turned to a theory as to the cause of the death of Barbara Jiminez (whether she had drowned or been strangled was not determined, so he was trying to establish murder):

Prosecutor:

> Was there anything else exceptional or remarkable or noticeable about the visual inspection of the body than what you have told us?

Dr. Anderson:

> At the time that the body was placed on the autopsy table and examination was begun, it became apparent that there was across the neck a *braid* of hair which was tightly drawn across the neck and had not been previously apparent because of the position of the body.

Prosecutor:

> Showing you Doctor, what we have had marked as State's Exhibit GG, it is a picture, and I will ask you if that picture does depict the *braid* of hair that you referred to?

Dr. Anderson:

Yes, it does.

A physician, of all people, should know the difference between hair that is *braided* and a *strand* of hair. The prosecutor inadvertently corrected him:

Prosecutor:

> Now, Doctor, you have told us that prior to the time that you had the body, in the examining room at the hospital . . . you had not noticed this *strand* of hair around the neck, is that correct?

Dr. Anderson:

> That's correct.
>
> . . .

Prosecutor:

> Could you describe for us the . . . approximate length of the hair of the body?

Dr. Anderson:

> It was in the 14 to 16 inch length, I should think.

Prosecutor:

> Can you describe for us generally, Doctor, the swelling or lack of swelling of the body and the members thereof?

Dr. Anderson:

> There was generalized swelling as part of the decomposition and decay process, and this involved the face, and the neck, and the chest, and the abdomen was quite bloated and the extremities also were swollen.

Prosecutor:

> Doctor, bearing in mind that you arrived at the scene

and observed the body lying there in the water and observed the hair as you described on the head floating freely around the head, and bearing in mind what you have told us concerning your observation of the swelling of the body and its various portions, directing your attention to what you have told us concerning the strand of hair around the neck, I will ask you if you have an opinion as to whether or not the hair could have been placed around the neck just by the normal water and swelling of the body?

Dr. Anderson:

It's my opinion that the hair could not have been this tightly about the neck with the remained of the hair floating freely.[148]

On cross-examination, defense attorney Wylde effectively questioned this family physician's qualifications in the area of forensic pathology and whether his conclusions were supported by scientific evidence:

Defense:

Now, I assume, Dr. Anderson, from your recitation of your education background, that you are not a pathologist. Is that correct?

Dr. Anderson:

That's correct.

Defense:

And as far as a determination of cause of death, time of death, et cetera, I assume you have to defer to the discretion and the judgment of a pathologist. Is that correct?

Dr. Anderson:

That's correct.

Defense:

> Now, *you list* on this death certificate as *the cause of death, apparent strangulation*, is that correct?

Dr. Anderson:

> *Yes.*

Defense:

> *You also indicate that the date of injury is unknown, the place of the injury is unknown, how the injury occurred, of course, unknown, and location unknown, is that correct?*

Dr. Anderson:

> *That's correct.*

Defense:

> *Tell me this, when you saw the strand of hair down at the morgue, how many times was it around the neck, once?*

Dr. Anderson:

> *Once.*

Defense:

> *Was it all the way around the neck or just partway?*

Dr. Anderson:

> *Just across the front.*

. . .

Defense:

> A bruise is a trauma of a sort?

Dr. Anderson:

> Would be a trauma, yes.

Defense:

> You didn't observe any of that-either at the scene or at the morgue?

Dr. Anderson:

> No, I didn't.

Defense:

> In your observation of the autopsy, did you notice- and this is probably not a very precise medical term-but *was the neck broken?*

Dr. Anderson:

> *No,* I do not believe that it was.

Defense:

> *There was no trauma to the thorax,* either, that you observed, was there?

Dr. Anderson:

> *None* that I could detect.

Defense:

> *Was the hyoid bone broken, fractured, or disrupted in any way?*

Dr. Anderson:

> No, it was not. This was particularly sought for, and it was intact.

Defense:

> *This is a very common symptom of strangulation cases, isn't it, that the hyoid bone is broken?*

Dr. Anderson:

> *This sometimes occurs.*

Defense:

> *Occurs quite frequently, doesn't it?*

Dr. Anderson:

> *I really don't know.*

Defense:

> *The trachea was also normal, was it not?*

Dr. Anderson:

> *I believe it was.*

Defense:

> *And the trachea is also something in the neck?*

Dr. Anderson:

> *The windpipe that goes down to the lungs.*

Defense:

> *Trauma to the larynx and trachea are also indicative of strangling, are they not?*

Dr. Anderson:

> *It could be.*

To make clear that the theory put forth by the prosecution-that Barbara Jiminez's death occurred within 24 hours of her husband's death-was not supported by the evidence, the attorney for the defense continued:

Defense:

> *Now, is it a fact, Doctor, that the decomposition which you noted would be indicative of about a two or three-day exposure to air and sun?*

Dr. Anderson:

I really don't know. I think this in an area that I am not familiar with, nor have expertise in.

Defense:

I'm sorry, you are not a pathologist, that's right. Are you the deputy coroner for Le Sueur County?

Dr. Anderson:

Yes.

Defense:

Who is the coroner for Le Sueur County?

Dr. Anderson:

Dr. A. E. Waldon.

Defense:

Is he a pathologist?

Dr. Anderson:

No.

Defense:

I assume, sir, as deputy coroner in an area that has a lot of lakes and summer visitors and things, people that visit for recreational purposes, you have been exposed to drowning cases before?

Dr. Anderson:

No, I have not.

Defense:

Have not?

Dr. Anderson:

No.

In preparation for submitting evidence should the BCA's assistant identification officer give false testimony, the defense attorney continued:

Defense:

> Basically now, it is true, is it not, Doctor, in the case of, let's say, victims of drowning, individuals who have been exposed to the water for . . . some period of time, it is possible to remove the skin of the hand almost like a glove? And thus fingerprinting impressions and things can be obtained by technicians, is that correct?

Dr. Anderson:

> Yes. It's my understanding that this is true, yes.

Prosecutor:

> Did you see Dr. Sanford perform any procedure such as this?

Dr. Anderson:

> Yes, he did. He removed all of the fingertips.

On redirect questioning, the prosecutor again implied that Barbara Jiminez was strangled:

Prosecutor:

> He [Wylde] asked you whether or not if they [the larynx, hyoid bone and/or trachea] had been damaged, if this is consistent or inconsistent with strangulation. Merely because they are not damaged, does this rule out strangulation?

Wylde interrupted: "I am going to object. I think the witness has already told me he is not competent to answer that question."

"I agree," said the judge, "Sustained."

The noon recess gave the prosecutor the opportunity to confer with the doctor about a time of death that would have allowed for my having committed the murder. So when the trial reconvened:

Prosecutor:

> Do you have an opinion as to whether the body had been there for some appreciable period of time prior to the time it was removed, or whether, say, it may have just floated in there recently prior to removal?

Dr. Anderson:

> It's my opinion that the body had been in this position for a considerable length of time prior to its being found.

Defense counsel challenged Dr. Anderson on this contradiction to his earlier testimony:

Defense:

> I asked you this morning, Doctor, if it were not a fact that the amount of decomposition you observed here, the elements you observed here, would be indicative of two to three days in that position, correct? You remember that question? You told me you didn't have an opinion.

Dr. Anderson:

> I don't remember the question in that specific sense, no.

Defense:

> Well, do you remember that I asked you a question along those lines this morning and you told me you didn't have an opinion?

Dr. Anderson:

> Yes, I told you that I did not have an opinion as to the exact length of time that it had been there.

Defense:

>You testified before, at least three days, haven't you?

Dr. Anderson:

>I don't recall.

Defense:

>You recall, I am sure, testifying in Mankato at another trial, do you not?

Dr. Anderson:

>Yes.

Defense:

>You recall being asked about this and saying "at least three days," in response to a similar question.

Dr. Anderson:

>I don't recall, but I recall the questioning.

Defense:

>Do you recall that Mr. Adamson asked this question: "*I take it from your testimony that the degree of decomposition that occurred could have occurred in as little as three days,* if I understand your testimony correctly, or am I putting words in your mouth or making a suggestion that is impossible?" Answer: "*I really must say that I think at least three days would have gone by.*" Do you remember that question and answer being put to you like that?

Dr. Anderson:

>Yes.

Raymond Sanford, M.D., the elected coroner for Blue Earth County who performed the autopsy on Barbara Jiminez, was called to the stand:

Prosecutor:

> Now, Doctor, you appreciate the matters under consideration here in this courtroom is concerning the deaths of Michael Jiminez and Barbara Jiminez? First of all, let's briefly allude to the Michael Jiminez situation . . . Were you called on or about the 23rd day of April, 1974, concerning the body of Michael Jiminez?

Dr. Sanford:

> Yes.

Prosecutor:

> Who actually performed the autopsy?

Dr. Sanford:

> Dr. Ohrt, my associate.

Prosecutor:

> Did you have an occasion to subsequently become involved in the case of Barbara Jiminez? You are actually the one who performed the autopsy in this case?

Dr. Sanford:

> On Barbara Jiminez, yes.

Dr. Sanford went into great detail in describing the autopsy while alluding to the colored photographs displayed to the jury. The prosecutor's questions then turned to the cause of death:

Prosecutor:

> At this time I am going to direct your attention to State's Exhibit GG and also HH. I will ask you if you recognize what those pictures depict?

Dr. Sanford:

The first picture shows the strand of hair intact around the front of the neck and shows some discoloration of skin and so on, and it is obvious that the victim has quite an abundance of hair. It's a heavy-headed scalp here. It shows my hands retracting the chin just to show that strand of hair. The hair was removed, detached from the scalp, and that I am holding that strand of hair in my hand.

Prosecutor:

Now . . . what if anything did you observe about the body of Barbara Jiminez that led to your ultimate decision as to how she died?

Dr. Sanford:

The strand of hair around the front of her neck.

To ease the impact should defense counsel demonstrate to the jury Dr. Sanford's questionable conclusion as to the cause of death, the prosecutor continued:

Prosecutor:

And what other factors do you normally consider in arriving at the cause of death?

Dr. Sanford:

Possibility of drowning.

Prosecutor:

In addition to the examinations that you have told us about here, for instance, how could you rule out poisoning or something of that nature?

Dr. Sanford:

Oh, stomach contents and portions of organs were submitted to the State Crime Bureau of Criminal

Apprehension Laboratory for their analysis.

Prosecutor:

Did you receive back from them results and findings?

Dr. Sanford:

I never received such a report, no.

Dr. Sanford's testimony that he did not receive the results of the test is suspect, especially since later testimony from a representative of the crime lab revealed that Barbara Jiminez's stomach did contain alcohols that could cause unconsciousness, even death.

Prosecutor:

Okay. Bearing in mind those additional things you told us about, I will ask you if you have an opinion as to a reasonable medical certainty as to the cause of the death of Barbara Jiminez?

Dr. Sanford:

My opinion is she died of strangulation from the *strand* of hair.

Prosecutor:

All right. Now, *you did mention possible drowning*. Did you seek additional consultation through one of your fellow professionals on this?

Dr. Sanford:

Yes, I did. *Dr. John Coe*. He is *medical examiner for Hennepin County* [Minnesota]. Dr. Coe *was of the opinion that it is not an absolute finding*.

Prosecutor:

So by that you mean *you could neither rule for or rule against either of the causes*?

Dr. Sanford:

Yes.

Prosecutor:

What other factors besides the presence of the braid or strand of hair around the neck of the body of Barbara Jiminez did you consider in rendering the opinion that it was apparent strangulation? Were there certain other microscopic findings or finding of tissue of the body that in any way support your opinion?

Dr. Sanford:

That wasn't helpful, no.

Prosecutor:

Was there anything that you found about the hyoid bone and the trachea injury or lack of injury to it that would cause you to rule one way or the other?

Dr. Sanford:

Those structures were removed and no injury was found to any of those structures.

Prosecutor:

But in view of that, did you rule out strangulation?

Dr. Sanford:

In view of that, I considered that the most likely cause.

The prosecutor then turned to the subject of sexual relations, with graphic description and displaying graphic photos to the jury, to insinuate as a motive, that Barbara Jiminez was raped:

Prosecutor:

Now, Doctor, did you examine the body of Barbara

Jiminez, specifically the reproductive organs, sexual organs?

Dr. Sanford:

> Yes.

Prosecutor:

> And what was the conclusion?

Dr. Sanford:

> My conclusion was that she could have had sexual intercourse within a period of time prior to death.

. . .

Prosecutor:

> Were you able to tell with any degree of certainty as to the time?

Dr. Sanford:

> No.

Prosecutor:

> And why was this? What is your reason for that?

Dr. Sanford:

> Period of time and also irrigation of the vagina, washing. Washing, irrigating effect of the vagina.

Prosecutor:

> Doctor, directing your attention to State's Exhibit KK, which is a picture of the body of Barbara Jiminez in the waters of Scotch Lake, does that picture and posture of the body indicate to you that it is possible that the forces of nature and the waters of the lake performed this irrigation action?

. . .

Dr. Sanford:

> Yes.

Prosecutor:

> Now, Doctor, so apparently at some point prior to the death of Barbara Jiminez, it is your opinion to a reasonable medical certainty that she in fact did have sexual intercourse with someone?

Dr. Sanford:

> Yes.

Prosecutor:

> Is there any way of knowing or do you have an opinion as to if you could ascertain as to who this was with?

Dr. Sanford:

> No.

Prosecutor:

> Are there tests that can be performed through use of the deposits of sperm that would reveal the identity?

Dr. Sanford:

> There are some tests, yes.

Prosecutor:

> But there were additional factors that were not available in this case that are necessary, is this correct? Could you tell the jury what those factors are?

Dr. Sanford:

> I'm not too familiar with the particular types of tests,

and it is not one that we do locally in Mankato.[149]

On cross-examination the counsel for the defense immediately attacked the prosecutor's implication that Barbara Jiminez was raped:

Defense:

> I assume, if I told you that the person you were examining was apparently a married woman and with no apparent difficulty, and, of course . . . there would be nothing in your mind that would be inconsistent with what you would expect to find in a young lady of that type, would there?

Dr. Sanford:

> That's right, yes.

Then defense counsel challenged Dr. Sanford's conclusion that Barbara Jiminez had been strangled:

Defense:

> Apparently the only evidence that you found during your autopsy which would indicate the possibility of strangulation was the strand of hair? At least, that is all you have told us about?

Dr. Sanford:

> Yes.

Defense:

> Now . . . if that assumption were correct, then you would be talking about some outside affect on the area of the neck, correct? As opposed to being smothered?

Dr. Sanford:

> Yes.

Defense:

But you have already told us also that there was no fracture or interference that you could see of the hyoid bone, the larynx, the trachea, or any of the organs of the throat, is that correct?

Dr. Sanford:

Yes.

Defense:

Now, is it not more likely that in the case of strangulation you would find a trauma, injury, or fracture to one or more of those organs or bones?

Dr. Sanford:

Not necessarily.

Defense:

Well, it certainly is common in cases of strangulation to find such evidence, is it not?

Dr. Sanford:

Yes, yes.

Defense:

And you did not find any such trauma or fracture in this case?

Dr. Sanford:

No.

Defense:

And apparently you consulted with Dr. Coe through correspondence, and you were particularly concerned with this mastoid area you talked about?

Dr. Sanford:

Yes.

Defense:

And where is the mastoid bone?

Dr. Sanford:

If I may point in the photograph, it is this prominent bone in the back of the ear.

Defense:

So we are talking about a hemorrhage of the bone of the ear. So he directed your attention to some authorities, in whose opinion presence of the mastoid hemorrhage would be specific for drowning, correct?

Dr. Sanford:

That's correct.

Defense:

Dr. Coe told you in his experience he had seen drowning victims who did not possess this mastoid hemorrhage, is that correct?

Dr. Sanford:

Yes, that's correct.

Defense:

He said, and even occasionally vice versa?

Dr. Sanford:

Yes.

. . .

Defense:

Alright, we will take it one step further. Now, you say

that the other factor that you took into consideration was the presence of the hair which you saw? Obviously the person whom you examined was in some state of decomposition? And for want of a better word, there is obvious bloating? And it is possible, is it not, Doctor, that the hair on the neck was caused by the placing of hair at any time and became part of the swelling process?

Dr. Sanford:

Yes.

Defense:

It was laying on the neck and then when the skin swelled it swelled around the hair.

Dr. Sanford:

Yes.

Defense:

Now, you have told us that after you detached the hair it was removed without too much difficulty?

Dr. Sanford:

Yes.

Defense:

There is one other symptom which we haven't talked about or one other finding which appears in your protocol, and that is edema. And could you tell us what edema is?

Dr. Sanford:

Edema means accumulation of water.

Defense:

Did you find certain amounts of edema in the lungs?

Dr. Sanford:

Certain amounts, yes.

Defense:

Now, the finding of edema in the lungs is consistent with drowning, is it not?

Dr. Sanford:

Yes.

Defense:

You have told us that you sent several specimens to the Bureau of Criminal Apprehension. Some fluids we have already talked about. We talked about one. I assume you sent blood?

Dr. Sanford:

Blood was obtained and sent.

Defense:

And other bodily fluids? Samples of tissues and things like that?

Dr. Sanford:

Yes

Defense:

Now, you did not personally run any of these tests, is that correct?

Dr. Sanford:

No.

Defense:

And you never received any reports from the BCA on stomach contents, is that correct?

Dr. Sanford:

No, I didn't.

Defense counsel then clarified the assumption as to the time of death, which the prosecutor had avoided during his questioning of Dr. Sanford:

Defense:

Doctor . . . I will show you particularly State's Exhibit K . . . Is it not true, Doctor, *based upon your experience, that the decomposition or the symptoms which you have observed on the back of the deceased would be indicative of about a two-day exposure to air?*

Dr. Sanford:

Yes.

Defense:

It is true also, is it not, Doctor, that in examining the body with an idea of diagnosing strangulation, one of the first things that is looked for is finger marks, or fingernail impressions, or some sort of bruising identification, that sort of thing, in the area of the neck on the back?

Dr. Sanford:

Yes.

Defense:

You didn't find any of that here?

Dr. Sanford:

No.

Defense:

You did not send your protocol to Dr. Coe?

Dr. Sanford:

No.

Defense counsel successfully challenged the testimony of Anderson and Sanford, demonstrating the alliance a locally elected coroner has with the prosecution. This caused the prosecutor to search for a medical examiner to support the testimony of coroners Anderson and Sanford.

An article in the *Mankato Free Press* headed "Strangled by Own Hair," nevertheless indicated that there was no evidence, other than the strand of hair across the front of Barbara Jiminez's neck, to support the theory.

Deputy Sheriff Pat Smith Jr. of Le Sueur County was summoned to the stand. The questions put to him could have been asked of Sheriff Pat Smith Sr. when he testified, but this was part of the prosecution's strategy-to bring in as many witnesses as possible, to sway the jury with sheer numbers, just as it had introduced more than 200 exhibits, regardless of evidentiary value. The prosecution proceeded:

Prosecutor:

Did your office continue its investigation after the body of Barbara Jiminez was found?

Deputy Smith:

Yes it did . . . we continued investigating different areas around Scotch Lake, because we were missing some articles of clothing yet.

Prosecutor:

What do you mean, you were missing certain articles of clothing?

Deputy Smith:

There were only two articles of clothing recovered from the female victim . . . the bandana, and one shoe at our crime scene, and the clothing she was wearing never was discovered.

The remainder of questions put to Deputy Smith by the prosecutor dealt with the lake and the area around the lake:

Deputy Smith:

> Scotch Lake . . . located in southern Minnesota [is] very shallow . . . the one cabin on the whole lake would be on the other side of the lake . . . last three or four years has been very unique to see a boat on the lake, period . . . I hunted ducks and geese on there . . . Primarily agricultural around the lake. There is pasture and farm land completely surrounding the lake.[150]

The cross-examination by defense counsel focused on items discovered that could have been evidence but that had not been introduced and were no longer available:

Defense:

> Deputy Smith, you said . . . you didn't find anything that was significant prior to the 4th of May, but I prefer to be the judge of that. When did you find the ripped blouse, the panties, the other brown coat, things of that nature?

Deputy Smith:

> There was a blue pair of panties found by one of our officers the next day, which would have been the 3rd of May, approximately six or seven miles from the crime scene.

Defense:

> How about the other brown coat, do you recall when that was found?

Deputy Smith:

As I recall, the other brown coat that was found was found by another officer and turned over to Blue Earth County prior to the discovery of the victim.

Defense:

How about torn blouses? Do you recall finding some torn blouses?

Deputy Smith:

I myself didn't find any torn blouses.

Defense:

How about the scarves?

Deputy Smith:

One of the posse men found some scarves. I would say it was in a field road 15, 18 miles from the scene.

Defense:

The coat belonging to Barbara Jiminez that has been received in evidence . . . was found, as you say, about 18 miles from the scene. Where, for example, were the blouses found?

Deputy Smith:

I believe the blouses were found . . . south and then west of Waterville.

Defense:

These other items that we have been talking about, the other brown coat and the torn blouses, the scarves, the panties, all these other items that were found along the highway at various parts of the county . . . were those items turned over to Blue Earth County as far as you know?

Deputy Smith:

    These items were turned over to Blue Earth County.

Defense:

    When you say nothing significant was found by you, what you mean is nothing that you have subsequently used for evidence was discovered during that –

Deputy Smith:

    That's correct. There was a great many items taken for identification that couldn't be identified.

Defense:

    Also, when you say . . . the only items of female clothing that Barbara was wearing, you are talking about those items that were portrayed in those pictures of the Jiminezes leaving Emporia, Kansas?

Deputy Smith

    That's correct.

Defense:

    So when you say "She was wearing," you are referring to the time those pictures were taken and only that time?

Deputy Smith:

    I was referring to the photograph.

Defense:

    In addition to the piece of cloth, the end gate rod and the shoe, all of which have been received in evidence, or at least identified, what other items did you find there that you took to the BCA?

Deputy Smith:

I don't recall any other items that were taken there. There was some-several sets of tire prints that were photographed at the scene. Outside of that, nothing was taken from the scene.

On defense counsel's instructions, Deputy Smith marked on the map where the panties were found:

Defense:

> That is on the other side of Scotch Lake?

Deputy Smith:

> That's correct. It would be on the east side.

Defense:

> Now, the box, did you at that time go through the contents yourself?

Deputy Smith:

> Yes, I did.

Defense:

> And it is true, is it not . . . that miscellaneous items such as . . . the box of pipe filters, the milk carton, the typewriter rental receipt and that sort of thing, were on the bottom of the box? Under the clothes?

Deputy Smith:

> That's correct.

With the jury from a metropolitan area, defense counsel made a point of showing the small size of the Le Sueur County Sheriff's Department, which wouldn't have the means to investigate like a larger police department:

Defense:

And you have identified yourself as the chief deputy of Le Sueur County, is that correct?

Deputy Smith:

That's correct.

Defense:

Pat Smith Sr. is your father?

Deputy Smith:

That's correct.

Defense:

And Chris Smith is a deputy, he is your brother, is that correct?

Deputy Smith:

That's correct.

Defense:

Okay. I believe your father testified he . . . had four deputies in the county?

Deputy Smith:

Probably wasn't counting me. I am five.

Defense:

Would you agree with the characterization that the public landing of Scotch Lake is a lover's lane area?

Deputy Smith:

Yes, I would.

Rebecca Stovall (formerly Rebecca Niehus), the sister of Michael Jiminez, testified on direct examination that her brother and his wife, Barbara, arrived and stayed with her and her boyfriend at her apartment over the weekend in Emporia, Kansas, and participated in their activities. She said the purpose of their trip was to purchase a car from her.

As in the first trial, Stovall identified items belonging to the Jiminezes-the sign giving their route back to Minnesota, Barbara Jiminez's coat found under the bridge of the Cannon River, her shoe discovered at Scotch Lake, and the clothing the Jiminezes were carrying in their duffel bag. On viewing the photo she had taken of the Jiminezes as they left Emporia, Stovall stated that the items of clothing Barbara Jiminez wore at the time had not been shown to her.[151] (These and other items never surfaced.)

On cross-examination, defense counsel asked questions that the public defender in the first trial should have asked in the first trial:

Defense:

> I believe, Mrs. Stovall, you already told us about two of those items, that is, some items of clothing in the last exhibit. Obviously a checkered blouse with long sleeves, and . . . you said a red top or something that is shown in that picture. What were some of these other items you have never seen?

Stovall:

> Cashmere sweater, Michael's gray-and-blue-plaid shirt. None of his clothing, I don't believe, except for his sweater.

Defense:

> Maybe I can help you out . . . How about personal items of toiletries, like toothbrushes or cosmetics, personal things of that nature?

Stovall:

> Yes. Barbara had a cosmetic type purse . . . That was missing. Her billfold was missing. Pictures I gave her were missing. Michael's medication I believe was never

found. Her ring. Her wedding band.

Defense:

    These were things that you have never seen since?

Stovall:

    No.

. . .

Defense:

    How about other items of jewelry, any earrings that you saw?

Stovall:

    Her wedding band. She had a copper ring.

Defense:

    Did they have hair brushes?

Stovall:

    Yes. I think one was a wig brush. Toiletries.

Defense:

    I know this is difficult for you, but I do have to ask. Now, they arrived, or you were aware that they were there about 9:15 on the 19th, you have testified. At that time I assume they had with them a duffel bag and knapsack as you described?

Stovall:

    Yes, sir.

. . .

Defense:

This visit was a surprise, you weren't expecting it?

Stovall:

No.

Defense:

Now, you went out to a couple of spots on Saturday night? You went shopping, I guess, with Barbara, to the shopping center. Did you notice whether she had a large amount of money?

Stovall:

No, she didn't. She had gotten a dollar out of Michael's billfold because she didn't have any money.

Defense:

And when all four of you were out socializing, did you notice that he had a lot of money, was he picking up the tabs?

Stovall:

They didn't pay for anything. We paid for everything.

Defense:

So you assumed they didn't have much money?

Stovall:

They told us they didn't. They had about enough money to get back home.

Stovall's testimony here, as in the first trial, brings to mind the questions of how the Jiminezes could pay for a car-title change, nor to mention the gas to return to Minnesota, with only six dollars between them, and why didn't they wait the extra day, until Monday, to get the title changed, instead of hitchhiking back to Minnesota? And what about the questions raised by defense counsel in this trial: What happened to

Michael Jiminez's medication, the clothing Barbara Jiminez was wearing when they left Emporia, Kansas, her identification, wedding band, and so forth?

The *Mankato Free Press* reported on Stovall's testimony in an article titled "Jiminezes Went to Kansas for Car, Sister Testified."[152]

BCA Agent Thomas Simonson was summoned to the stand. He stated as he had in the first trial in Mankato that before working for the BCA, his experience had been with the Mankato Police Department. Simonson testified that he was at the crime scene where Michael Jiminez's body was discovered, that he observed evidence and measured the distances from one object to another as well as the width of the tire tracks. He cited the distance between the road and the railroad tracks as approximately 80 feet. He said he took soil samples and testified as to the evidence allegedly found at the scene:

Prosecutor:

    And these items were ultimately transported to where?

Simonson:

    I took them into my possession and kept them in my possession with the exception of the . . . cartridge case. At four o'clock I turned that over to Sheriff Wiebold. He then returned it to me at approximately six P.M., at which time I locked everything in my desk and maintained it in my custody.

Simonson testified that the tire tracks at both crime scenes were measured and that photographs were taken of the tracks. He said the tire tracks measured 65 inches from outside track to outside track- a half-inch less than the measurement of the tires of the Bronco, taken by investigators in California. Twenty-eight photos of tire tracks were then introduced, apparently to overwhelm the jury by sheer numbers rather than actually incriminate me.

Simonson's testimony continued:

Prosecutor:

> Directing your attention back to the tracks that you observed and told us about at the Blue Earth County scene, and now the ones at the Le Sueur County scene, were you able to form any conclusions as to the similarity or dissimilarity of any of the tracks?

Simonson:

> Well, we-there is nothing outside-there is a similarity between the dimension of the tracks but there is somewhat of a difference in the measurements, but they are similar.

Prosecutor:

> That would be width?

Simonson:

> Yes, sir.

Prosecutor:

> But other than that, from your observation there is really nothing that you can do to identify the tracks?

Simonson:

> No. There is no identifiable characteristics in any of the tracks.[153]

That answer was false. Le Sueur County Sheriff Pat Smith wanted a plaster cast made of the tracks, which obviously left clear tire-tread impressions in the dried mud (I also had observed that when, during the first trial, we toured the area where the bodies were discovered.) The following cross-examination reveals that the crime lab eliminated my vehicle as the source of the tire tracks, a conclusion possible only through comparison with distinguishable tracks found at the crime scene.

Defense:

It is fair to state that there were many, many tracks all over this area?

Simonson:

Oh, yes, sir.

Defense:

And these photographs show these tire tracks being measured. I assume you took measurement of all tracks, or the ones you could?

Simonson:

Yes, sir.

Defense:

Have you preserved any of those measurements?

Simonson:

Outside of the photograph? No.

Defense:

So the only measurement of any of those tire tracks you preserved are the ones that just happened to come close to coinciding to the measurement of the two tracks that you found at the Blue Earth County crime scene? Is that a correct statement?

Simonson:

No, sir. There was also some tracks-*there was a track here that would be about the same width, in the mud and snow designs, but that tire track has been eliminated by the lab technician. It is not of the suspect vehicle. So that measurement means nothing.*

Since the vehicle I was driving had mud-and-snow tires, the authorities had been of the mindset that the Bronco made those tracks, leading the jury in the first trial to believe that as well, and since there would have been a lab report stating elimination of the Bronco as the source of the tracks thought to be from the assailant's vehicle, the prosecutors must have removed the report before their files were subpoenaed at the appellate hearings.

Defense:

> One more question ... referring to the photo exhibits. These, you say ... portray a four-wheel-drive vehicle with snow tires?

Simonson:

> Well, they portray a mud-and-snow-type tire.

Defense:

> Those are the ones that were eliminated?

Simonson:

> *Those have been eliminated.*

Defense:

> You didn't take plaster casts of any of these tire tracks you found?

Simonson:

> No, sir. The rest of them are, well, I feel, obviously are not mud and snow tires, but they were, like I say, it's just tire tracks all over and you just took what was plain and measured what you could.

Defense:

> You are not saying you discounted these other tracks because they were not mud and snow tires?

Simonson:

> Oh, no, no, but, like I say, *the mud and snows are positively*

eliminated.

Defense:

> You didn't take any casts of tire tracks at the Highway 14 Blue Earth County scene either, did you?

Simonson:

> No, sir, I did not.

As to the "evidence found at the Blue Earth crime scene" to implicate me, defense counsel continued:

Defense:

> You investigated several homicide cases, have you not, in your career? Anything strike you as odd at finding so much evidence just lying on the ground at the so-called crime scene?

Simonson:

> I would have to state, sir, that is sometimes a very messy business. I-

Defense:

> You must admit, based on your experience, this is a little bit unusual- two ballpoint pens, a book of matches?

Simonson:

> I would state it is a very large amount of evidence, yes, sir.

Defense counsel completed his cross-examination regarding dirt and mud removed from my Bronco for comparison:

Defense:

> You testified that you picked up soil samples, did you not, at both sites?

Simonson:

>Yes, I did.

Defense:

>There are tests that can be run in that regard too, isn't there?

Simonson:

>Yes, they can run some tests on them.

Further questioning revealed that no tests were conducted (at least no one admitted tests were done), just as the BCA's micro analyst later testified that no tests were conducted on the hair in the knot of cloth found at the Le Sueur County scene:

Defense:

>I believe there is a photograph in here, or [a] couple pictures that have been received in evidence, showing the cloth being measured with a tape measure, the distance from the tree-do your notes reflect that you measured actually the length of the cloth?

Simonson:

>No, sir, I did not.

Defense:

>You found something in the knot that you though were hairs. Of course, you know as part of your training it is possible to identify hairs? There was evidentiary value to that, so that could be identified perhaps as to source or compare with known hairs of-like fingerprints can, right?

Simonson:

>Yes, sir.

Defense:

So you tried to preserve that evidence?

Simonson:

Yes, sir.

Helen Troxel, the waitress at the café in Blairsburg Corners, Iowa, testified as she had in the first trial, that she waited on the Jiminez couple on April 22 between 11:00 A.M. and noon-initially reported by the sheriff of Blue Earth County as around 4:30 P.M., which coincided with the time of my phone call from Belvidere, Illinois, at 5:03 P.M. On cross-examination by defense counsel, Troxel stated that the Jiminezes were alone and that they were not carrying a duffel bag.[154]

Wallace Sorum, the BCA's micro analyst, was called to the stand. He said his current employment was with the Highway Patrol Crime Lab in Spokane, Washington. His subsequent testimony not only contradicted what he had stated in the trial in Mankato, but also his answers to repeated questions at this trial:

Prosecutor:

At the time you originally received the smaller item, the one that was tied in a knot, did you examine it for the presence of any foreign materials?

Sorum:

There were hairs integrally involved in the knot of the piece of cloth.

Prosecutor:

Did you later, then, attempt to make any type of analysis of the hairs found entwined in the knot and any other hairs?

Sorum:

No, I did not.

Prosecutor:

Any hairs at all?

Sorum:

> *I did some hair comparisons,* yes, sir. I found hairs from two sleeping bags and one pillow and pillowcase. These items were said to have come from California, and I attempted to compare these particular hairs with hairs-known hairs from the head of Barbara Jiminez.

Prosecutor:

> And how did you do that? Would you briefly describe that?

Sorum:

> *It's a microscopic examination . . . the hairs did not compare.*

Sorum claimed, as he had in the first trial, that hair was a poor type of evidence:

Sorum:

> I could take a dozen hairs from your heads, each one of your heads, and somebody else could hand me an unknown, and I could probably not make a conclusive identification that it did come from your head or any one of your people's heads.
>
> Hair generally is-probably the most positive thing you can say concerning hair is in a negative aspect. In other words, you can say that hair did not come from a person's head, but you cannot say that hair definitely came from a person's head.

Sorum then contradicted himself again, giving a different answer to the same question put to him by the prosecutor:

Prosecutor:

> Were you asked or did you attempt to make a

comparison between the hairs found in the knot, with the known hairs of Barbara Jiminez?

Sorum:

> *A cursory examination was done. That is strictly visual, naked eyeball examination of gross colors, and this is all . . . they were comparable as far as gross color is concerned.*[155]

On cross-examination, defense counsel probed:

Defense:

> Let me understand your testimony, Mr. Sorum, you received some items from California, a pillow and pillowcase, and you removed hairs from those?

Sorum:

> Yes, sir.

Defense:

> That is a painstaking process. I assumed you have to go through and select hairs and all that, right?

Sorum:

> It's a visual examination.

Defense:

> So you have to select the head hairs from any other hairs that might be present, and then you compared those hairs to the known hairs which you had received from Barbara Jiminez?

Sorum:

> That's correct.

Defense:

> Then you went to this sheet [cloth], which is an item

presented to you as coming from the alleged scene of a crime, in which you found human hairs, head hairs, and you only made a visual comparison, a gross visual comparison between those hairs and the known hairs you had from Barbara Jiminez?

Sorum:

Yes, sir.

Defense:

Did you, before you untied that piece of cloth, Mr. Sorum, make any measurements of how long [length] it was tied together?

Sorum:

I don't believe I did. No, sir.

As stated in chapter 5, regarding Sorum's testimony in the first trial, if he had measured the cloth-an issue not probed until the second trial-the fabric would have proven too short for use as a gag. Defense attorney Wylde argued this point in his closing statement to the jury.

The attorney for the defense then turned to the partial book of matches allegedly found at the Blue Earth County crime scene and to the examination of the used matches found in the Bronco's ashtray:

Defense:

You attempted to draw a comparison between the fibers present in this matchbook and the matches you found in the ash tray. And your conclusion was no match, is that correct?

Sorum:

That is correct, yes, sir.

Defense counsel then asked about the results of tests Sorum would have been expected to make on debris and soil samples from the Bronco, including those that the BCA's Simonson said he had sent to the crime lab:

Defense:

> Now, apparently you also had submitted to you several other bags of debris in addition to the ashtray debris you have already discussed?

Sorum:

> Yes, sir.

Defense:

> You were given some bugs that were removed from the radiator of the car in California, and different other containers of debris, soil, dirt, that sort of thing, said to come from a car?

Sorum:

> Yes, sir.

Defense:

> And I assume you would have received at some other time soil samples that had been taken from the Blue Earth and Le Sueur Counties.

Sorum:

> *I don't recall if I did.*

Defense:

> Did you perform any tests on these debris and soil?

Sorum:

> No, I did not.

Defense:

They were not all given to you for tests?

Sorum:

That is affirmative.

Defense:

Now, it is possible, is it not, let's say the bugs you received, some time comparison can be made regarding wild life of a particular area, correct?

Sorum:

Comparisons of that nature could be made, I am sure.

Defense:

Soil can also be compared, can it not?

Sorum:

Yes, sir, it can.

Defense:

And *it is still your testimony that you conducted no microscopic analysis* of the hair found in that knot, is that correct?

Sorum:

That is correct.

Defense:

What basically, as far as a microscopic analysis goes, what do you look for when you analyze hair?

Sorum gave a lengthy outline on what can be determined through such tests, *which he said he didn't perform*, contradicting his first trial testimony wherein he said he *did conduct a microscopic examination of the hair found in the knot.*

Defense counsel's cross-examination of Sorum concluded with

questions about the two brown coats that were discovered and turned over to the Blue Earth County Sheriff's Department:

Defense:

> There has been testimony about two brown coats, and I wonder if this is the one of Barbara Jiminez's that was submitted, or another one?

Sorum:

> Yes, sir, it is.

Defense:

> Is that the only coat that you examined?

Sorum:

> It's the only coat *I recall*.

If indeed, the "other brown coat" was the one covering the contents of the box I discarded, which would support the existence of a third hitchhiker, it was in the prosecution's interest not to turn it over to the crime lab for analysis-or, if it *was* turned over to the crime lab, to deny it. Sorum's answer that Barbara Jiminez's coat was the only one he "recalled" was evasive.

A few years later I became acutely aware of Sorum's testimony in two other murder trials that also were related to one another. He testified then that he "positively" identified hair at the crime scene as coming from one of the defendants. (This was before DNA testing was available and admissible as evidence in court.)

The first trial resulted in a conviction and life sentence. As a result of getting to know the convicted man in prison, I became convinced of his innocence, as like me, he was in another state and thus had an alibi for the time the crime was committed.

When the man's wife subsequently went on trial in the case, I contacted her attorney to say I had read Sorum's testimony from her husband's trial. With my transcript, the attorney impeached Wallace Sorum, and the jury came back with a "not guilty" verdict.

After five years of imprisonment, the husband was finally granted a retrial. Released on his own recognizance, highly unusual for an individual facing another trial in a murder case, he was allowed to move back to his home state of Pennsylvania. After about a year of freedom and notification of a new trial at which he was to be represented by a public defender, he felt he could not risk or face another prison term and so made a plea bargain: his testimony at a hearing that he was guilty for a sentence of five years, which he had already served. When his mother heard that he was forced to say he was guilty, she suffered a heart attack and died. Then he took his own life!

By the time Sorum performed an analysis of the evidence in this other man's case, he apparently had transferred back to Minnesota. Perhaps his findings in Washington had also come under scrutiny.

Now that DNA testing to identify hair as coming from a specific individual is recognized as scientific evidence, numerous cases of innocent people convicted on the testimony of experts for the prosecution have come to light.

A recent case is that of Washington State Patrol scientist Arnold Melnikoff, who engaged in scientific fraud during his tenure as the director and hair examiner for the Montana State Crime Laboratory from 1970 to 1989. Melnikoff's false testimony about hair comparisons led to at least two wrongful convictions of innocent men in Montana. A more recent exoneration involved Jimmy Ray Bromgard, who was released from prison when DNA testing established his innocence. Bromgard had served 15 years of his 40-year sentence.

The appendix of this volume-"Government's Prosecutorial Misconduct-Harmless Error?"-treats in greater depth both fraudulent testimony by experts for the prosecution and its consequences.

Janis Seestrom, the firearms examiner with the BCA, had testified in the first trial that she was "100 percent sure" the spent cartridge allegedly found at the Blue Earth County crime scene was ejected from my rifle. She said she determined this through "breech face markings" caused by the shell slamming against the breech of the rifle.

She also testified she examined the head wound of Michael Jiminez but found no signs of powder burns to indicate he had been shot at close range and no foreign matter in the wound. She stated that she did not test-fire the gun to see how far from the victim the shooter would have to be to avoid leaving powder burns on the body.[156]

On cross-examination, Seestrom was challenged about the firing test she claimed to have made and about her ballistics qualifications:

Defense:

> Now, let's go to the firearms identification. You made a statement-first of all, *that gun, rifle is clean at the present time. I assume you cleaned it after you test fired it?*

Seestrom:

> *No.*

Defense:

> *Do you recall what condition it was in before you fired it?*

Seestrom:

> *It looked very much as it did right now.*

Defense:

> *Well, no, because you fired it and if you haven't cleaned it, there is going to be powder residue and things in the barrel.* I am asking before you fired it, did you check the barrel?

Seestrom:

> *I couldn't tell you to be certain.*

As she had not test-fired from my rifle, Seestrom must not have performed the test she claimed.

Defense:

Now, you said that there were-one of the first things you noticed about the shell, was the presence of extractor marks, or an extractor mark, ejector? Therefore, not a revolver, but perhaps a semiautomatic pistol or automatic semiautomatic rifle?

Seestrom:

Yes.

Defense:

You did not compare extractor marks?

Seestrom:

No, I did not.

Defense:

Now, did you take any pictures of what you saw through your microscope when you were comparing-

Seestrom:

No, I did not.

Defense:

Therefore, the only evidence of what you saw is that which is now in your memory?

Seestrom:

That's correct.

In essence, Seestrom admitted the BCA crime lab had the means to use comparison photography as support for her testimony, but at the first trial, she had stated, "We do not photograph in our laboratory."

Since the defense counsel in the first trial challenged Seestrom's alleged performance of the one test, why did she not then perform the other two tests to prove her findings conclusively for the second trial?

If she had done those two tests, she would not have been able to say she was "100 percent sure" that the spent cartridge allegedly found at the crime scene came from my rifle, and in fact, the tests she did not do would have proved the spent cartridge did not come from my gun.

After the trial, I ordered a book on the subject of forensic evidence. On the topic of ballistics, it states that ejector marks and firing-pin impressions are the most reliable means for determining which specific firearm has ejected a spent cartridge. These are the two tests Seestrom did not perform.[157]

The U.S. Bureau of Alcohol, Tobacco and Firearms make such identifications through firing-pin impressions. Further, I sent the transcript of Seestrom's testimony to an independent firearms-consulting firm, which, based on her testimony, questioned her findings.[158]

Defense counsel also challenged Seestrom's qualifications in another area: On direct examination, as to Barbara Jiminez's body containing traces of ethyl alcohol (present in intoxicating beverages) and isopropyl alcohol (a rubbing alcohol), Seestrom claimed they could have been the result of decomposition rather than as a means of subduing her or as evidence of her own substance use. The cross-examiner probed:

Defense:

You are not a toxicologist or a pathologist?

Seestrom:

No. I never claimed to be.

Prosecutor Christian finally located someone to support the opinion of the coroners and now of Janis Seestrom, regarding the alcohols in the body of Barbara Jiminez. Ironically, though, the deputy medical examiner for Hennepin County-Garry Peterson, M.D.-contradicted the opinion of his superior-chief medical examiner, John Coe, whom the coroners had contacted. Garry Peterson took the stand.

Referring to the correspondence addressed to Dr. Coe and to his response, the prosecutor asked questions only in regard to what caused the death of Barbara Jiminez, carefully avoiding Dr. Coe's conclusions as to the time of death of Michael Jiminez:

Prosecutor:

> Do you recall what, if any, particular area of inquiry the letter was addressed to Dr. Coe and what the response was, just the area under consideration?

Dr. Peterson:

> As I recall, the basic question was with respect to hemorrhage in the mastoid ear cells. There are some areas in the bone of the skull behind the ear, in under the scalp, and those are sometimes seen to have blood in them in cases where the individual has drowned. The slide came and we examined the slide and found some areas of hemorrhage and the question was, is this always seen as drowning? And the other side of the coin is, when this is seen, does it always indicate drowning? . . . Our answer was that it is not always seen in drowning, and that when it is seen, other causes of death can be, in fact, the actual cause of death. It is not necessarily drowning.

Prosecutor:

> I gather that, then as it applied to this particular case . . . that it was your opinion and that of Dr. Coe that it wasn't particularly evidence of drowning in the particular case.

Dr. Peterson:

> That the individual had not necessarily drowned, yes.

Prosecutor Christian went into the testimony given by Drs. Sanford and Anderson on direct examination, using Dr. Peterson to back their conclusions. In closing:

Prosecutor:

Well, Doctor, you have considered all of the information that was made available to you. I will ask you, just as you in conclusion, in your opinion would . . . Dr. Sanford and Dr. Anderson be correct?

Dr. Peterson:

I think it is consistent with the evidence that is here.

Prosecutor:

You find nothing inconsistent with their reasoning or their conclusions?

Dr. Peterson:

No.

Defense attorney Wylde leaned back in his chair so that the jurors sitting in the front row could hear what he said and remarked to me, "He sure has changed his story from when I talked to him last night."[159]

On cross-examination, Wylde attacked the change in Dr. Peterson's conclusion:

Defense:

Now, I think it is important, Doctor, that we do not let the investigating tail wag the diagnostic dog, so to speak, and I think we better get down to a few facts. First of all, how long have you had to study the information that you have been testifying from today?

Dr. Peterson:

I think the material was given to me the night before last.

Defense:

You did not visit the scene in this case?

Dr. Peterson:

No, I didn't.

Defense:

In fact, the only thing you actually saw prior to receiving this material was the slide that you received?

Dr. Peterson:

That is correct.

Defense:

Now, apparently the findings that you have classified as being controversial today are those articles by a forensic pathologist that you referred to in that letter, correct?

Dr. Peterson:

Yes.

Defense:

And your letter indicates that the material you sent to Dr. Sanford regarding this middle-ear hemorrhage would indicate that the findings were diagnostic, that is, exclusive of any other cause except drowning?

Dr. Peterson:

I'm not familiar with any articles that say that they completely exclude other causes of death.

Defense:

Both of these articles, the author feels that such lesions are diagnostic?

Dr. Peterson:

I am not familiar. I do not know which two articles were sent. The articles I am familiar with are not quite that 100 percent certain.

Defense:

>And isn't it a fact, Doctor, that in Dr. Coe's letter, he agrees with the articles?

Dr. Peterson:

>*That appears to be what Dr. Coe is saying, yes-*I don't like to speculate on his interpretations of someone else's article.

Defense:

>*I think you both told-both came to the same conclusion?*

Dr. Peterson:

>*That's correct.*

Defense:

>*In effect, you even asked-agreed to write the letter, but he said he would?*

Dr. Peterson:

>*That is my recollection.*

Defense attorney Wylde quoted directly from Dr. Coe's letter:

Defense:

>". . . which would seem to indicate to me certainly the major and probably the vast majority of drowning cases which you investigate have this hemorrhaging."

Dr. Peterson:

>I would say the vast majority. I would say certainly the majority. Usually the majority.

With Dr. Peterson supporting Janis Seestrom's testimony, that is, that the presence of foreign substances of alcohol in Barbara Jiminez's body was part of the natural process of a body decomposing, defense counsel continued:

Defense:

> Now, when we talk about alcohol, you say-you didn't sound too convinced of this answer. *You said you thought both forms of alcohol could be the product of the decomposition?*

Dr. Peterson:

> I am sorry if I didn't sound-*yes, they both can. I am certain of that.*

Defense:

> *Would it surprise you, too, that Dr. Coe would offer a contrary opinion?*

Dr. Peterson:

> *Yes, it would.*

Defense:

> Alright, but of course, in this situation, you cannot-you are just speculating, you don't know whether this alcohol occurred through injection or through decomposition, you are saying it is possible it could occur either way?

Dr. Peterson:

> That's correct.

On food discovered in the stomach of Barbara Jiminez, indicating that she ate at a later time than her husband did, defense counsel inquired:

Defense:

> ... that finding clearly is consistent with the theory that this individual ingest some food before death, sufficiently close to death so that digestion did not occur?

Dr. Peterson:

> That's correct.

And challenging the prosecution's claim that Barbara Jiminez was strangled, defense counsel asked:

Defense:

> *Now, in cases of ligature strangulation, would you not expect to find trauma to the trachea and the larynx?*

Dr. Peterson:

> *Generally you would, yes.*

Defense:

> And, of course, you did not perform the autopsy?

Dr. Peterson:

> No, nor was I able to examine that.

Defense counsel Wylde began to question Dr. Peterson on the fact that he and Dr. Coe had agreed on the original time of death of Michael Jiminez, thus supporting my alibi defense. The prosecutor, however, objected. In the judge's chambers, the prosecutor argued that defense counsel was using the prosecutor's witness as his own witness. The judge sustained the objection.

Why did Dr. Peterson change his conclusions from those of his superior on behalf of the State? For personal gain? Deputy medical examiners don't rise to the position of chief medical examiner (a promotion Peterson later received) by testifying against the State for the defense-especially not in high-profile cases.

Walter Rhodes, assistant identification officer with the BCA, took the stand, and the prosecutor asked him about his experience in fingerprinting. Rhodes responded that he had been with the BCA for seven years, with the Minneapolis Police Department for 20 years, and for the last ten years there was in the ID Department. So Rhodes had a long history of testifying for the prosecution. On his formal training in fingerprint identification:

Rhodes:

Well, while [I was in the Minneapolis Police Department, it] was on-the-job training as far as classifying fingerprints. Latent work [in this case, identification of fingerprints] there is no schools that you go to. You learn this by experience or working with people who are involved in latent work. I have gone to the BCA Fingerprint School of Classification, and that is about all that is left to people in our type of work.

Rhodes stated that he was able to positively identify the body of Michael Jiminez through fingerprints on file with the Mankato Police Department. He also said he had dusted my rifle for fingerprints but found none-not even mine. Moreover, Rhodes said, there weren't any fingerprints on items allegedly found at the Blue Earth County crime scene-not even on the matchbook, and this didn't make sense, unless someone had purposely wiped the items clean.

Like the BCA's micro analyst Wallace Sorum, Rhodes contradicted himself during direct questioning by the prosecutor (emphasis is added to statements countering what would be revealed under cross examination and to statements designed to mislead the jury into thinking there were only two hitchhikers):

Rhodes:

> We processed over 100 pieces of evidence ... mainly paper. We developed only eight latent prints that we thought could be used for identification, and these latent prints were photographed and then enlarged. *We compared the prints with Michael Jiminez and Mrs. Jiminez and Edward Clark and they did not belong to any of the people involved.*

Prosecutor:

> You indicated that you did find, as I recall, one print on the box [that Ed Clark discarded], two prints on a shopping bag, the Jiminez's sign indicating their route and destination, and three on a sheet of paper. And what if anything, did you do in an attempt to identify the prints

that you did discern?

Rhodes:

> Well, we had three people involved in this. We had the prints of Michael Jiminez, we had the prints of Mr. Clark. *We weren't able to find any recorded prints of Mrs. Jiminez so the only comparison that we could make was with the finger impressions of Michael Jiminez and with Mr. Clark.*

Prosecutor:

> *You said that you did not have a record or were unable to develop any prints of Barbara Jiminez?*

Rhodes:

> *That's right.*

By claiming there weren't "any *recorded* prints of Mrs. Jiminez," Rhodes misled the jury into thinking that the investigators did not have Barbara Jiminez's classification for comparison.

Prosecutor:

> Why was that, or what effort was made?

Rhodes:

> All effort was made, sir. We even had some of her personal belongings brought to the lab, such as tablets and notebooks that she might have handled, and I couldn't tell you how many pieces of paper that we processed trying to find latent fingerprints, and we were unsuccessful.

Prosecutor:

> Was any effort made to take prints from the body itself when it was recovered?

Rhodes:

> . . . We did take prints. The body was so badly

decomposed, that *I don't know whether it would have been possible for us to make a positive identification or not.*

Prosecutor:

... You have indicated the number or potential number of prints that you found and what you thought might be identifiable, or at least had some significance ...

Rhodes:

Roughly about six or eight latent prints that we developed that we thought we might use for identification.

Prosecutor:

And then did you attempt to identify those prints that you found? ...

Rhodes:

... To make an identification, first of all, you have to have another set of prints to compare, and *as I have stated before, the only two prints that we had to compare belonged to Mr. Clark and Mr. Jiminez.*

Prosecutor:

Was any effort made to, let's say, *check those prints against the public as a whole, or is it impossible* to conduct such type of identification process or search?

Rhodes:

... *I have to have the name of the suspect before the latent print becomes of any value to me.*

Prosecutor:

So are we to conclude, Mr. Rhodes, that of the six or eight latent prints that you discovered in all of your work in this case, *you were unable to reach any conclusion as to the identification of the source of the print?*

Rhodes:

> Only conclusion, sir, that I could make, that *they did not belong to Mr. Jiminez or they did not belong to Mr. Clark.*

Prosecutor:

> Incidentally, did you compare those six or eight prints among themselves? Did they compare to one another?

Rhodes:

> There were two prints that were similar, but they were not identical.[160]

Cross-examination by defense counsel revealed that Rhodes did not do a thorough job in seeking the identity of the person whose fingerprints were discovered; it also impeached him:

Defense:

> Were these prints that you raised on the box on the outside or the inside of the box?

Rhodes:

> Outside.

Defense:

> However, also included in the items from the box were prints from the shopping bag, and the piece of paper. They were inside the box when you got them. So you succeeded in raising and listing about eight.

Rhodes:

> That's right, sir.

Defense:

> You were not asked to process any automobile in

connection with this case . . . nor did you send any of the prints you raised and developed out to California, did you?

Rhodes:

I don't recall sending any prints to California.

Defense:

You didn't send any prints to the Federal Bureau of Investigation?

Rhodes:

I did not.

Defense:

Now, you have told us that you, in order to perform an identification, [you] have to have not only the unknown print, but you would want an identifiable named print or print with which you could compare it.

Rhodes:

That's true.

Defense counsel had the bailiff set up a chalkboard and picked up a piece of paper for reference in questioning Rhodes:

Defense:

Now, I am just using the board because it is easier to see than the piece of paper. Now, the purpose, Mr. Rhodes, of classifying, according to Henry's-it is Henry's what?

Rhodes:

Henry System, we call it, classification.

Defense:

>Modified FBI system, is it not?

Rhodes:

>Well, you call it the Henry Classification System, sir.

Defense:

>The purpose of classifying prints is an attempt to take a latent and give you a guide to get into a group or a possible category which you could compare, is it not?

Rhodes:

>No, sir.

Defense:

>It is not?

Rhodes:

>That is not what classification is about.

Defense:

>Now, classification, you begin with a key, do you not? That is the first number in your classification? It would be a figure of some kind? [He writes on the board: "19."]

Rhodes:

>That's right. [As in the first trial, Rhodes thought he was being given the opportunity to show off his "expertise."]

Defense:

>Okay. Next would be the major classification, or the major item, would it not? And that is represented by letters, correct? [He writes on the board: "L" and "M."]

Rhodes:

That's right.

Defense:

And then you go to the prime right, that's numbers, "9" [and] "2."

Rhodes:

That's right.

Defense:

Letters, capital letters, or could be if it is ulnar. It's a slash and direction of the loop, or to the right or to the left. If it is to the right, then it is a capital R. [He writes: "R" and "R."] Then you go to a sub-secondary. That is usually three numbers? [He writes: "000" and "001."]

Rhodes:

That's right.

Defense:

And then you come up with a final. [He writes "15" and "14."]

The full entry on the chalkboard reads:

19 L R 000 15

M 2 R 001 14

Rhodes:

That is right.

Defense:

And therefore, if you get a figure like that, that is a classification of the print which you can catalogue?

Rhodes:

That is right. That is classification, sir, of ten fingers.

Defense:

And you were given at some point for Michael Jiminez and for Mr. Clark a full set of prints? On a card, rolled set of prints?

Rhodes:

Controlled prints, that's right.

Defense:

You said you weren't able to raise the prints of Barbara Jiminez?

Rhodes:

That is right.

Defense:

Does that figure I put on the board, Mr. Rhodes, mean anything to you in relation to this case?

With a startled look, Rhodes paused, then responded:

Rhodes:

Does that mean anything to me?

Defense:

Yes.

Rhodes:

I think it is what we kind of arrived at as Mrs. Jiminez's classification.

Defense:

That is what I thought. Thank you.

On redirect questioning, the prosecutor continued to mislead the jury even though Rhodes had admitted that they had Barbara Jiminez's fingerprint classification:

Prosecutor:

> Did that classification or potential classification have any bearing on your ability to identify the latent prints that you found?

Rhodes:

> We could not find anywhere any *recorded* prints of Mrs. Jiminez. We didn't have them in our file, or no other agency we could find that recorded any prints of Mrs. Jiminez.

Prosecution:

> So they would have no significance in helping you find a positive print to identify some of the latent prints that you have?

Rhodes:

> That's right, sir.

The prosecutor in his attempt to deceive the jury-made up of laypersons-implied that the researcher must check an actual print only against prints on file. As shown through cross-examination by defense counsel, however, prints are classified by numbers and letters, and it's not necessary to have a name to go along with the print.

Defense counsel again asked a question of Rhodes related to this subject, to emphasize that an established and thorough effort was not made to identify the unknown prints:

Defense:

> I asked you if you sent the prints to California and did you send the prints to Washington to the FBI?

Rhodes:

No, I did not, sir.

How Wylde learned that Rhodes had Barbara Jiminez's fingerprint classification, I do not know, but in the file of the prosecutor, subpoenaed during appellate hearings, there was a memorandum dated five months before the first trial, listing Barbara Jiminez's fingerprint classification. It revealed more:

> HOMICIDE 734-1831
>
> Victims: Michael and Barbara Jiminez 5-7-74: *Epidermal skin from fingers of victim, Barbara Jiminez were inked, recorded and classified.*
>
> Classification was found to be:
>
> 19 L 9 000 15
>
> M 2 001 14
>
> Due to the vast amount of physical evidence to be processed, the latent work, at this time, has not been completed. Of the partial latent prints found so far, none match the finger impressions of the *two victims* or Edward R. Clark.
>
> Walter A Rhodes
>
> Assistant Identification Officer[161]

At the appellate hearing, defense counsel Wylde, when asked by my appellate attorney whether he had seen the memorandum, responded that he had not. In the appeal, my attorney stated:

> Because this would mean that the fingerprints . . . were those of a third person, Mr. Wylde naturally felt that was even more significant than Barbara's classification. If counsel had this report prior to the trial he surely would have brought this to the jury's attention.[162]

When the prosecution's experts testify with questionable and challengeable evidence, the defense should bring in its own experts.

That occurs, however, only in cases in which the defendant can afford expert testimony. I doubt that if defense attorney Wylde had petitioned the court to do so in my case, Judge Fitzgerald would have approved the funds. He had already denied funding for an investigator to search the Michigan Department of Motor Vehicles for the motorists I gave assistance to the night I arrived home.

I do believe that absent the funds needed to bring in rebuttal expert witnesses, my attorney did a good job of challenging the findings of the State's witnesses on forensics. At one point defense attorney Wylde asked to approach the bench. There he stated:

> At this point we are apparently to the point in the trial where there is going to be introduced a group of exhibits, physical evidence found at the scene of the death of Michael Jiminez which were depicted in photographs which went in yesterday over defense objections.
>
> I would like the record to note a continuing objection with respect to any of these items for the grounds already alluded to, that I feel any evidence in the death of Michael Jiminez should be inadmissible.

Judge Fitzgerald overruled this objection.

Sheriff Wiebold of Blue Earth County took the stand. He described the crime scene at which Michael Jiminez's body was discovered, just as had BCA Agent Simonson. Through the sheriff, numerous additional photographs of the crime scene, along with allegedly discovered physical evidence, were introduced.[163]

During cross-examination, defense counsel pursued a line of questioning regarding items that were found in Le Sueur County and turned over to the Blue Earth County Sheriff's Department but *not* introduced by the prosecution. These included a "brown jacket" that Wylde suspected was the brown suede jacket (in my opinion likely belonging to the third hitchhiker) that had covered the contents of the box I discarded:

Defense:

>Could you describe some of those items that were found?

Sheriff Wiebold:

>There was another old brown jacket, a pair of women's panties... There are numerous other articles of varying sizes and descriptions which I don't recall exactly.

Defense:

>What did you ultimately do with the other items... that were found?

Sheriff Wiebold:

>Some of the items-many of the items that were failed to be identified after the trial in Mankato-were discarded.

Since the items were not discarded until "after" the first trial, public defender Adamson could and should have investigated the items, particularly the brown coat, for that trial.

Referring to photos taken of the crime scene and the surrounding area, defense counsel proceeded:

Defense:

>There is a house across the street, and what appears to be a barn down the road... Could you estimate the distance for me, let's say, this railroad crossing to this house?

Sheriff Wiebold:

>I'd say probably three-quarters of a mile, sir.

Defense:

>Who lives in that house, do you know?

Sheriff Wiebold:

> I don't recall . . . Offhand, it was a rental property.

Referring to additional tire tracks found at the scene:

Defense:

> Is it a fair statement, Sheriff, that there were a lot of tracks, on both the north and south side of Highway 14?

Sheriff Wiebold:

> Oh, definitely.

Reflecting on a lack of established investigational procedure:

Defense:

> You did not direct that any search be conducted for a bullet?

Sheriff Wiebold:

> I directed only that a search be conducted of the area, to find anything else that might pertain.

Defense:

> Did Mr. Simonson BCA field agent, while you were there, produce any magnets, metal detector, or anything of that nature?

Sheriff Wiebold:

> No.

Defense:

> Did you take any plaster casts or impressions of any of the tire tracks?

Sheriff Wiebold:

> No, sir. I used the photographic technique in lieu of

that.

Defense:

    Now, did you find anything at the scene of Highway 14 that did not ultimately connect with Mr. Clark?

Sheriff Wiebold:

    Oh, yes.

Defense:

    Such as?

Sheriff Wiebold:

    Oh, I can recall one thing in specific. It was a receipt from a Sherwood Auto Parts of Mankato. I don't recall for sure where it was found.

Defense:

    You said that a penny was found on Michael Jiminez's body. You subsequently searched the apartment, and found about $150 didn't you?

Sheriff Wiebold:

    I didn't. Two of my men did.

Defense:

    The watch, Sheriff, that you mentioned, was that running or not running?

Sheriff Wiebold:

    As my memory serves me, sir, it was not running at the time that I observed it on the body of the deceased.

Defense:

    Do you recall the time that was on the watch?

Sheriff Wiebold:

> I believe it was somewhere around eleven. It was pointed at eleven on the watch.

On redirect examination, prosecutor Christian asked Wiebold:

Prosecutor:

> Sheriff, I assume as a law enforcement officer you have a gun that you often times carry on your person. Other than that particular gun, are you familiar with other guns? For instance, do you own other guns?

Sheriff Wiebold:

> Numerous other weapons. I collect weapons. At this point in time my collection would run in excess of 100 pieces.

Prosecutor:

> Do you possess or own any guns of the caliber that is reflected in State's Exhibit OO [the cartridge casing allegedly found at the crime scene]?

Sheriff Wiebold:

> I do.

Prosecutor:

> What type of weapon is it?

Sheriff Wiebold:

> I have three revolvers in that caliber and one carbine.

Prosecutor:

> Specifically directing your attention to Exhibit OO, after it was taken from the crime scene, did you perform any visual examinations of it? What, if any, observations

did you make of that that were pertinent to you?

Sheriff Wiebold:

> I found pertinent to my observation, the fact that the markings on the rim of this cartridge indicated that it had been fired from an automatically ejecting weapon.

Prosecutor:

> Is that the same type of weapon that you personally own?

Sheriff Wiebold:

> Yes.

Prosecutor:

> What type of weapon is it that you own?

Sheriff Wiebold:

> A 44 Ruger Carbine.

Defense attorney Wylde objected and at the bench argued against the introduction of any more evidence from the Michael Jiminez case. Judge Fitzgerald sustained the objection, but with the prosecutor about to give a lengthy argument, both attorneys and the court reporter followed the judge into chambers. The prosecutor argued:

> Well, I just wanted the record to reflect that . . . the court summoned myself and counsel for the defendant up to the bench and indicated that he felt that in his opinion that the prosecution was attempting to offer too much evidence concerning the crime scene on the death of Michael Jiminez and accordingly instructed the prosecution to stay away from that area . . . the whole case of the State being built, so to speak, on circumstantial evidence and the State taking the position that the killings or the deaths of Michael Jiminez and Barbara Jiminez being part of one episode, that in order for the State to

effectively prove intent on the part of the assailant to kill Barbara, is also a necessary part to show the facts and circumstances of the death of Michael Jiminez.

The judge again ruled that no more evidence or photos relating to the Michael Jiminez crime scene could be introduced, but this was like closing the barn door after the horses were out-the jury had already been exposed to it.

Continuing his testimony, Sheriff Wiebold erroneously testified, as he had in the first trial, as to my utterance upon being informed of the indictment brought against me by the Le Sueur County Grand Jury:

Prosecutor:

> Could you tell us, the best you can recall, your words, or what you told him at that time?

Sheriff Wiebold:

> To the best of my knowledge, there were three indictments brought forth by the grand jury in Le Sueur County, one of them being first-degree murder, the other being another first-degree murder with the intent to commit rape, and then second-degree murder, which would have been murder without premeditation.

Prosecutor:

> Did you relate to Mr. Clark this in the conversation?

Sheriff Wiebold:

> I did.

Prosecutor:

> Did you have an occasion to visit him, then, later that day in his cell?

Sheriff Wiebold:

Yes, a short time later.

Prosecution:

Tell us your observations of his demeanor at that point, if you can?

Sheriff Wiebold:

When I entered the cell, Mr. Clark had his head pillowed in his arms. Seemed visibly shaken and upset.

Prosecution:

And did Mr. Clark say anything?

Sheriff Wiebold:

He said, "That girl wasn't raped"

Prosecutor:

Was he looking at you?

Sheriff Wiebold:

No, he wasn't.

. . .

Prosecutor:

And then what, if anything, did he say?

Sheriff Wiebold:

I believe he said, "Oh, I thought you were the minister," or something to that effect.

Prosecutor:

Had you said anything to him prior to that, or at that time? What did you say?

Sheriff Wiebold:

I said, "Is there anything I can do for you, Ed?" upon entering the cell.

Prosecutor:

And was this before or after he said this statement about the girl?

Sheriff Wiebold:

As I recall, it was before.

"You liar," I thought, and we certainly weren't on a first-name basis. On recross-examination, the defense attacked Wiebold regarding this allegation:

Defense:

Now Sheriff, with respect to this statement you claimed to have overheard, I am going to ask you to search your mind. Is it possible the statement was "The girl was raped"-did he say, "The girl was raped"?

Sheriff Wiebold:

That's not what I heard.

Defense:

You realize it is a very thin line between "was" and "wasn't"?

Sheriff Wiebold:

I realize that.

Defense:

Now, when you went into that cell pursuant to the SOP, operating procedures which you employ in Blue Earth County, you were being monitored sight and sound, were you not?

Sheriff Wiebold:

> As my memory serves me, the jailer was standing in the doorway, yes.

Defense:

> Then, you also have a sound-monitoring system?

Sheriff Wiebold:

> We do.

Defense:

> So therefore when somebody goes down in the cell area, the person in the control room can monitor him through the devices where sight are available and sound throughout, and that is a security device?

Sheriff Wiebold:

> That's right.

Defense:

> And therefore when you went into the jail, I assume you were being monitored for security?

Sheriff Wiebold:

> I presume so.

Defense:

> Alright, now, let's get back to the distinction between the words "Was" and "Wasn't". Now, you have testified today, Sheriff, that after the statement where you came in and said something you believe, the statement was made to you, and that Mr. Clark looked up and said, "I thought you were the minister," something to that effect. Now, considering the frailties of memory being what they are, and considering the distinction available here, there was a

hearing that was held the very next day?

Sheriff Wiebold:

I believe so.

Defense:

That was the day after you alleged you heard this conversation that you testified to?

Sheriff Wiebold:

That's right.

Defense:

You testified to the same series of events in that situation, didn't you?

Sheriff Wiebold:

To the best of my memory, I did.

Defense:

And you gave a different version of what occurred at that hearing, did you not?

Sheriff Wiebold:

I don't have the transcript. I don't recall my examination version.

Defense:

Do you remember testifying to the effect that after he made that statement to you, "He looked up, recognized me, and said no more"?

Sheriff Wiebold:

Quite possibly said that. I don't recall exactly my words.

The headline in the *Mankato Free Press* regarding Sheriff Wiebold's testimony announced "Wiebold Bites Bullet in Clark Trial".[164]

While defense attorney Wylde did a good job raising the question as to the truthfulness of the sheriff's allegation, Wylde could have impeached the sheriff if he had been aware that the jail log carried the entry "Recording, Max. South" for the time of the incident. He could have subpoenaed the tape and played it to the jury, and most certainly he would have impeached the sheriff if we had had at that time the signed statement from Deputy Joseph Hauer, which I obtained in 1979 *after* appellate hearing (and quoted from in chapter 9 of this volume). Hauer stated: "If Clark did say anything the tape was to be saved and given to either Jerry Wersal or Sheriff Wiebold."

For the second time, Christian attempted to introduce the statement I had made during interrogation in California-not an admission of guilt but that I had not been in Minnesota in three years. The prosecution was not above trying, through erroneous statements, to deny a defendant his constitutional rights for the sole purpose of winning a conviction.

This occurred in judge's chambers in one of the long conferences, during which the prosecutor also expressed concern about costs related to the trial:

> *It is my interpretation that he would sign the Miranda form* that was presented to him . . . that *at no time did he ever indicate that he wanted to see an attorney* before he would make a statement or comment to them, and *the fact he did make a statement or comment to them that I felt was in the nature of an admission*, but, in any event, the Court felt otherwise, and it is my opinion from that point I have to make a decision to appeal the Court's Order or proceed. *Based upon the fact there is an economical factor, certainly could not afford to stop the proceedings* at this point and go to the Supreme Court [to appeal the judge's ruling].

Judge Fitzgerald again ruled the statement inadmissible. Nevertheless, it eventually came into evidence. After the trials, both the Blue Earth and

Le Sueur County District Courts acknowledged that it had been obtained illegally and therefore was inadmissible.

The *Mankato Free Press* reported on another long conference-on whether the prosecution should be allowed to call the prosecutor from the first trial to the stand-in the judge's chambers:

> Action in the first-degree-murder trial of Edward R. Clark ground to a halt this morning as the attorneys were having it out in judge's chambers.
>
> Court convened on time in the Hennepin County Courthouse in the ninth day of the trial, but broke immediately for the private talks . . .
>
> An investigator for the defense said that an ad which was run in the *Free Press* and the *Daily Reporter* [legal publication] seeking any knowledge about the deaths of Michael and Barbara did net some results.[165]

The prosecution intended to read my testimony from the first trial out of context, omitting all references to my innocence. With defense counsel arguing against this ploy and the manner in which it was to be introduced, Judge Fitzgerald questioned the prosecutor:

> Why isn't it just as good for you to read questions and answers and the court can make a statement that this presentation is evidence that the jury can use in connection with their arrival at their verdict in this case, period? I don't know. Maybe I am just putting too much emphasis on bringing the prosecutor in the first trial in, in view of the fact you have got this first trial in this thing up to your eyeballs already. Do you have any violent objections to-

"Yes, I certainly do," interrupted the prosecutor. "I do not feel that I should have to myself read the questions and the answers."

"Well, it is your case. You do what you want," said the judge. "In view of the posture of the case as of now, I am going to let you do it the way

you want to."

"There is nothing that I can-I am not going to be allowed to cross-examine on any questions as it is in the transcript?" asked defense counsel Wylde.

"That is what it amounts to, yes," answered the judge.

John Corbey, the prosecutor from the Michael Jiminez trial, took the stand as the last witness of the day and of the prosecutor's case. Introduced through Corbey were weather charts for the Mankato area during the time in question as to the slaying of Michael Jiminez. This served no purpose but to throw in more "evidence" to overwhelm the jury.

The questioning then turned to who Corbey was and to my testimony in the Blue Earth trial:

Prosecutor:

>What is your occupation, Mr. Corbey?

Corbey:

>I am an attorney.

Prosecutor:

>And among your other duties as attorney, are you, like I am in Le Sueur County, part-time county attorney for Blue Earth?

Corbey:

>Yes, sir, I am.
>
>. . .

Prosecutor:

>And were you present in court in Mankato at which time there was proceedings concerning Edward R. Clark? And did you observe during the course of those

proceedings that Mr. Clark took the stand and testified in his own behalf?

Corbey:

Yes, sir, I did.

Prosecutor:

And prior to his taking the stand, did you observe that the clerk administered the oath to him?

Corbey:

Yes, sir, I did.

Prosecutor:

At this point, Mr. Corbey, we are going to be referring to a portion of that testimony of Mr. Clark, and I will direct the question, I will indicate who asked the question, I will further indicate the page of the transcript and the line or folio of the transcript so the testimony can be found, and that I would like you to respond with the answer . . .

Referring to page 920, continuing through the page to 921, there is a question by Mr. Adamson: "Now, Mr. Clark, as you were on Highway 80 and going through the State of Iowa, did you have occasion there to pick up any hitchhikers?"

Corbey:

The answer is "Yes, I did."

Prosecutor:

Question: "And could you state for the record and for the benefit of the jury where it was that you picked these hitchhikers up?

Corbey:

"It was along Interstate 80, west of Des Moines, Iowa."

. . .

Prosecutor:

Now, referring to page 961 . . . questioned by yourself, Mr. Corbey: "have you ever been in Wisconsin before?"

Corbey:

Answer: "Yes, sir."

Prosecutor:

Question: "When?"

Corbey:

"February of '74 was the last time. No, I'm sorry. You wanted the last time?"

Prosecutor:

"Yes."

Corbey:

"The last time would have been after I left this area. After picking up the hitchhikers and all this had happened. I would have gone through Wisconsin."[166]

I was stunned at the way the prosecution was presenting my testimony in the Blue Earth trial. The prosecutor took my statements out of context so the jury would hear only what he wanted them to hear. His presentation omitted nearly 40 pages of my testimony, including that about picking up *three* hitchhikers, falling asleep while one of them drove for me, waking up the next morning and finding that I was alone in the Bronco, making the phone call to my home later that day near Belvidere, Illinois, and the time I arrived home. And Corbey's manner of answering was giving the jury the impression the answers had been forced from me. The jury was obviously affected by this.

Juror Danials interrupted the testimony: "Your Honor, could I ask for a short recess? I just don't feel well." (I thought, "Neither do I.") The judge replaced Juror Danials with an alternate juror.

I was infuriated. That evening I tried to contact the media to complain that my testimony had been taken out of context to mislead the jury, but my calls were intercepted. The next morning, this attempt was brought up in chambers. The prosecutor responded: "I think the court should advise the defendant or order him that he shall not conduct any press conference. In the event he does, he should be held in contempt and suffer whatever possible consequences there might be."

I was summoned, and the judge warned that I would be "held in contempt of court" should I go public. This was ludicrous-I was already serving a life sentence. From the look on Judge Fitzgerald's face, I could tell he knew this as soon as he said it. Nonetheless, I had no opportunity to publicly complain.

We returned to the courtroom. The judge said nothing, sitting for a few moments deep in thought. Then he summoned both attorneys back into chambers, this time without the court reporter. Apparently he wanted to discuss something that would not be on the record.

John Corbey later was summoned back to the witness stand. And Wylde was allowed to elicit from him my testimony including that there were three hitchhikers, not just the Jiminezes, that when I awoke the next morning there was no lake in the vicinity, and that I had discarded the box, in which the typewriter receipt was found, because it was full and used only for trash.

I believe Judge Fitzgerald reversed his ruling and allowed defense counsel to cross-examine Corbey out of concern that I would otherwise raise hell about it whenever I had the chance to complain publicly, but overwhelming damage had been done. Hearing a fuller account did not abate the shock of the jurors at hearing during Corbey's direct examination only what the prosecution wanted them to hear.

My appeal addressed the prejudicial tactic of the two prosecutors:

> Defense counsel objected quickly and strenuously to the introduction of the transcript of appellant's testimony given at the Blue Earth County trial. He argued that the transcript was hearsay evidence and that its introduction would violate appellant's Fifth Amendment privilege against self-incrimination. The court ruled against appellant . . .
>
> Appellant testified [at the appellate hearing] that he was compelled to take the stand in the first trial for two reasons: a television commentator the night before had reported that appellant was going to testify, and the State had introduced a statement which he had made to the California police officers . . .
>
> Appellant explained: [T]here was reference during the trial by the State regarding a statement I had made in California to the authorities, and I felt that I would then have to testify also in regards to that to clear up the matter.
>
> Appellate Attorney: That was the testimony by one of the California police officers to the effect that you had said to them you haven't been in the state of Minnesota for three years?
>
> Appellant: Yes, sir.
>
> Appellant Attorney: And you felt that was something you have to rebut, something you have to explain to the jury?
>
> Appellant: Yes, sir.
>
> Defense counsel objected also to the way in which the prosecution planned to present the testimony from the prior trial. The trial court turned a deaf ear to his objection and allowed the State unfettered discretion in presenting

the prior testimony. Specifically defense counsel objected to two prejudicial elements of the manner in which the prosecutor intended to present the evidence:

> First, the transcript was read in dialogue from by two prosecutors: Mr. Christian, the one handling the second trial, read the question, and Mr. Corbey, the one who had handled the first trial, read the answers. The jury was fully aware of Mr. Corbey's connection with the case from preliminary questions asked of him by Mr. Christian. In addition to speculating as to appellant's reason for taking the stand in the first but not the second trial, the jury must have wondered at the choice of the former prosecutor to read appellant's part of the transcript-a procedure that even the trial court labeled "peculiar". Moreover, the jury's duty to weigh the credibility of the witness was confused by the inflection given portions of the transcript by the two prosecutors. Defense counsel's suggestion that the transcript or a summary of the testimony be read by the clerk would have had far less prejudicial impact on the jury.
>
> Second, defense counsel objected to the prosecution's taking the prior testimony out of context by reading only selected portions of the transcript. He urged the trial court to rule that either all or none of the transcript be read into evidence. Again, the trial court overruled the request.[167]

The State rested its case. A United Press International (UPI) headline proclaimed: "Prosecution Rests in Jiminez Trial." Defense counsel Wylde moved for a directed verdict of acquittal on all three counts of the indictment, stating the reasons, including that no evidence had been presented as to how Barbara Jiminez died.[168]

Such a motion is routine at the conclusion of a prosecutor's case, but judges rarely grant it.

Chapter 12: The Case for the Defense

Defense attorney Wylde made his opening statement to the jury, in part:

> The purpose of an opening statement is to put into perspective for you in some degree the evidence which we expect to produce, what it will show. Now . . . the State's theory is that these two young people were killed on or about the same time.
>
> The defendant's evidence will simply show, number one, that the death of Michael Jiminez occurred around midnight on April 23, and that Edward Clark could not have been the agency of the death of Michael Jiminez. He wasn't there.[169]

Delvin Ohrt, the pathologist who performed the autopsy on Michael Jiminez, was called to the stand. In the first trial, Dr. Ohrt had testified for the prosecution, but since Michael Jiminez's death was determined to have occurred at a time that made it impossible for me to have committed the murder, he was now testifying for the defense.

After preliminary questions, defense counsel Wylde proceeded:

Defense:

> Now, sometime, I believe it was April 23 . . . you were asked to perform an autopsy on an individual identified to you as Michael Jiminez, is that correct?

Dr. Ohrt:

> Correct.

Defense:

> Did you, in addition to other things, have occasion to inquire into the possible time of death?

Dr. Ohrt:

> This was requested by the law enforcement people.

As in the first trial, Dr. Ohrt outlined how he had come to the conclusion as to the time of death. Then:

Defense:

> *Doctor, based on your observations and the information which you had, did you have an occasion to form an opinion concerning when Michael Jiminez met his death, the time?*

Dr. Ohrt:

> The opinion that we gave *in the past* was somewhere in the vicinity of 15 to roughly 20 hours prior to the time of our examination.

Defense:

> You examined him at four o'clock in the afternoon. Do you know what that comes out to?

Dr. Ohrt:

> *It was between nine o'clock on the 22nd and 3 A.M. on the 23rd.*

Defense:

So that would be three hours either side of midnight on the 23rd of April 1974.

Dr. Ohrt:

Yes.[170]

On cross-examination, however, Dr. Ohrt exaggerated, wavering on the time of death for the benefit of the prosecution. He emphasized that his conclusions were "in the past" to suggest he had since altered his findings. He did this in spite of his having confirmed his findings with the leading forensic pathologist in the state:

Prosecutor:

Doctor, you indicated this was an opinion that you were asked to give sometime previously? And it was originally asked you by law enforcement people, I assume?

Dr. Ohrt:

Correct.

Prosecutor:

And the purpose, I assume, was to give them some idea of approximately how long the body may have been there?

Dr. Ohrt:

What they wanted to know was roughly what time he was killed. We tried to give them that, with certain other factors taken into consideration.

Prosecutor:

Well, using that term, then, was this opinion that you gave us a rough guess or estimate?

Dr. Ohrt:

Time of death is always a rough estimate . . . We can

give a minimum time much better than we can give a maximum time.

Prosecutor:

So then the minimum time of death was 15 to 22 hours?

Dr. Ohrt:

I would say the minimum time to give you an hour figure would be roughly 15 hours, give or take a couple.

Prosecutor:

How about the maximum time?

Dr. Ohrt:

This stretches out into the vicinity of, oh, roughly 40 to 42 hours. There is a lot of individual variation in this particular situation.

Prosecutor:

And the autopsy again was performed at about 4 P.M. on April 23?

Dr. Ohrt:

Correct.

. . .

Prosecutor:

So that would take us back to, oh, possibly even Sunday night, is this correct?

Dr. Ohrt

. . . Sunday night, very possibly. The reason that we rule out death during the day is Highway 14 has a steady stream of traffic.

Prosecutor:

But that was just sort of a logical approach on your part?

Dr. Ohrt:

Yes . . .

Prosecutor:

Okay. *So you don't particularly want to give us the impression here that it is your opinion that it was 15 to 22 hours?*

Dr. Ohrt:

Statistically it would be most likely within that period of time, but not necessarily so.

Prosecutor:

So there really was nothing inconsistent, then, with your finding at the time of autopsy that would be inconsistent with a death 20 to 30 hours prior to that time the tests were conducted?

Dr. Ohrt:

That's correct.

Prosecutor:

Probably even longer than that?

Dr. Ohrt:

Possibly.

Defense attorney Wylde, just as he had confronted Dr. Peterson on changing his position in favor of the prosecution, now challenged Dr. Ohrt on extending the time of Michael Jiminez's death:

Defense:

It would be statistically unlikely, however, is that correct?

Dr. Ohrt:

The statistics, from the relatively small amount of date we have got . . . would put us in the time range I gave, again, with the daylight sequence and everything else, for the law enforcement people.

Defense:

It would be less likely he laid there all day Monday and all day Tuesday, would it not?

Dr. Ohrt:

But it is possible.

Defense:

Oh, it's possible, but you consider it unlikely in your opinion?

Dr. Ohrt:

Yes.

Because of Dr. Ohrt's double-talk, defense counsel now became assertive in his questions:

Defense:

And I talked to you yesterday, and I asked you at that time if you still felt your opinion, plus or minus three hours at midnight, the 22nd, was valid?

Dr. Ohrt:

Yes.

As he stated in the first trial, the grand jury had asked Dr. Ohrt to be even more specific than three hours either side of midnight. He put the time of death at around midnight, before the discovery of Michael Jiminez's body and the autopsy. Midnight was the time of my arrival at home, 700 miles to the east, in Michigan.

Since Wylde told the jury that the "death of Michael Jiminez occurred around midnight on April 23" and that "Edward Clark could not have been the agency of the death of Michael Jiminez. He wasn't there," the jury was much concerned as to the time of death. During deliberation, the jurors asked to review Dr. Ohrt's testimony, but Judge Fitzgerald denied them the opportunity.

The next witness, Elizabeth Pastor, was a representative from the American Automobile Association (AAA or "Triple A"). As in the first trial, and as part of the State's case in this trial, she gave the average mileage from Reno, Nevada, to Des Moines, Iowa, then north to Minnesota. The prosecutors wanted to jury to hear only those figures, as additional measures coincided with my alibi. As a defense witness, she now gave the distance from Rochester, Minnesota, near the Iowa border, to the Rockford-Belvidere area in Illinois where I made the phone call, as 270 miles. And from Rockford to my home near Detroit, Michigan, as 385 miles.[171]

During another of the many conferences in this trial, a juror abruptly stood up and headed to judge's chambers. There, juror Oberlin voiced his frustration over the long conferences. Then he asked, "Can members of the jury ask the witnesses questions?"

Judge Fitzgerald put his response on the record:

Judge:

> The question was, "Do you allow jurors to ask questions of the witnesses?" The Court answered, "No."

Oberlin:

> Just for my own personal information, is that ever allowed?

Judge:

As far as I am concerned, never allowed.

Oberlin then expressed his reasons for asking, indicating that the jury was confused about why evidence from the Michael Jiminez case was being introduced in this trial:

Oberlin:

> Now I heard testimony, excruciating details between distances . . . in Blue Earth County crime scene. This week we have heard a lot of detailed testimony [as] to other distances . . . We have not been able to review any of the maps, for instance . . .

Judge:

> The maps will go to the jurors at the time the case is turned over to the jury, along with all the rest of the evidence.

Oberlin:

> But there is a lot of detailed testimony that was given. It's very hard for me to understand because the map wasn't right before us, and these weren't pointed out. The second problem I am having, not seeing the evidence in a timely fashion . . . *We have had a lot of information thrown at us. For instance . . . testimony from the Michael Jiminez trial . . . well, a lot of details on the Michael Jiminez murder. In fact, half the testimony I have heard has been concerned with that . . . Right now it is very confusing in my own mind what the relevant relationship is between a lot of this evidence.*
>
> Now, my understanding is that the trial is . . . in terms of evidence and testimony and facts to prove the innocence or guilt of Mr. Clark . . . now I am probably revealing my ignorance of the judicial process. I hope that a lot of this testimony is tied together by the attorneys here because, quite frankly, and I haven't discussed with the other jurors-but I suspect that they may be confused by a

lot of the testimony as much as I am.

Now, gentlemen, I am by education and vocation an engineer, and I am an engineering manager, and . . . I have had more of my share of experience solving problems, and identifying, examining evidence, so I think I know something about communicating and, quite frankly, I hope it improves.

Another point that has been bothering me, you gentlemen have access obviously to *the Michael Jiminez [trial] transcript*, a lot of other information we don't have access to. Please put yourselves in our shoes. We are hearing this for the first time, and *we don't understand the relationship between a lot of stuff that is being presented*, and I think maybe at times maybe you gentlemen forget this . . .

Judge:

That's alright. I appreciate your calling these points to our attention . . . I will give complete instructions to all the jurors at the close of the trial.

After juror Oberlin left the chambers, the prosecutor, recognizing that he could be quite persuasive during deliberations, stated, "I would move to have him dismissed, but I, to be quite frank, don't know the legal basis for."

Judge Fitzgerald answered: "Sure spotlights the Michael Jiminez trial decision. I mean, the decision to allow evidence in, and the fact of that trial and conviction.[172]

Defense counsel Wylde walked into the courtroom to explain to me the reason for the long delay, including that juror Oberlin had voiced his dissatisfaction over the prosecutor bringing in all the evidence from the Michael Jiminez murder trial, that it was confusing the jury. And that the prosecutor wanted Oberlin dismissed from the jury panel. We agreed that it was in my best interest to have Oberlin remain. Wylde then returned to chambers:

Defense:

The thoughts he [Oberlin] expressed are probably thoughts that many jurors have in a trial. He has come forward and stated them to the court and counsel, which is contrary to what most jurors do, because I have never heard that comment from a juror, but I see no basis for removing him at this point . . . simply because he voices his thoughts. He also did indicate that he hadn't conferred with the other jurors about this at all, which is some indication he is following the court's instructions. As far as highlighting the Michael Jiminez matter, we fought about this and it is on the record and I don't see anything special in that comment that-

Judge:

Well, I have already told counsel that it strikes me that the juror's statements just indicate to me the recent anti-lawyer, anti-judicial process campaign in the media and elsewhere seems to have struck home in spades with Mr. Oberlin, and that although I have never been confronted with the problem, either, I don't see any valid basis for . . . removing him at this stage just because he had the gumption to speak up and voice his thoughts at this stage.

Prosecutor:

I believe that he indicated that in view of the fact that he is an engineer, he should have something above natural, perhaps supernatural power to analyze and digest this material, consequently he is not qualified.

Judge:

All right. The record will show that the court doesn't find anything . . . which would require his removal or is a basis for challenging him, and for that reason the State's motion to remove the juror is denied.[173]

With the jail located in the same building as the courtroom, the escorting deputy stopped putting handcuffs on me during the defense portion of the trial. Apparently he was confident I wouldn't attempt anything stupid. I wondered whether he had heard enough of the proceedings to generate some doubt about the defendant's guilt. I certainly appreciated his gesture. Also, in this trial, there was no personal reason for the Hennepin County Sheriff's Department to portray me as "dangerous" as had the Blue Earth County Sheriff in the earlier trial.

Having grown weary in the more than a year of doing everything I could to defend myself, I was now in somewhat of a stupor, oblivious to my surroundings, including the people we passed in the corridor. But one day, on the way to the courtroom, I heard my wife's voice, "Hon," and then my mother's trembling voice, calling me as she always did, regardless of my age, "Eddie."

Escorting deputies are wary of anyone approaching a defendant, but the deputy stopped and allowed me to approach my family. My wife and I embraced, and with difficulty, my elderly mother raised up from where she sat and threw her arms around me. It was the first time I had seen my wife and mother in ten months. The minister whose family had befriended my family when they were in Mankato also stepped forward, shook my hand, and said his congregation was praying for me. Although the deputy didn't say anything, as he moved closer, I understood that he didn't want to stand in the corridor any longer than necessary.

Walking away, I said, "Don't worry, Mom. Everything's going fine." I would reassure her no matter how bad things looked.

I recognized another familiar face in the corridor. We waived. It was Dr. Robert Bailey, who had performed the hypnosis on me at the state prison. He made the trip from Wisconsin at his own expense and was going to testify that he believed I was telling the truth when I testified at the first trial about picking up three hitchhikers. Judge Fitzgerald, however, ruled Dr. Bailey's testimony inadmissible.

A UPI headline in Twin Cities announced: "Relatives Testify in Clark Trial" on July 24, 1975, the day my wife, Jere, took the stand, and after preliminary questions, defense counsel proceeded:

Defense:

> Mrs. Clark, calling your attention to the 22nd of April 1974, did you at some time receive a telephone call from someone whose voice you recognized as that of your husband?

Wife:

> Yes, I did.

Defense:

> Could you tell us about what time that was on the 22nd?

Wife:

> It was about five o'clock in the afternoon.

Defense:

> And after that call was terminated, did you make another telephone call to somebody in Michigan?

Wife:

> Yes, I called his mother.

Defense:

> And how do you recall the date as being the 22nd?

Wife:

> Well, I know it was a Tuesday.

Defense:

> This is the 22nd, Tuesday morning?

Wife:

Yes. Now, the 22nd is a Monday. It was a Monday . . . Monday night around dinnertime. He came home on Tuesday morning.

The prosecutor would capitalize on her simple, self-corrected mistake during his cross-examination, implying that she was lying as to when I arrived home. The defense attorney continued:

Defense:

And you saw your husband on Tuesday. Was that the following day?

Wife:

Yes. Early in the morning.

Defense:

About what time, do you remember?

Wife:

One-ish.

Defense:

How do you recall it was one-ish?

Wife:

Because I looked at the clock.

Defense:

What is your phone number?

Wife:

. . . . -8443

Defense counsel asked my wife about the return trip I made to California and what was in the U-Haul trailer. She said it was filled with household goods, furniture, including the washer and dryer, freezer, beds, dressers, and so forth.

> Defense:
>
> Was Ed alone when he left?
>
> Wife:
>
> He had our daughter with him . . . She was seven and was going to stay with her grandparents until we completed the move to California.

Because I had initially assumed my arrest in California was related to the civil lawsuit of my former business partners, defense counsel proceeded:

Defense:

> Mrs. Clark, were you made a party to any lawsuit in the State of Michigan?
>
> Wife:
>
> I was served papers.
>
> Defense:
>
> Mrs. Clark, where do you now reside?
>
> Wife:
>
> In Ferndale, Michigan.
>
> Defense:
>
> With whom do you live?
>
> Wife:
>
> Just myself and three children.
>
> Defense:
>
> Are you employed?

Wife:

Yes. Ten hours a day, six days a week.

Defense:

And you need that occupation in order to support yourself?

Wife:

Yes, I do.[174]

My wife hadn't told me about the long hours she had to work or about her hardships, and all this time, for more than a year, while raising three children, she had had to do without, other than what our friends had given or lent her, because most of our household items were sitting in storage in California. This made my situation even more unbearable.

The prosecutor was hostile and disrespectful simply to imply she was lying. His rudeness mounted with each question-to the point that Judge Fitzgerald had to warn him twice to back off, but the prosecutor hammered away with questions that implied things totally unfounded and untrue, regardless of her answers. I was boiling inside, and Wylde knew it.

"Stay calm. Don't fall for it," he advised. The prosecutor's attitude towards my wife was an attempt to rile me into displaying anger to support his characterization of me in his closing statement to the jury, as a "Dr. Jekyll and Mr. Hyde." To say that in a fit of rage I killed the Jiminezes for whatever reason. Still, to this day I regret that I remained silent during the prosecutor's disrespect towards my wife.

The prosecutor, despite the independent evidence of the phone company records as to when she received the call, pushed in his cross-examination:

Prosecutor:

And yesterday afternoon, prior to the recess, you told us that you were *sure* that this call at five o'clock in the afternoon was on Tuesday, did you not?

Wife:

I don't believe I did. It was on Monday.

Prosecutor:

Well, you wouldn't deny it if the record so showed that, would you?

Wife:

No, but if I did, it was a mistake.

Nevertheless, the prosecutor had the court reporter read that excerpt from her previous testimony. He challenged her again:

Prosecutor:

So you were more sure, yesterday afternoon, that it was on a Tuesday than you were it being April 22nd, which was Mr. Wylde's question to you?

Wife:

Well, the dates are confusing, but it was a Monday night, early Tuesday morning that he arrived home.

Prosecutor:

[Angrily] I move to have the answer stricken as not being responsive.

Like the prosecutor in the first trial, prosecutor Christian also implied we were having marital problems:

Prosecutor:

Now, you have indicated that your husband then got home about one o'clock in the morning and you are sure of this because you looked at the clock. And he stayed there three or four hours and then he went to his mother's. And the reason he left is because you and he were having marital problems, is it not?

Wife:

Not, it is not.

Prosecutor:

Do you deny, Mrs. Clark, here under oath, that you ever told anybody the reason he left after only staying there a short time was because you were having marital problems?

Wife:

Yes, I do deny that.

Prosecutor:

You deny telling anybody else that was the reason regardless of whether it was or was not, that was my question.

Wife:

I am sure I didn't ever tell anybody that. That wasn't the reason.

During cross-examination, numerous long conferences took place because the prosecutor wanted to bring in BCA Agent Simonson as a rebuttal witness who gave his testimony against my wife in the first trial-including his erroneous allegations as to exactly what I had told her regarding picking up the hitchhikers.

Defense counsel Wylde objected because of the marital privilege that prevents a spouse from testifying as to communications with a spouse. The public defender in my first trial should have made this objection as well.

Prosecutor:

> Mrs. Clark, you were present in Mankato last fall for a trial, were you not?
>
> Wife:
>
> Yes, I was.
>
> Prosecutor:
>
> And you observed your husband testifying? You heard everything he testified to?
>
> Wife:
>
> Yes.
>
> Prosecutor:
>
> And you yourself testified, did you not?
>
> Wife:
>
> Yes, I did.

The prosecutor was laying the foundation to bring in my testimony from the first trial through my wife, and out of context, just as he did by calling the prosecutor from the first trial to the stand. To imply that I had concealed from her the details of picking up the hitchhikers and subsequently ended up in Minnesota, he asked her whether I had told her anything beyond picking up the hitchhikers. At the time I mentioned it, our problems related to the lawsuit and final preparation for moving our family to the West Coast were our concern-I had no idea then of what had happened to any of the hitchhikers.

When leaving the witness stand after her testimony, my wife spontaneously came over and hugged me in front of the jury. Out of the corner of my eye, I could see the dirty look on the prosecutor's face. He intended to make her life more miserable if he could.

In chambers, prosecutor Christian moved to have my wife kept available until the defense had presented its entire case so he might call her back to the stand *if* he could establish grounds to do so. Defense counsel Wylde argued that to do so would place her job in jeopardy, that he would go along with her agreeing to fly back to Minnesota if needed. Judge Fitzgerald denied the prosecutor's motion, and she was not required to return.[175]

The judge, however, also disallowed defense counsel's questioning of her as to what I had testified in the first trial, which would have put the rest of my relevant testimony in context. Wylde tried another approach:

Defense:

> Because of the cross-examination of Mrs. Jere Clark . . . the defense should be allowed to subpoena from the first trial any witness who listened to the testimony of the defendant and could therefore testify to anything the defendant testified to at the first trial . . . Once again, we have a portion of the . . . testimony elicited at the former trial in evidence which is, I submit, misleading . . . Of course, being consistent with the position I took at the time Mr. Corbey testified, I submit that this enables me to inquire into the entire context of the testimony given by the defendant in the first trial, I don't retreat from that position.

Prosecutor:

> Well, I take the position that the testimony elicited by me on cross-examination does not permit the defense of doing anything further concerning the testimony at the Blue Earth trial either through the transcript or through other independent witnesses.

Judge Fitzgerald ruled that the defense could not bring in other witnesses to testify as to what I stated in the first trial.[176]

The prosecution's tactic of asking my wife to testify to anything we said and implying what was said between us, was raised on appeal:

> Appellant's wife supported the alibi defense by establishing that he called home about 5 P.M. on April 22,

> 1974, and arrived home approximately eight hours later . . . This was consistent with the telephone company record showing a call from the toll-way to appellant's home at 5:03 P.M. on the 22nd . . .
>
> On cross, the prosecutor's question concerning her conversations with appellant about the hitchhikers . . . caused a discussion in chambers, resulting in the trial court's ruling that appellant had not waived the marital privilege concerning communications with his wife . . . However, the court later ruled that by taking the stand in the Blue Earth trial *and testifying to communications with his wife, appellant did waive the statutory privilege* . . .
>
> Appellant submits that the trial court erred in ruling that he waived the marital privilege against disclosure of confidential communications simply *because his attorney in a prior trial failed to object* to cross-examination that required his wife to disclose such communications.[177]

I saw my wife, Jere, for the last time at that trial. So that she could get on with her life, we divorced four months later. No matter how painful, it was something we had to do.

My mother took the stand and again testified to receiving the phone call from my wife on that Monday, the same evening my wife received the phone calls from me. My mother said again that I visited her early the next morning. On cross-examination, she was asked again whether the clothing I wore contained any blood. She responded that it did not.

Christian knew the jury would not tolerate the disrespect towards my 76-year-old mother that he had shown my wife, so he attacked her credibility in a more subtle way:

Prosecutor:

    Mrs. Clark, like any mother, you love your son?

Mother:

Certainly.

Prosecutor:

And you would like to do anything to help him, wouldn't you?

Mother:

Young man, the one thing I would not do for my son or any of my children is lie for them!

Christian had no further questions.[178]

Like my wife, my mother stopped to give me a hug as she left the witness stand. The prosecutor complained to the judge over this display of affection. He told me, "Refrain from that kind of behavior!" My mother visited me every year in prison as long as she was physically able to travel. She lived to age 93, still holding out the hope of seeing her son a free man.

William Martin, security director for General Telephone Company of Illinois, testified from the phone record as he had in Mankato. On cross-examination, however, the prosecutor initiated a ploy to discredit Martin, the key independent witness in my alibi defense. The prosecutor claimed inconsistencies, especially as to my home phone number, between Martin's testimony in the first and second trials.

The prosecution obviously planned this in advance of Martin's testimony, knowing it would differ from the altered transcript of the first trial. Martin's testimony, as it appeared in the appeal brief, with relevant text emphasized by the appellate attorney, follows:

Martin:

A toll call was made on April 22nd of 1974, at 5:03 P.M. The call lasted approximately two minutes and 50 seconds, and it was placed from 815-5431-9034, which is the telephone located at the oasis in Belvidere [Illinois]. It was placed to area code 313- . . . -8443, which is a number in Royal Oak [Ferndale], Michigan. The charge for the call was a dollar ten cents, four quarters and one dime was deposited for the call.

Defense:

Now, this was a station-to-station call?

Martin:

Correct.[179]

On cross-examination, Martin was discredited through use of the altered Blue Earth trial transcript:

Prosecutor:

The to-number is what?

Martin:

The to-number was 313- . . . -8443.

Prosecutor:

Mr. Martin, you indicated that you personally were at Blue Earth Court last fall, is that correct?

Martin:

Yes, sir.

Prosecutor:

I am going to hand you, Mr. Martin, a copy of a transcript, a portion of your testimony, I will ask you here just to read this question and then turn the next page and read the question and answer . . . page 567. Have you read it, sir? Does that appear to be a correct and accurate copy of the questions or answers put to you at that time?

Martin:

No, sir, it is not.

Prosecutor:

Well, *the transcript would show that apparently the testimony at that time was that the number that the call was placed to was different,* does it not?

Defense:

I am going to object. The witness has stated the transcript does not accurately reflect the testimony.

Judge:

Sustained.

Prosecutor:

Well, in what way, sir, would you say that this does not reflect your testimony?

Martin:

The testimony indicates the number called was 313- . . . -8663 . . . I did not testify that the number was 313- . . . 8663, but that it was 313- . . . -8443.

Prosecutor:

Well, I appreciate, Mr. Martin, that *none of us, our memories are that good or bad,* but are you sure that what is in the transcript was not your testimony under your recollection at this point?

Martin:

[Rising from his chair] Yes, sir. That is what I would say. I have no reason to give contradictory testimony. I have no interest in this case. As a matter of fact, I-

Judge:

Just a minute, just a minute.

Martin:

-have appeared here-

Judge:

Just a minute. There is no question to the witness. You have a question?

Prosecutor:

I think you would agree, would you not, that *this copy of the transcript that I have given you reflects testimony different than what you have given to here today?*

Martin:

Yes, sir. I agree with that. I have never seen that transcript prior to this time.

Prosecutor:

And you indicated that this was a station-to-station call? Is there any way that you identified the caller or the recipient of a call by your records?

Martin:

No, sir, not on a station-to-station call.

Prosecutor:

Well, again, Mr. Martin, I appreciate that you have, of course, have no interest in this case at all, but *are you absolutely certain that you didn't testify this way at Blue Earth Court last fall?*

Martin:

I would say so, yes, sir.

Prosecutor:

And that is based upon your looking at this number

and not looking at those documents now, though, is it not?

Martin:

That's right. And at my previous testimony I testified from the same document and I would not have confused the numbers because those numbers were read off of this ticket just as I am reading them off to you now, sir.

Prosecutor:

But apparently there are two different places that the receiving number is referred here as 8663. Now, I have given you an opportunity to review the transcript, have I not?

Martin:

Just now, yes. Sir.

The prosecutor then quoted from the transcript to emphasize to the jury his claim that Martin had testified differently at the Blue Earth trial. And the prosecutor again took advantage of the transcript alterations to impeach Martin:

Prosecutor:

If a call were made person to person, would it show the name of the person called as well as the person that received the call?

Martin:

If a person made a person-to-person call, the information on the ticket would show the name of the person being called.

Prosecutor:

Wouldn't show the person making the call, name of the person making the call?

Martin:

No.

Prosecutor:

Well, again, referring to this transcript, page 571, there is a question: "Now, if a person-to-person call was made, Mr. Martin, would your records reflect at least the name given to the operator and the person called?" And the answer, "It would reflect the name of the party making the call and also the party receiving the call." Do you recall that testimony?

Martin:

I don't recall that, sir. If I made that statement, then I misunderstood the question from the standpoint of whether it was a person-to-person or person-collect call, but on the station-to-station call, there will be no names on the ticket.

The prosecutor again capitalized on a discrepancy in Martin's testimony from what was recorded in the Blue Earth transcript:

Prosecutor:

Well, in essence, then, Mr. Martin, your testimony is that the records of the General Telephone Company of Illinois reflect that approximately-did you say "5:03"-[the call was placed]?

Martin:

That's right.

Prosecutor:

Well, again, if I may interrupt there. This transcript would show that the previous time was 5:30. Did you note that when you reviewed this [transcript]?

Martin:

I saw that when I reviewed it, but that is not what I testified to.

After Martin finished testifying, another conference took place in judge's chambers. Wanting to get as much mileage out of impeaching Martin as he could, the prosecutor asked the judge, as quoted in the appeal:

Prosecutor:

Can I have a copy of that testimony introduced without any further foundation from this man [defense counsel Wylde]?

Defense:

Well, I don't know. You impeached him with it. You read it in. You got the Q and A. He admitted that is what the transcript shows. Is it necessary to memorialize it?

Judge:

He didn't deny that the transcript shows what you read to him. He admitted it shows that, so your evidence is he testified one way-the transcript shows another. By this admission it shows a different number. Mr. Wylde has agreed that his transcript shows the same figures that yours do, the ones that you used. I don't think you need-

Prosecutor:

Okay. That is what I am getting at. I am certainly going to yell about this.

Judge:

The evidence is there.

Defense:

It's there like any other impeachment.

Mr. Christian carried out his threat to "yell about this" in his closing statement to the jury, as was argued on appeal:

> During the trial in the instant case, Martin again testified that the phone number called from the toll way was 313- . . . -8443, appellant's phone at his Royal Oak [Ferndale], Michigan home. On cross-examination Martin was thoroughly discredited through the use of the Blue Earth trial transcript . . .
>
> At the Blue Earth post-conviction hearing, it was established that the transcript was in error, and that Martin's actual testimony was that the call was placed to . . . -8443, appellant's home. In fact, the reporter also incorrectly transcribed appellant's own testimony regarding his telephone number. These errors in the transcript were stipulated during the Blue Earth post-conviction proceeding.
>
> Mr. Wylde's testimony [at the hearing] that Martin was a very important witness to the defense was surely accurate in view of the fact that he provided the only alibi evidence. Appellant's sole defense was that he was not in Mankato when Michael Jiminez was killed because approximately ten hours earlier, depending on actual time of murder, he was in Belvidere, Illinois.
>
> Mr. Wylde testified that he was unaware that the transcript was incorrect until Martin testified. Although he assumed it was a mistake, he was not alarmed because he thought Martin's records were the best evidence. In this assumption he was totally mistaken, for the records are so technically coded that their use by laymen is highly unlikely.
>
> Appellant has not been able to present direct evidence that the prosecutor knew the transcript of Martin's

testimony was in error. We do know that Mr. Christian was aware that Martin was going to testify, that his testimony was important to Clark's alibi defense, and that he read the transcript twice by the time Martin took the stand.

Although Mr. Christian testified that he did not know that the transcript was inaccurate when he used it to impeach Martin, it is so obvious that both he and the trial court should have been aware of it. What significance would there have been to Martin's testimony that a stranger received a call from the toll way? Why wouldn't the Blue Earth prosecutor have argued to the jury that the evidence was of no significance because the call was to the home of some unknown person in Royal Oak? Why would appellant's wife have been brought from Michigan to testify that she received a phone call from her husband if the location of the phone from which that call was made was not shown?

Moreover, in spite of Mr. Christian's denial of having gone through Corbey's Blue Earth file, Corbey testified that he reviewed his whole file with Christian on several occasions prior to the second trial.

Appellant was denied due process and a fair trial because he was deprived of the alibi evidence which he was clearly entitled to present, and upon which his entire defense rested. Whether the prosecutor acted willfully or not is insignificant, for the effect upon appellant's defense was the same in either case.

Judge Fitzgerald's Findings.

Judge Fitzgerald concluded that prejudice could not

have resulted from the impeachment of Martin because the record . . . went to the jury . . . Appellant submits that the exhibit is so difficult to interpret that it is pure conjecture to conclude that the jury was able to decipher its meaning.

The finding that the prosecutor was aware of the mix-up in testimony *when he started his cross-examination* requires a conclusion that the prosecutor improperly used the Blue Earth transcript to impeach Martin's testimony.[180]

Since the Blue Earth trial transcript had also been altered as to my testimony about my home phone number, the prosecutor apparently would have tried to impeach me as he did Martin. The Minnesota Supreme Court subsequently ruled that the transcript was "in error", but that it was "harmless error."[181]

After the trial, I found out that the Blue Earth trial court reporter, a substitute for the initial court reporter killed just before start of the trial, had moved to Phoenix to work for a law firm. In seeking evidence as to *who* was responsible for altering the transcript, I mailed the court reporter a certified letter, asking whether she still had her original notes from the trial. She did not respond.

A United Press International story announced the end of the trial: "Defense Rests Case in Jiminez Slaying."[182]

Chapter 13: Prosecution's Closing Statement

A UPI story announced: "Final Arguments Today in Slay Trial."[183] The prosecutor's closing statements to the jury took several hours.[184] Below, with my comments, are the particularly pertinent excerpts of his statement:

> You have heard evidence concerning Barbara Jiminez's death, and you have heard evidence concerning the trial involving Michael Jiminez . . . It is the State's position that this is all one episode or sequence of events . . . when you consider that Michael and Barbara Jiminez were seen standing together on the highway in Emporia, Kansas, on Sunday, April 21st.
>
> The next positive identification or time sequence that we have in the finding of Michael Jiminez . . . about noon on Tuesday, April 23rd.
>
> Now, I appreciate that in doing that, that *you have to disregard the testimony of Helen Troxel, the lady that worked in the café at Blairsburg.* She says that it is her recollection, being shown the pictures, "Yes, that is the people I saw.

I am quite sure that it was Monday, sometime between eleven and noon."

So, this, of course, *is inconsistent with the body being there Sunday night* . . . I am sure that this lady did not come in here and lie to us. On the other hand . . . *she could well have been mistaken first of all as to the identity of the people.*

One thing that makes me think that is because *she said she didn't see them have any luggage, or if we say that she did in fact see them, it could have been a different day. I suppose it could even be possible she may have saw them stop there on the way down to Iowa and Kansas.* I think Helen Troxel could have been mistaken, and so you might say, "Well, if that is what you think, why did you bring her up here and have her testify?" But again, I *feel as prosecuting attorney that I have the obligation to bring before you any and all evidence* that might have some bearing on the case.

For the prosecutor to say Helen Troxel could have been mistaken about seeing the Jiminezes on their way from Emporia, Kansas, to Minnesota because "she didn't see them have any luggage" was ludicrous. The prosecutor was aware that if he did not call Troxel as a witness, the defense would, as she had testified in the Blue Earth trial.

The prosecution *did withhold evidence*, as revealed in chapter 3 and 4, including Ernest Ties, the attendant at the service station adjacent to the café, who also saw the Jiminezes. This evidence-the existence of Ernest Ties along with that of Glen Bjorklund, who saw me alone in my Bronco-was *discovered by appellate attorney Ronald Haskvitz in this prosecutor's file* during appellate hearings.[185]

As quoted from my Le Sueur appeal: "Appellant Was Denied Due Process of Law . . . by the Failure of the State to Produce Certain Evidence Vital to the Defense," the sections related to Glen Bjorklund and Ernest Ties:

C. The statement from Glen Bjorklund.

During a review of the *Le Sueur County prosecutor's file*, a supplementary offense report dated May 13, 1974, was found. Attached to the report was a statement taken from Glen Bjorklund, owner of a service station in Alden, Minnesota (P.C. Exhibit 21). According to Bjorklund, a man driving a Ford Bronco stopped for gas on a day late in April. His description of the vehicle closely fit appellant's Bronco and he indicated from a photograph shown to him that the man driving was Clark. Bjorklund stated that the driver was alone in the vehicle.

Mr. Wylde was never advised of Bjorklund's identity nor of the fact that a statement had been taken from him (P.C. 92). According to Wylde, the defense had hired an investigator to locate witnesses with the precise information that Bjorklund had provided the State (P.C. 94).

The significance of Bjorklund's statement was that it would have established Clark was alone in his Bronco at a place in southern Minnesota (P.C. 94). This would have made it highly unlikely that he was at Smith's Mill during the time Michael Jiminez was murdered. In addition, the statement would have supported the testimony of Helen Troxel, the waitress at the "M & M Café" in Blairsburg Corners, near Ames, Iowa. She testified that she waited on the Jiminez couple on Monday, April 22, between 11:00 and 1:00 o'clock in the afternoon (vol. 6, pp. 133-39). The couple was alone when they left the restaurant and returned to the highway. Because this testimony was not consistent with the State's theory that Michael Jiminez was dead the night before, the prosecution asked the jury to disregard it (vol. 14, pp. 25, 41, 48). Bjorklund's statement would have supported Troxel's version and made it impossible for the prosecutor to ask the jury to disregard the crucial facts to which she testified.

D. The interview with Ernest Ties.

The supplementary offense report of the Blue Earth County Sheriff's Office, *located in the Le Sueur County County prosecutor's file* (Ex. 21), indicates that the investigators contacted Helen Troxel and one Ernest Ties. While Troxel was called as a witness at the trial, no mention was made of Ties. According to the report, ties, a service station attendant at the truck stop adjacent to the M & M Café, *saw Barbara and Michael Jiminez at the café, but did not see appellant or his Bronco.*

Ties would have supported the testimony of Helen Troxel to the effect that Barbara and Michael Jiminez were in the M & M Café. He would [also] have supported her testimony that *they came in alone and returned to the highway alone* (vol. 6, 133-39).

As the appellate attorney pointed out, if the defense had been aware of this information at the first or second trials, neither prosecutor would have been able to claim that Helen Troxel was mistaken.

The prosecutor's closing statement continued:

> So far as the defense establishing, as it claims it would, that the death of Michael Jiminez occurred about midnight on the 22nd, I submit they did not, by the testimony of Dr. Ohrt. So then what else did they offer to attempt to show that Ed Clark could not have been in Minnesota?
>
> *One essential step is missing here. What do the records from the telephone company show?* . . . Mr. William Martin-You recall I pointed out to him . . . the transcript of the Mankato trial says this other number was called, and, well, *he says,* "I didn't say that." But then you turn a couple pages, same darn mistake.
>
> But *is it possible that there was a mistake somewhere along the line in his recollection or his memory of the items that he is testifying to?*

> . . . let's now get Ed Clark home. He comes home, spends a brief time with his wife. Then he goes and stays with his mother. Does he tell his wife about picking up any hitchhikers and traveling up to Minnesota? No. What does he tell her? *"From Lake Tahoe to Ferndale, I stayed on [Interstate] 80."* She says he did mention hitchhikers, but I guess it was a hitchhiker. *Nothing about female hitchhiker or a pair of hitchhikers.*

My wife never testified that I said I "stayed on 80." She did testify that I told her I had picked up "hitchhikers."

> He doesn't tell his mother that, and obviously she was telling us the truth. *She said she would like to get him out of this mess.*

To the contrary, my mother never made such a statement. She unequivocally stated she would not lie.

> What else does he do while he is in the Michigan area . . . ? *Hide the Bronco.* Puts it in his mother's garage . . . Why is he hiding it?

We were keeping the Bronco out of sight because of the lawsuit, as my wife testified.

> . . . Any one of you might have been able to ask questions better and develop the evidence better than I did, but unfortunately you weren't given the opportunity . . .

> Now, there might be some claim made that some of the evidence was not properly preserved. You remember, you heard testimony about, gee, *wasn't there a brown coat found?* Wasn't there a torn blouse found? Wasn't there a bra found? Wasn't there a pair of panties found?

> . . . You also heard the explanation what happened to those items. They were all taken in possession by the law enforcement people, they were taken to relatives . .

. Identification process was attempted. They could not associate them with . . . either Michael or Barbara. They were then taken to the crime laboratory. They attempted to make tests on them. Nothing could be developed, and so later they were just discarded.

As testified by the prosecution's witness BCA micro analyst Wallace Sorum, the crime lab never received the brown coat for testing.

I don't think that you can short the law enforcement people for the efforts that they made in this case. Ladies and gentlemen, I can tell you that I as the part-time county attorney for Le Sueur County, am extremely proud of the law enforcement people and the job they did in this case. You heard about the size of their staffs. Le Sueur County, four or five deputies, and the sheriff, Blue Earth County, 16 [or] 17 deputies and their sheriff. We don't have homicide divisions out in rural areas.

We don't have specialists. We have just got a bunch of guys trying to do a job. They darn well might not know anything about Henry's classification of fingerprints.

The Minnesota's Bureau of Criminal Apprehension and its crime laboratory (whose assistant identification officer erroneously claimed the bureau did not have the fingerprint classification of Barbara Jiminez) assisted the sheriff's departments from the beginning of the investigation.

My recollection is that it was approximately 65 inches, *65 inches being the same width of the set of tracks that was found near the railroad tracks at the Michael Jiminez death scene and consistent with the width of a set of tracks found at the Scotch Lake scene . . . You couldn't see what kind of tire tread was there because the ground was hard and dry, but they were able to measure the width from one to the other.*

The prosecutor minimized the importance of the tire tracks, claiming there was no identifiable impressions because "the ground was hard and dry," but when asked whether plaster casts had been made of tire tracks at the Blue Earth County scene, Sheriff Wiebold did not say they couldn't be taken. He said he "used the photographic technique in lieu of that."

The prosecutor ignored the facts that the distance between my vehicle's tire tracks was half-an-inch wider and that Sheriff Smith wanted plaster casts taken of the tire-tread impressions left in the dried mud at the Le Sueur County scene. For reasons unknown, the investigators took photographs only, when there were obvious, clear tire-tread impressions. More important, as revealed during agent Simonson's testimony, the crime lab eliminated my vehicle as to making the tire tracks. The lab would not have been able to do that without clear tread impressions for comparison.

> Remember when you were brought in the . . . courtroom here and selected as jurors, and the judge told you, ". . . we have got for your consideration the case of the *State of Minnesota vs. Edward Clark*." He read the indictments to you, said this is a murder case.
>
> At that time, myself, Mr. Wylde, and Ed Clark were sitting at the table . . . I am willing to bet . . . that many of you wondered, well, just which one of those three people are supposed to be the murderer.
>
> . . . I thought the same thing a year ago . . . when I first saw Ed Clark. I said to myself, "Man, there has got to be some mistake, that fellow doesn't look like a murderer." Very pleasant looking, very neat, conducts himself well. Beautiful manners. What does a murderer look like?
>
> . . . Carrying this one step further, *does Ed Clark look like a mechanic? No. I think he looks too refined, too well educated, too well mannered to be a mechanic.*

This was a direct slap against anyone who is an automotive technician or who is in any other vocational trade. And, as argued by the appellate attorney, quoted later in this chapter, "The prosecution's final argument must be based upon reference to the evidence," not personal opinion.

What, if any, explanation have we heard at all? You recall the testimony at the Blue Earth County trial when Mr. Corbey was here? . . . [Clark] admitted he picked up hitchhikers. He admitted he had been in Minnesota. Mr. Wylde developed, weren't there three hitchhikers picked up? . . . What about this third hitchhiker? . . .

"Did Ed Clark at any time describe this third hitchhiker to anybody?"

"Yes, once."

"To whom?"

"An investigator for Mr. Adamson."

And as you know, Mr. Adamson was his attorney in the Blue Earth trial. That is the only person that ever received a description of a third hitchhiker, which means he did not describe him to the police. He did not describe him to his wife. He did not describe him to his mother . . . We don't know whether the hitchhiker was tall, short, fat, young, old, black man, Indian, white man, or what have you. Ed Clark would want us to believe the third hitchhiker got in the car by Des Moines.

Quoting the above text on my appeal, the appellate attorney argued: "The prosecutor created a prejudicial inference of guilt by introducing certain testimony which should not have been admitted because it could serve no purpose other than to penalize appellant for the exercise of a fundamental right-his right to remain silent and to request an attorney."[186]

Any attorney will advise his client not to say anything to the police, partly for the reason that the police might take statements out of context or lie about what a suspect says, just as I had experienced. And talking to the police may provide them the opportunity to learn about exculpatory evidence-evidence that would clear a suspect-that they might then withhold.

The prosecutor continued:

That third hitchhiker . . . took two railroad ties and piled them on the body of Michael Jiminez in the form of a cross . . .

That third hitchhiker is the person who put the shoe of Barbara Jiminez in the tree near her body . . . He is a figment of the imagination of the evil and deceitful mind of Ed Clark. He is the Mr. Hyde of our Dr. Jekyll. He put the railroad ties maybe on the body of Michael Jiminez and the shoe in the tree at Scotch Lake to tell the world, "Catch Ed Clark."

. . . you cannot logically reason why those railroad ties were placed in the form of a cross, or why that shoe was planted on the tree. Logically, only one person or two persons can tell us that. One is Ed Clark and the other is this third hitchhiker . . . That is why this third hitchhiker was invented.

He picked up hitchhikers. He admits this. He cashed a check at Ames, Iowa. He admits that . . . This means that in Ames, Iowa, he was out of his way. He was not on his most direct route home. He was something less than 100 miles already going out of his way . . .

Ladies and gentlemen, I think the only reasonable explanation that can be attributed, or motive that can be attributed to the death of Michael and Barbara Jiminez is sex . . . you can see from the pictures when you observe that Barbara Jiminez was a very attractive girl . . . The type of person that someone with that type of inclination might want to do something with and about.

. . . I think, *this is my personal theory of the case* . . .

So when we are approximately ten miles from Mankato . . . we come to a field driveway . . . pull in the field driveway, drive up to near the railroad tracks . . .

... The shooter wanted to do something with Barbara Jiminez. *I can't answer where she was at that time,* and the only offering that I can show is that chunk of pink cloth that was found out at Scotch Lake ... be it a gag or something the hands were tied up with or what. It had human hair in it, hair consistent with the color and type that Barbara Jiminez had.

... why was the body of Barbara Jiminez devoid of clothing? Why no jewelry, no wedding ring? What possible motive could anyone have for killing Michael and Barbara Jiminez except sex? ... As a scientific fact we know from the tests performed on Barbara Jiminez's body that sometime prior to her death the act of sexual intercourse had been conducted ...

The judge will tell you that the alternate count of first-degree murder, that of killing during the course of rape or attempted rape, has been dismissed by him ... Now, as I mentioned in this case, *the court has ruled that the State has not shown beyond a reasonable doubt that Barbara Jiminez was raped. I agree. That doesn't mean the State hasn't proved she was raped, but it means that she was not raped and killed, I should say, beyond a reasonable doubt.*

The prosecutor misled the jury with double-talk and a contradiction: It is not the duty of the court to determine whether there is reasonable doubt-that is for the jury to decide. The judge determines whether there is evidence enough supporting the prosecution's claim for a jury to consider. Apparently, the judge ruled the evidence did not exist, so it was improper for the prosecutor to state: "That doesn't mean the State hasn't proved she was raped."

Mr. Wylde is one of the finest gentlemen I have had occasion to try a case against or with of [*sic*] any attorney ... he is going to point out various things to you and these things are going to be in the light of his client ... Mr. Wylde is a very experience and capable attorney so he is going to deliver to you some very logical reason or some arguments . . .

. . . I submit to you that *if the evidence in this case was actually any different than what the State presented, you would have been presented with rebuttal evidence.* If a man with the capability of Mr. Wylde had thought that there was medical testimony to prove or disprove something about the death of Barbara Jiminez different from what the State's doctor testified, you would have heard about it. If he had thought that there was some other identification could be made between that rifle and the shell, we would have heard about it. The same way with the pink sheet.

As shown previously and as outlined in chapter 16 ("Exculpatory Evidence Discovered"), the prosecution withheld evidence supporting my innocence.

The balance of the prosecutor's closing statement to the jury was included in the appeal:

Appellant Was Denied Due Process of Law and a Fair Trial, as a Result of the Prosecutor's Prejudicial and Improper Closing Argument.

During his closing argument the prosecutor admonished the jurors *not to get hung up* and warned them that appellant's attorney [defense attorney Wylde] would try to get them hung up . . .

He went on to present the highly prejudicial and improper "get him or he will get you" warning:

. . . You recall when you were all chosen as jurors . . . you were asked, "*Do you believe in law and order?*" . . .

. . . *Every day, nearly every day, on the front page there is something about crime and violence.* And I am sure that some of you . . . say, "Why don't they do something about it? . . . Why don't the police go out and catch those guys? . . .

Why are they left out running around?

> ... *Ladies and gentlemen, later this afternoon in this case, the "they" is going to be you.* You ... will be at that point, one link in a chain of the justice system of the United States ... *we all have to seize the bull by the horns* ... and do our job ... This is what society deserves ...

It is an elementary rule of law that the prosecution's final argument must be based upon reference to the evidence. Matters which cannot be regarded as evidence and which serve to divert the minds of the jurors from the facts to which their consideration should be given in determining whether the accused is guilty or not may not be introduced into the closing argument.[187]

A UPI article finally announced: "Prosecution Rests in Jiminez Trial."[188]

Chapter 14: Defense's Closing Statement

The defense's closing statement took several hours as well.[189]

At the outset there are a couple of things that I . . . would like you to keep in mind throughout the course of my summation. One is that you are not here to determine whether in this case the investigating officials did the best they could, nor are we particularly interested in *someone's personal conclusions or thoughts* that they may speculate or postulate the evidence shows.

You are here to do one thing and one thing only, and that is to analyze the evidence that has been presented to you in the light of your reasoning, your judgment, and your common sense and determine whether . . . the State has proven their case beyond a reasonable doubt.

Now, there are four things that I would like to call to your attention. Number one is the nature of a criminal prosecution. We haven't heard too much about the title of this case is the *State of Minnesota v. Edward R. Clark* . . . . that title, I submit to you, is a precise delineation of the forces that are against each other in this particular matter. On the one side we have the State of Minnesota. We have the people that they have presented, the facilities, which you are aware of now after four weeks of trial, which they have at their disposal . . . And all these . . . forces are geared to one objective and one objective only, and that is to bring this prosecution to a successful conclusion.

On the other hand, we have the accused, Edward R. Clark, and I submit to you . . . he has one thing and one thing only, and that is the presumption of innocence . . .

. . . You are going to have them in the jury room . . . 200 some exhibits that have been introduced in this case. Everything from the time records of Edward Clark at Burke Chevrolet up to and including that gun, most of which I submit should have very little influence on your deliberations in this case because . . . most of them are meaningless except in so far as they support a conclusion, a supposition . . .

It used to be in England, for example-it was the law that you could not go to trial accused of a criminal offense unless you entered a plea, so many people who were accused of felony offenses rather than stand the risk of possible trial and conviction refused to plea . . .

Well, the authorities to prevent this situation devised this idea of *piene forte et dure*, and the accused who refused to plead was taken out into a courtyard . . . and a large board was placed on his chest and rocks were heaped upon the board one at a time until one of two things happened. As the result of the pain, he was forced to plead and hence go to trial, or he died, crushed to death . . . and I submit to you that that is exactly the situation we have got here.

We have got 211, 212, exhibits in this case . . . and

someone is hoping, I think, through the sheer weight and volume of the evidence, that you are going to conclude that it adds up to what they say it does . . .

. . . it is possible during the course of this trial that the questions have been asked in such a way that the answer that was given was not particularly responsive to the question . . . and you realize it was and you think about it. Let me give you an example.

When Mrs. Clark was being cross-examined, the question was asked, didn't you say, or didn't you tell . . . that when you saw the Bronco, it was too full for anyone else to be in it? Or words to that effect. The answer was denied. That is where it sits. That is the state of the evidence. There is no evidence to the contrary.

Now, before I begin to speak about the evidence in this case, I think I should be flattered by the remarks of opposing counsel, and if this were the first courtroom I had ever appeared in . . . the first case I ever tried as a young lawyer, prosecuting attorney, I said the same thing to the jury . . . we have to put that in a little bit of perspective.

. . . the charge of murder in the first degree committed while attempting to commit rape with force and violence . . . has been dismissed by the court.

Now we are left with two charges, murder one and murder two . . . key in this definition are the words . . . "Premeditation" and "Intent." They both have to exist in the situation of first-degree murder, and one, that is, the element of intent, in the situation of second-degree murder . . . I don't think based on . . . the scientific evidence that they presented here, [they] have proved either case . . .

. . . They have speculated that the cause of death was

strangulation, and they grudgingly admitted it might have been drowning . . . You have got to have a death which occurred about the same time as the first death . . .

Now, what evidence has been introduced concerning time of death? Ten days more or less a few. Dr. Peterson says ten days is one possibility. Dr. Anderson, at least three days. There is no precision . . .

Cause of death. It is probably strangulation. And upon what is that conclusion based? Two types of strangulation . . . Manual strangulation is in a majority of cases accompanied by rupture of the hyoid bone accompanied by exterior trauma. Ligature strangulation is, as Dr. Peterson told me on cross-examination, he would expect to find trauma to the trachea, trauma to the larynx . . . None of these facts are present in this case. None.

At this point, defense attorney Wylde quoted from a page attached to the autopsy report, which was Dr. Coe's opinion:

"Certainly we see cases of middle ear hemorrhage secondary to trauma of which there was none in this case, or in other cases in people who have not drowned, and occasionally we do not find any significant bleeding in persons that we know have drowned."

They haven't proven a murder.

They have talked about the so-called admissions which they elicited through Mr. Corbey by way of reading portions of prior transcript referred to them as admissions. The admissions consisted of "I picked up hitchhikers west of Des Moines, six or 6:30 on the 21st of April. I woke up at a truck stop. I cashed some traveler's checks. When I woke up, I was in Minnesota. About seven, eight o'clock in the morning I got gas. I drove back through Wisconsin after this was over." And then, through Mrs. Clark, that he had driven to Belvidere, and hence home to Ferndale . . .

What did we have to show you through cross-examination?

They didn't even tell you in their questions and answers that there were three hitchhikers. That was something that we had to bring out. We had to bring out the fact that when he woke up there was no lake around. They were perfectly willing to let you rest with the admission that anything is possible . . .

It was up to the defense to bring out questions and answers, "Why did you get rid of the box?" "I thought it was trash."

. . . It was up to us to bring out the fact that the ballpoint pens were in a tray laying in the car, things of that nature, when you begin to analyze the circumstantial evidence. Pens were accessible to anybody that is in the car . . .

Are we to assume from the evidence that the only place these people went was up 35 to the north? Now, that is what one sign on that bag says, "35 north" but there are two other signs on that bag . . . written with green magic marker, one of which says "35 Minnesota," the other of which simply says "Minnesota." Mrs. Stovall testified that she assisted in putting on only the red mark, the "35 N."

Now, where did "Minnesota" come from? If "35 N" is sufficient to get you up to wherever you are going, say Mankato, why do you have to write, "Minnesota"? And, then, if you got a green magic marker, how did it get there? Who put it on?

Can't we assume from that there was a detour? Isn't that just as logical, that someplace else, not just up 35,

> that they went someplace else, perhaps meeting this third person? It's all there.
>
> Mrs. Stovall would have us believe that there was no money. Didn't have any money. Hence, I suppose in an attempt to exclude robbery as a possible motive for this. But yet there was $150 in their apartment when the police went there.
>
> Perhaps the most important piece of evidence which I would like you to really consider when you get in the jury room is that attempt to talk about tire tracks.
>
> Now you can look at these pictures . . . 25 [or] 30 pictures in there with tire tracks, and you can look at these impressions.

The Sacramento Sheriff's Department had rolled the vehicle over paper to get clear tread impressions of the Bronco.

> You are not going to find any tire track in any picture that matches those impressions . . . I went over this in some detail with Sheriff Smith as well as Mr. Simonson. There are three or four photographs in here that depict what is probably the track of a snow tire, or also some sort of deep tread . . . the sheriff tried very hard to say a four-wheeled drive vehicle . . . this is what they measured, and right now I am referring to State's Exhibit I . . . Got another one here. State's Exhibit H. These are two of the Exhibits I talked to Thomas Simonson about, and that is the tire track he told me the crime lab eliminated [where the vehicle had driven through the mud hole, up the incline, in the direction of the body].
>
> I asked him the question three times and he gave me the same answer, this was eliminated . . . you can ponder for days . . . and you are not going to see any track in any of those pictures that comes close to looking like the track on that piece of paper . . . not only does it not prove

their conjecture, but it proves exactly the contrary.

. . . We can trace the route that Mr. Clark took across the United States with the traveler's checks. Is that what a guilty mind does? Is this the act of a culprit, in endorsing traveler's checks that can be traced, like fingerprints . . . Harrah's; Cheyenne, Wyoming; Nebraska; Ames, Iowa . . . You don't leave that kind of evidence . . .

How about the scientific tests that paid out in the negative? Sure, you can compare dirt, debris, soil samples. They took three or four bags from the car in California, they brought it back. What happened? Nothing . . .

. . . Now, someone had used some of the matches that were out of that matchbook that was found at Smith's Mill . . . Did they find matches that matched that in the ashtray? No . . .

Most important, you heard the description of the things that were in the Bronco when he left California: . . . Everything was tested for the presence of blood or the presence of semen and everything was negative. Negative.

Is it the act of a guilty mind to take a thing like this [the sheet Ed Clark had used as a dust cover] . . . Here, look at it. It has got a patch in it. It is just an old piece of cloth. And to carry that back to California without any attempt to secrete it whatsoever . . . What is one of the first items they found when they went in? The sheet and the gun . . . Is that the act of a guilty mind? No, no, no.

Now, then . . . We come back to the fact, which the prosecuting attorney wants to laugh away as insignificant . . . the telephone call. What he didn't deal with is the fact of the accused arriving in Ferndale 1 A.M. on the 23rd. His mother's house shortly after three o'clock on the 23rd. We have got roughly, I believe, 700 miles is the rough figure that was put in evidence with respect to . . . Belvidere, Illinois, and to Ferndale, Michigan.

We have got a 14-hour trip, approximately. Now, *this is where it becomes important when we talk about the time of death of Michael Jiminez* . . . the ultimate answer . . . given to that question that was asked by the prosecuting attorney, was . . . *midnight plus or minus three hours, is based on pretty sound scientific evidence. I think that was an exact quote from Dr. Ohrt,* "*Pretty sound scientific evidence.*" He said it was in the 15-20 to 22 hour range before the autopsy . . .

. . . Dr. Ohrt speculated that the death of Michael Jiminez could not have been effected in the daylight? . . . I think it is the only logical inference that can be drawn from the evidence, that this occurred after dark on the night before, and that fits solid scientific evidence.

. . . He said he had begun his autopsy at 4:30. Fifteen hours back from 4:30 brings us to 1:30 in the morning on April 23 . . . And if we go to the outer limits where it is 6:30 P.M. on the 22nd.

At none of those times could Edward Clark have been in the State of Minnesota because he was in Michigan at one o'clock that morning . . . They haven't attacked that. They haven't impeached it, nor can they.

His mother testified that she looked at the clock. It was sometime after three o'clock that he came to her house. Now, that is there and that is in evidence and that is a fact . . .

. . . they want you to forget Mrs. Troxel . . . they brought her in here. She testified unequivocally that she saw Michael and Barbara between eleven and one o'clock on Monday, the 22nd . . . They want to say she must have been mistaken. "We brought her here because we wanted to give you all the evidence." They want to forget her because it doesn't fit their theory . . . their supposition.

. . . They want to go way out to the outer limit and pick 10:30 P.M. on the 21st, when their own witness whom they called, for whose credibility they vouch, and they brought her in here to testify that she saw these people alive at noon, between 11 and one . . .

There are a lot of questions that have to be asked about some of the evidence in this case . . . I would refer you to State's Exhibit F. This is a picture of the rag that was found and it is before you in evidence in two pieces, I measured it when Mr. Sorum was on the stand. Now, the prosecutor asked you to speculate that this was used as some kind of a restraining device, a gag or a bond. Well, I submit to you that there is probably only about 17 inches of cloth . . . I have a 17 inch neck. Why not rip a whole piece off? Why not rip two or three or four, or how many you need, to do what the prosecuting attorney suggests to you was done? That didn't happen [here].

There is another Exhibit I . . . This is the bill of sale that he gave to Mr. Martin at Burke Chevrolet on Automotive Services, Incorporated, stationary. The address, and "Hazel Park, Michigan." That is the business that had been, and that is what he used. Here is a person that is trying to be deceitful, trying to cover his identity?

Look very carefully at the exhibit that is depicted in State's triple Z, and if that looks like a piece of paper that was folded up and found under a flap . . . It's wrinkled, it's crumpled, and I submit to you that it was found exactly where the other was found. That is, in the pile of debris in the bottom of the box.

The "piece of paper" was the typewriter rental receipt found in the box I discarded, which made me a suspect. The prosecution had claimed it was "folded" beneath a flap at the bottom of the box-to make it appear

EVIDENCE OF INNOCENCE

I didn't know it was there.

Do you really believe that Mr. Sorum did not subject that hair sample to a microscopic analysis? Now, he sat here and he told us why they analyze hair, all the different ways you can compare it, the pigmentation, the different layers of hair, the scales. He told us why they performed those tests. He microscopically analyzed every hair sample that was sent to him from California . . . and yet here is the crucial piece of evidence that they think they have. This is the piece of rag or piece of sheet that was found at Scotch Lake, he said he could look at them. He says they are head hairs, they appear to the observation to correspond with the known hair of Barbara Jiminez, and do you really believe he didn't subject those to microscopic analysis after all else that he told us he did? . . . I don't think that is logical. I think he compared them and he got a result that he didn't want to use in his report.

About the impeachment of Mr. Martin from General Telephone Company. I don't particularly care what numbers they threw around. You have got the exhibit here. He says he has no interest in this case. There it is. There is when the call was made, there is the time it was made, and there is the number that was called, and there is the card. It's a fact.

Let's ask some questions about the investigation, and as I told you, I think in this case the conclusion was formed as early as the 6th of May [the day Ed Clark was arrested]. The prosecuting attorney told you a good deal this morning about human nature, the human condition. Well . . . we have had a good example of it in this case . . . . To illustrate that point . . . once you form a conclusion, once you have made up your mind, then you only see those things which tend to support your conclusion, and you tend to exclude those things, too, that do not support your conclusion.

What goes on, let's say, on the 7th or the 8th of May, whenever that second conversation that was with Mrs. Clark, where she testified that one of those people out there told her that they would have her for perjury if she testified . . . This is the day after the accused is in custody. You are supposed to be conducting an investigation, you are not supposed to have had those conclusions formed at that time.

Sergeant Kelley from Sacramento, California, what did he tell Mr. Hart? "We have a warrant out for the arrest of Mr. Clark." . . . They didn't have a warrant out for his arrest. All conclusions.

Now, what has happened to all those other items of clothes . . . the second coat, the blouses, the kerchiefs, the panties, anything else they told us about . . . The prosecuting attorney told you, "Anything that wasn't identified in the first trial we threw away. Well, didn't fit our conclusion."

. . . Good case in point, the questions that I asked Mr. Sorum when he was reading from his notes, "Well, my notes reveal that on such and such a date I received a pair of panties found at the Scotch Lake scene" . . .

We have got a pair of woman's undergarment over here on Scotch Lake on the opposite side of the lake, because somebody didn't identify it, we get rid of it. We get rid of everything after the first trial. I submit that is a pretty good characterization of the investigation . . . We haven't heard anything that was done since the first trial. We got rid of the evidence that didn't fit our theory. Now we are going to come in here and ask you to rubber stamp.

Let's talk about this route again that the prosecuting attorney directed you to. He speculates that the person left Smith's Mill, drove up and took a right on the first hard surface road which, by the way, happens to be Route 60. Now, he has asked you to speculate that this person drove in a circle. But if that supposition is correct, the individual is already on Route 60 when he left Smith's Mill. Why drive all over, particularly someone whom the prosecutor would have us believe is unfamiliar with the terrain, is unfamiliar with the country? He would speculate that somebody drove all over and actually came back on the same route where they started from in the first place. That doesn't make a good deal of sense . . .

Where are these other clothes? On the one hand, they ask us to say that Mr. Clark is a murderer and that he is so meticulous and so careful that somehow he has managed to, without a trace, get rid of many of the clothes and many of the items that were in the possession of the people that they claim he murdered. And yet on the other hand he was so careless as to throw a box with incriminating evidence out of the car, and yet so careful that he managed to get rid of other evidence without a trace despite all the work by the mounted posse in this area during the week or ten days or two weeks that intervened. And yet, again, he was so careless and so stupid that he took back to California for no apparent reason an old sheet and gun which he knew was a murder weapon. No, no. It's illogical.

There are a lot of other items that aren't presented here, not only the clothes that Barbara was wearing when she disappeared. Toilet articles, purse, toothbrush, cosmetic bag. They talked about a wig brush in the search warrant, they talked about rings and jewelry in the search warrant, none of which they found in California . . . Where are these things?

You have to ask the question because on the one had they want you to believe that Ed Clark . . . drove around this territory throwing things out of the automobile and yet was so clever that he managed to conceal these things from their observation and discovery.

. . . The fingerprints-we went through this Henry's classification formula with Mr. Rhodes. Do you really think that people go to all the trouble to classify hundreds of thousands and millions of fingerprints that they retrieve unless you know who it belongs to?

That is why they have catalogues, that is why they have classification, so they can go back and compare. Now, it is very easy to say, well, the elements are going to affect the fingerprints. That is, fingerprints that were not Michael Jiminez's and the fingerprints that were not Edward Clark's that were found on some of those other items. And Mr. Rhodes said, "Well, I guess the likely supposition should be that these fingerprints could have belonged to Barbara Jiminez . . ." He said, "We weren't able to come up with a set of fingerprints," and yet we could go through the classification chapter and verse with him, put it [Barbara Jiminez's finger print classification] upon the blackboard . . .

Do you believe he can't match? Do you believe they didn't get a set of fingerprints from Barbara Jiminez? If they did not, why would they have the classification in their files?

There were very important items . . . one was the sign . . . here is Walter Rhodes's initials down here in the lower left-hand corner with what appears to be a very nice fingerprint which didn't belong to Michael Jiminez, which doesn't belong to Edward Clark . . .

You would . . . expect that if a fingerprint appeared on here, it would [be] Ed Clark's but . . . it belongs to someone else . . .

He was able to raise prints from the box. He was able to raise prints from items that were inside the box, prints that did not belong to Edward Clark, prints that did not belong to Michael Jiminez, as well as prints that were taken from the car when it was searched in California . . .

He said he didn't send them to California. There were obviously a set of fingerprints from Michael Jiminez in California because it was in Sergeant Kelley's report, none of which were compared to BCA prints, none which were sent to Washington . . . If they have got a print, maybe eight prints from different people, maybe eight prints from the same person, but there are prints of somebody else . . . where you wouldn't expect to find them, and we have heard the entire extent of the classification process that they went through to identify them.

When I asked Sheriff Wiebold, "Did you find other things at Smith's Mill that did not connect to Edward Clark?" He told me, "Oh yes, there were lots of other items." . . . Where are they?

The prosecuting attorney told you that I would be trying to raise a lot of questions and that is true . . . This is the only thing that is available to an accused, particularly a person in Edward Clark's position at this point . . . A person cannot prove he is not guilty. He can attempt as best he can to explain something, and hence we have got the time of arrival in Ferndale, and, by the way, this is going to be referred to in the judge's instructions as an alibi. Now, that is a Latin word . . . but the judge's instructions is just going to be that an alibi is a contention that the defendant was not present at the time-at the place where he was alleged to have committed the offense, so, as I say, it's a legal word that is used in the law, but I ask you not to give it the sinister connotations which tend to attach to it.

This case is unique because . . . you know the situation that Edward Clark is in, and you are here as citizens of the State . . . and you are here as the people's line of scrutiny between an accused and between the police, and you are probably the last group of citizens . . . that is ever going to have a chance to look at this case.

The judge is going to tell you that you are not to consider the consequences of your verdict in terms of penalty or punishment, and, of course that is the law, and you should not. But, again, this case is a little bit unique, because just as in the Blue Earth County, one thing is certainly going to happen if you should return a verdict of conviction in this case . . . they are going to close this file like they closed the other one, and not going to investigate this case anymore, just like they didn't investigate the other case, and you are . . . the last people that are ever going to have a chance to pass judgment on Edward Clark.

Chapter 15: Judge's Instructions, Jury Deliberations, Sentence

In his instructions to the jury, the judge noted, among other things:

> This is the case of the *State of Minnesota v. Edward R. Clark*. It is before you on an indictment returned by the Grand Jury of the County Le Sueur, State of Minnesota. The indictment accuses the defendant of the crime of murder in the first degree and the crime of murder in the second degree. Here, let me advise you that the alternate count of first-degree murder while committing or attempting to commit rape has been dismissed by this court and should not concern yourselves further with regard to that alternate count.[190]

As the jury went into deliberation, the newspapers aptly announced in headlines: "Clark Trial Jury to Begin Deliberations," "Clark Trial Goes to Jury," and "Jury Deliberating Clark Case Retire."[191]

Defense attorney Wylde came to see me during the deliberations. He said the jury had requested Dr. Ohrt's testimony as to the time of death of Michael Jiminez, the scientific data used to determine it, and a blackboard and chalk. Wylde said this was a good sign, indicating the jury was discussing my alibi defense, that I was not in Minnesota when Michael Jiminez was murdered or when Barbara Jiminez met her demise. I was optimistic.

The judge, however, refused to turn over to the jury Dr. Ohrt's testimony and the scientific data, stating they would have to rely on their own recollections. He refused despite his having told juror Oberlin, on record, "The maps will go to the jurors at the time the case is turned over to the jury, *along with all the rest of the evidence.*"

I was later summoned to the courtroom. Wylde was pacing in the corridor. He approached me and in a sullen voice said the jury was coming back in to ask the judge to repeat the law giving the difference between first- and second-degree murder. When the jurors filed into the courtroom, none looked at me. Their faces were expressionless.

Judge Fitzgerald quoted the law on the elements of murder in the first and second degree. The jury then went back to deliberate. Later that evening, the jailer came to get me again. There was total silence on our way to the courtroom.

Filing into the jury box, every juror avoided eye contact with me. The judge asked me to rise. Defense attorney Wylde stood beside me as the verdict was read: "Guilty of murder in the first degree."

Wylde asked that each juror be polled, to ensure each shared the opinion. One by one, their names were called, and each answered "Guilty." Two of the women jurors sobbed. Despite their sealing my fate, I felt compassion; it appeared they gave in under pressure.

After the jurors were excused and left the courtroom, the judge asked me whether I had anything to say before he pronounced sentence. In part, I stated:

> If I had competent counsel in my first trial, I know I wouldn't be standing here today. And you can tell a jury to disregard this and disregard that, but they are human and I know it has been a trying experience for them as it has for a lot of us. I have no ill feelings towards the jury

... I will say that I will continue to fight it the best I can, as long as I can. I had hoped to win in a court of law . . . but it just seems that a fair trial is an illusion as to what I think it should be. It doesn't exist. You can't be in two places at one time. Like I said, I am not guilty."[192]

Judge Fitzgerald asked the prosecutor whether he had any recommendation. That was a foregone conclusion-I had been warned what it would be if I did not plead guilty. He recommended a life sentence running consecutive to the first life sentence, and that is what I am doing now.

Twin Cities newspaper headlines on my conviction read: "Michigan Man Convicted in Second Jiminez Death" and "Convicted Slayer Gets 2nd Life Term." The *Mankato Free Press* dramatized the scene, erroneously reporting: ". . . and tears streamed down his face."[193]

My attorney moved for a new trial, saying that Judge Fitzgerald had contradicted his own conclusion-"strangulation by two strands of her long hair" in saying that the death could *possibly have* been caused by drowning. Also, the pathologist had relied primarily upon the finding of hair across Barbara's neck, though he admitted it may have lodged around the neck as part of the swelling process. Finally, Sheriff Wiebold's testimony that I had said, "That girl wasn't raped" was a clear indication Wiebold misunderstood this remark.[194]

In response to my appeal regarding the consecutive sentence, Judge Fitzgerald made it clear that he wanted me never to be released:

> This court was influenced passing sentence on the petitioner by the fact that two separate juries had heard essentially the same evidence and that both had concluded that the petitioner was guilty as charged; that the murders were unusually brutal and bizarre; and that the defendant was 36 years of age. Having these facts in mind, the Court was of the opinion that a consecutive sentence was called for.[195]

On appeal to the higher court, my attorney argued that there was no evidence to support the claim that the murders were "brutal and bizarre" since there was no trauma to the body of Barbara Jiminez and it could not be determined with certainty how she died.[196]

The appellate attorney also argued (and the jury must have wondered) as to why I testified at the first trial but not in the second. Attorney Wylde and I had decided that with Judge Fitzgerald giving the prosecutor free rein, it would serve no purpose. The judge had told the prosecutor upon his taking my testimony out of context: "[I]t is your case. You do what you want." His doing so had an irreversible negative effect on the jury—especially with the prosecutor's repeated reminders that I had been found guilty in the murder of Michael Jiminez.

In defense attorney Wylde's mistaken opinion, my convictions would be overturned on appeal and a new trial ordered upon his impeachment of the State's expert witnesses on forensics, who had withheld evidence of my innocence (exculpatory evidence). He thought the Minnesota Supreme Court would set down guidelines for the trial courts so that I would receive a fair trial. I don't fault my attorney for the suggestion; it certainly seemed logical at the time. But the result was different from what we expected!

In seeking a new trial, the appellate attorney argued *11 separate violations of my constitutional rights in the first trial*, In Mankato, *and 12 in the second*-everything from my illegal arrest, the eavesdropping on privileged attorney-client conferences, jury intimidation, and denial of effective counsel in the first trial, to unfairly impeaching my key defense witness with an altered trial transcript in the second trial, and the withholding of exculpatory evidence in both.

On five of the blatant constitutional violations, the Minnesota Supreme Court made no comment, despite their being supported by the evidence and despite precedence of relief in cases with a single such violation. The court ruled simply: "Defendant raises various other issues on appeal, which we have considered and find to be without merit."[197]

Part IV: Exculpatory Evidence

Chapter 16: Discovery

During appellate hearings, Ronald Haskvitz, the attorney handling my appeals, subpoenaed the prosecutors, their files, and the police investigation reports related to the case. On the witness stand, the Blue Earth County prosecutor, when asked whether he had brought his file, said he had. But he objected to revealing its contents, as it contained his "personal notes".[198] Apparently Haskvitz, an expert in this area of law, had run into this problem before.

Haskvitz answered, "You are a witness. You cannot object. Only the attorney representing the state [attorney general's office] can object." From memory he quoted the rules of appellate procedure. The judge then ordered the prosecutor to turn over his file.

As revealed earlier, in that file was the statement by Edward Newberg, formerly an employee of my business, who had been interviewed by Minnesota authorities in Michigan after my arrest. In the statement, Newberg said he had seen me in Michigan at a time that made it impossible for me to have been in Minnesota when Michael Jiminez was killed.

Asked about when he had received the statement, Corbey responded that he "couldn't recall" ever seeing it. But then he admitted that he had underlined some of the text. Newberg's statement was also found in the subpoenaed files of the Blue Earth County sheriff.

Also discovered in the Le Sueur County prosecutor's file was a memo from Walter Rhodes, the crime bureau's identification officer, dated five months before the start of the first trial, in Mankato. It listed Barbara Jiminez's fingerprint classification, which Rhodes had testified did not exist. It also noted that the fingerprints discovered were neither mine nor those of the Jiminezes, thus lending support to my claim of picking up three hitchhikers. Given the prosecutors' testimony that they had shared their files with one another, the Blue Earth County prosecutor apparently removed his copy before the appellate hearing.

Another document discovered in the Le Sueur County prosecutor's file was the Blue Earth County sheriff's investigation report revealing the existence of Ernest Ties, the attendant at the service station adjacent to the café in Blairsburg, Iowa. Ties supported waitress Helen Troxel in seeing the Jiminez couple alone at the café about the time I made the phone call home from Illinois. The investigation report also revealed that Glen Bjorklund, in Alden, Minnesota, near the Iowa border, had recognized me and my vehicle at his service station (at a time prior to the death of Michael Jiminez). He said I was alone.

The appellate attorney argued that Ties would have supported Helen Troxel's testimony as to seeing the Jiminezes at the café in Blairsburg, Iowa, which supported my alibi defense, as well as the importance of Bjorklund's observation of me *before* the death of Michael Jiminez:

> Ties would have supported the testimony of Helen Troxel to the effect that Barbara and Michael Jiminez were in the M & M Café. He would [also] have supported her testimony that *they came in alone and returned to the highway alone* . . .
>
> Ties' testimony would have made it impossible for the prosecutor to ask the jury to disregard the crucial facts to which Troxel testified. Ties may even have been able to establish the time and day that he saw the couple at the café, and thereby corroborate Troxel's testimony that the Jiminez couple came into the café on April 22, about 11:00 to 1:00 in the afternoon.

> The significance of Bjorklund's statement was that it would have established Clark was alone in his Bronco at a place in southern Minnesota at 7:30 to 8:00 in the evening . . . This would have made it highly unlikely that he was at Smith's Mill during the time Michael Jiminez was murdered (between 9:00 P.M. and 3:00 A.M. according to the medical evidence) . . . Bjorklund's statement would have supported Troxel's [account of seeing the Jiminezes alone in the café in Blairsburg Corners] and made it impossible for the prosecutor to ask the jury to disregard the crucial facts to which she testified.[199]

When John Wylde, who represented me at the second trial, took the stand at the appellate hearing and was asked whether he had been supplied with Walter Rhodes's memo listing Barbara Jiminez's fingerprint classification, he said, "No." Asked whether he had been given the investigation report revealing the existence of Ernest Ties and Glen Bjorklund, he answered he had not, though he was entitled to see it. He stated that an investigator for the defense had been hired to locate witnesses with the precise information Bjorklund had provided the authorities.

The *Waseca Journal* reported the existence of additional evidence of which I was unaware during the two trials. This included that Michael Jiminez's wife, Barbara, was seen in the café in Waseca in the company of a man two days after the discovery of Michael Jiminez's body. Until the authorities learned I had an alibi, the prosecutors apparently planned to call as a witness Bob Guthrie, who owned a local café and had seen Barbara Jiminez-the judge had announced at the start of the first trial that a "person from Waseca" would be called.

The Third Hitchhiker?

In 1984, ten years after I was convicted, another prisoner, Terry Stacey, approached me for advice regarding his sentence, as by this time I knew more about the law. He asked whether I was the "Edward Clark convicted out of Mankato." Stacey claimed he had information implicating other people-his "former drug partners"-in the murders.

I was skeptical. Was this just another case of a prisoner wishing to associate with someone of notoriety, someone involved in prison and sentencing reform? I asked Stacey questions about the Jiminezes-things that I had learned during the trial but that had not been reported by the media. Stacey had the answers, including knowledge of the place where the Jiminezes had resided in Mankato. Adding more credibility was the fact that Stacey was in for a drug-related offense. Having lived in Mankato, he knew much about the drug scene there.

Stacey was reluctant to reveal information to anyone but me, as he was afraid of being labeled a "snitch" among drug dealers in the prison. He also feared it might affect his parole-prison authorities have been known to assist the prosecution. I had to obtain assurance in writing from the state's releasing authority that there would be no retaliation before he finally agreed to give a deposition. Even then, I had to agree not to go public with the information until after his release.

I hired an attorney to conduct the deposition, and since "a picture is worth a thousand words," I arranged through the attorney to have the deposition videotaped. From the deposition (emphasis added):

Attorney:

>What did you tell him [Clark] you knew about this particular case?

Stacey:

>Well, I told him . . . that I had known some people that I thought were responsible for it . . .
>
>At that time *Jerry Jacobloski and Craig Cook* were doing business together, which was *selling drugs and dealing in drugs* . . . I met them down *around the Mankato area*-at that time. Over some business.

... they had mentioned that *they had been ripped off*-at that time it was considered a nice chunk of money, it was $8,000 or something like that, *over a drug transaction. And they had mentioned . . . Jiminez . . .*

... They were going to get their money back one way or another from those people . . . I believe it was *they went to buy some drugs and lost the money in the process or something like that.*

Attorney:

The Jiminez people went to buy some drugs and lost Jacobloski's money?

Stacey:

Money in the process, you know. And so I know that they were quite excited about that . . . I remember after hearing . . . *these hitchhikers being killed down there* . . . and it registered that *that was the people . . . Jerry and Craig was talking about at that time . . .*

I think Jerry had died out in New York sometime right around that time period . . . but his partner Craig, I know I talked to him because he lived in Minneapolis. I talked to him after that, after I heard about these people getting killed . . . I . . . asked him what was going on there . . . he said that they had taken care of business . . . That left me with the impression that they had killed them . . .

Attorney:

Do you think Craig Cook or Jerry Jacobloski would have the capacity to carry out that?

Stacey:

Oh, I would say either one of them were capable. And Jerry was hooked out of Buffalo, New York, and some of the people that they were dealing with from out there were quite capable, too.

Attorney:

Were their drug connections out on the East Coast?

Stacey:

Yes . . . between New York and California and Minnesota and Iowa. That's some of the states that I know that they were carrying on business at.

Attorney:

Where is Craig Cook now?

Stacey:

I think he killed himself or that he was killed . . .

Attorney:

Did they talk about any drug transactions or any business of any nature they might have had in any place in the state of Iowa?

Stacey:

Yes . . . well, Jerry and Craig and those people were involved with people out of several of the college towns down there . . . Iowa City, Ames . . . there are several small college towns down there . . .

Attorney:

. . . And would you know from any information that they would take trips to Iowa or-

Stacey:

Oh, sure, they would take trips down there . . .

Attorney:

. . . And do you know . . . did either Jacobloski and Cook have any legal employment or were they going to school or anything?

Stacey:

When I first met Jerry Jacobloski he was going to the Albert Lea College, I believe, at that time . . .

Attorney:

. . . You indicated . . . *there was some kind of commune or something in the Mankato area.* Did you actually live there yourself?

Stacey:

. . . *It was a few miles south . . . on Highway 22 out of Mankato . . . Jerry Jacobloski and I lived there with a number of other people.*

Attorney:

Have you ever been interviewed by, say, the DEA [Drug Enforcement Agency] or any state officials on associations you had with Cook and Jacobloski?

Stacey:

. . . the only time I was confronted by the police was that one time in Albert Lea, Minnesota . . . and *I was surrounded by the Albert Lea police with their guns drawn . . . They were looking for Jerry Jacobloski* at that time for something . . .

Attorney:

I want to focus on this Jiminez couple again . . . What was their relationship, as far as drugs went with Jacobloski and Cook, were they just users or were they dealers or what was your understanding of that?

Stacey:

Oh, definitely. *They were definitely dealing drugs.*

Attorney:

... *Did you, by chance, ever know either Jacobloski or Cook to wear brown suede-type or brown leather-type jackets?*

Stacy:

Oh yeah ... either one of them had worn jackets like that on and off through the years. At one time period that was kind of the style was a suede-brown suede.

Attorney:

Okay, Mr. Stacey, I would just *finally to ask you if you're convinced or at least of the strong opinion*, after the conversations you had with Mr. Cook, and the prior conversations you had with *Mr. Cook and Mr. Jacobloski, if they are the persons that murdered the Jiminez couple?* Now is that the impression you're left with and is that why you approached Mr. Clark?

Stacey:

Yes, it is ... *that's what they told me, that they had taken care of them.*

Attorney:

Would you have been more reluctant to bring that up if they were still alive?

Stacey:

Yes, I would.[200]

It is ironic that Stacey would not come forward while Cook and Jacobloski were still alive because he feared being labeled a "snitch", but that's the world of drugs-and a prisoner's code-and I had to accept it.

To summarize-Jerry Jacobloski and Craig Cook accused the Jiminez couple of losing $8,000 of their money, which was to have gone towards the purchase of more drugs, and they would get their money back "one way or another." After the Jiminezes were murdered, Cook told Stacey they had "taken care of business." That is they were responsible for the deaths of the Jiminez couple.

Jacobloski and Cook had drug connections on both the East and West Coasts. They took trips across the country, dealing in drugs at college towns, including some in Iowa, and in the vicinity of where the Jiminezes had last been seen alive together. The police in the college town of Albert Lea, Minnesota, near the Iowa border, were looking for Jacobloski with guns drawn, as he was considered dangerous.

Both Jacobloski and Cook were now dead, one allegedly by suicide and the other from a drug overdose.

Once learning that Jacobloski died before the slaying of the Jiminezes, I asked Stacey about it. He said Jacobloski and Cook had told him about the Jiminezes owing them money before Jacobloski's death, that Cook and someone else likely carried out the murders. Stacey said that Cook's criminal record included armed robbery.

I then focused on getting as much information about Jacobloski and Cook as I could-and since Waseca is located between Mankato and Albert Lea, to inquire of Robert Guthrie, who identified Barbara Jiminez in his café, about why he had not testified. Had someone suggested he not testify, or was it simply a case of the prosecutors intentionally neglecting to call him? Seeking this information required the services of a private investigator.

In Albert Lea and Waseca, the investigator met with the police chiefs. Both chiefs said they believed Mankato was a drug problem for the entire state. Without the investigator revealing the specific reason for his presence, both chiefs recognized he was taking a look at the Jiminez case, even though the murders had taken place ten years earlier. Both said that their law enforcement in the area had led them to suspect drugs were behind the slaying of the Jiminez couple. When the investigator revealed that I was his client, both chiefs appeared sympathetic and wanted justice served. They would help if they could-so long as it did not jeopardize their positions.

They told the investigator, in summary, that in Albert Lea, the police had a thick file on Jacobloski, who had a criminal record that included kidnapping. With some officials unaware that Jacobloski was now dead, there were still outstanding warrants for his arrest. The college in Albert Lea where Jacobloski allegedly had been enrolled had since closed. The college "had drug dealers swarming over it like locusts."

The date of birth given for Jacobloski put him at the age of 27 when he was attending college, lending credibility that being a student gave him access to the campus for selling drugs.

The birth date for Craig Cook put him at about the ages of the Jiminezes and the third hitchhiker. Cook was sentenced to Minnesota's state prison (there was only one at the time) for selling a controlled substance-cocaine-about four years after the Jiminezes were killed. Cook allegedly committed suicide on November 29, 1981.

When I read the report on Cook having served time at the state prison, I thought, "That bastard passed me in the hallway, perhaps even lived in the same cell hall, knowing that his actions put me in prison for what could be the rest of my life. And he didn't give a damn." Or did he? Did his conscience bother him to the degree that it led to his suicide? And if so, was suicide the final act of a coward, to choose death over spending the rest of his life in prison should he step forward and admit to the killings?

The Waseca police chief informed the investigator that Robert Guthrie had closed his restaurant and moved to Newton, Iowa. Provided with the address, the investigator attempted to reach Guthrie, but family members refused to allow the investigator to talk with him.

The investigator also went to the location along Route 22 where Jacobloski and Stacey had lived at a commune on a farm. It was close to where the body of Michael Jiminez was discovered south of Mankato along Highway 14-Route 22 running parallel to Highway 14. The owner resided in Mankato, but people living adjacent to the property were more than willing to cooperate with the investigator. They told him approximately 16 people had taken up residence at the farm and were a continuous problem, implying they may have been responsible for the farm burning down in 1976, two years after the death of the Jiminezes.

Not just through Stacey did I learn of the Jiminezes' involvement with drugs or that my public defender in Mankato had previously represented Michael Jiminez on drug charges. Another prisoner from the Mankato area told me he had purchased drugs from Barbara Jiminez and that she had a reputation on campus as "the Avon lady for drugs."

As I had new evidence-particularly the names of those who could be responsible for the killings of the Jiminezes and their likely motive-the reader might ask why I did not attempt to have my case reopened. Considering that the appellate court had ignored the flagrant violations depriving me of a fair trial in both cases, and knowing that the same justices ruling against me remained on the bench, I had little faith in the system. The result would be just another letdown for me and a reopening of emotional wounds for the families of the Jiminezes, ten years after the fact.

To test one theory about what transpired surrounding the deaths of the Jiminezes, I brought together four inmates who were drug dealers. Two were federal prisoners convicted of drug-related murders. With not much to do in a maximum-security prison and the subject of the meeting related to their "profession", the federal prisoners were eager to participate. So that they wouldn't show favoritism, I used no names and did not say that anyone had been arrested and convicted of the murders in question. Only one of them knew I was the one. We discussed the couple's movements in sequence and looked at excerpts from Stacey's deposition. Here is the information they reviewed:

The Jiminezes hitchhiked 300 miles to attend a wedding in Le Mars, Iowa, but continued to hitchhike another 240 miles to Emporia, Kansas, arriving unannounced on a Friday evening, allegedly to buy a car from a sister. They had only six dollars with them, but had left $150 in cash in their apartment in Mankato. Because they couldn't get the vehicle's title transferred on a Sunday, the Jiminezes chose to hitchhike the 540 miles back to Mankato rather than remain until the following day to register the car and drive back.

The Jiminezes picked up an Iowa road map when leaving Emporia, Kansas, though they were planning to hitchhike back to Minnesota on a direct route. They made a sign that read "35N," later discovered to display additional writing–"35 Minnesota" and "Minnesota," suggesting they took a detour off Interstate 35 before reaching Minnesota. The Jiminez couple comprised two of the three hitchhikers picked up in the Des Moines area on Sunday evening. Des Moines is the Home of Drake University, and the University of Iowa is close to Des Moines.

The Jiminezes did not return to Minnesota directly, as they were seen in a café in Blairsburg, Iowa, on Monday afternoon. Blairsburg is approximately 125 miles south of the Minnesota border, in close proximity to Ames, home of Iowa State University.

The Jiminezes, according to Stacey, at some point had "ripped off" drug dealers Jerry Jacobloski and Craig Cook for $8,000, who were "going to get their money back one way or another." And, "Jerry and Craig and those people were involved with people out of several of the college towns down there . . . Iowa City, Ames . . . "

Michael Jiminez's body was found in an open area, laid out to draw attention, with railroad ties placed across the body in the form of an X. The location of his wife's body, discovered 12 days later, was isolated. One of her shoes was placed in the crotch of a tree's branches with the toe pointed towards the body.

Two days after the discovery of her husband Michael's body, Barbara Jiminez was seen in Waseca, Minnesota, near the Iowa border, in the company of another man; both had seemed nervous.

At some point while she was missing, Barbara Jiminez ran to a farmhouse in Le Sueur County in fear for her life, where she made a phone call. She didn't call the police, but an individual who must have been involved with her and whom she trusted in some way. At some point afterwards she was killed by the people revealed by Stacey in his deposition: "I talked to him [Craig Cook] and asked him what was going on there and, to me, he said that they had taken care of business, you know . . . That left me with the impression that they had killed them."

We also looked at a series of articles on the drug trade in Mankato that examined violence and unsolved murders during that time. On discussing this information, the foursome agreed on this scenario:

The Jiminezes may have been used routinely as "mules" to bring drugs up from Emporia, Kansas, a known drug route from Kansas City to Mankato and other destinations north. Where low-level drug dealers can purchase drugs cheaper out of state, they regularly use college students, who need the money, to transport the drugs. As hitchhikers, they don't draw the authorities' attention that vehicles with out-of-state license plates do. Perhaps on a previous trip, the Jiminezes had lost the $8,000.

The Jiminezes may have been expected to pick up drugs and meet the third hitchhiker at some point after leaving Emporia, Kansas, to pay back the $8,000. The Jiminezes most likely knew the third hitchhiker; he wasn't someone who just happened to be hitchhiking along the same route towards Minnesota. He might very well have been Craig Cook, implicated through the deposition, or someone connected to Cook. Perhaps there was a prearranged meeting to take place somewhere along the Jiminezes' return route. Whoever it was perhaps deliberately did not mention the $8,000-to make them believe he was helping them get started as independent dealers-until the schemers could get their hands on the money, or drugs in lieu of the money.

Making a drug connection neither in Emporia, Kansas, nor in the Des Moines area, the Jiminezes stayed in or near Ames the rest of Sunday night through Monday evening. That would explain their presence at the café at Blairsburg Corners around noon on Monday. On Sunday evening, the third hitchhiker continued driving to Minnesota, while the man who picked them up near Des Moines, who had driven 1,600 miles in 34 hours, slept. That the vehicle ran out of gas may have saved his life.

Since the Jiminezes apparently did not have their duffel bag at the café in Iowa, they must have left it in the hitchhike vehicle; the third hitchhiker rummaged through it. Then, he put the duffel bag and its contents in the trash box, followed by his brown suede jacket. He replaced it with a sports jacket he found in the suitcase he took with him. The man who had picked the three up near Des Moines discarded the box as trash after he woke the next morning.

When the Jiminezes returned to Minnesota, they must have been forced to stay at the commune alluded to in Stacey's deposition instead of returning to their apartment: "There was some kind of commune or something in the Mankato area . . . it was a few miles south . . . on Highway 22 out of Mankato . . . Jerry Jacobloski and I lived there with a number of other people."

Michael Jiminez's sister revealed in her testimony that her brother took medication for his seizures, so his mental capacity may have been somewhat impaired. This may have made it easier to force or deceive him into temporarily leaving the commune. Since his medication was never found with other items belonging to the Jiminezes at their apartment, he may have left it at the commune.

Driving along Highway 14 in the middle of the night, the assailants, now with Michael Jiminez in another vehicle, turned onto an access way to the railroad tracks. Someone forced or tricked him into walking a short distance, then shot him from behind. The assailants then removed two railroad ties, one weighing 120 pounds, from a stack 18 to 25 feet away, and placed them on the body so that it would be discovered after dawn.

After driving the vehicle back to the highway entrance, the perpetrators scattered on the access way (if indeed these items were found at the crime scene) a matchbook and pens from the West Coast, formerly in the Bronco. They did this to divert the authorities' attention from local suspects, from their "concentrating on three separate persons that may have been in the area or known to frequent the area," as stated by the sheriff soon after discovery of the body.

A question. What was Barbara Jiminez doing as her husband was being shot? She could not have been left alone in the vehicle without restraints. We discussed three theories: She was not present, there was more than one person involved and one of them restrained her, or she was drugged. The third possibility is plausible-the autopsy revealed two types of alcohol in her system that could have incapacitated her. With Barbara Jiminez biding time for herself, she convinced the abductors she could make the connection and would be the dealer' best chance at making it. Days later, they used incapacitation again, to drown her.

Given that Barbara Jiminez' body was discovered in a different setting from her husband's, her assailants likely chose the remote lake and removed all her identification so that the authorities would not find or identify her body for some time. Placing it there would put across an ominous message, emphasized by the position of her shoe, to anyone else who might consider double-crossing these drug dealers.

So that is the theory developed by four men in prison experienced in the business of dealing drugs.

The credibility of Terry Stacey's deposition, which implicated Jerry Jacobloski and Craig Cook in the murder of the Jiminez couple, was summed up by Sheriff Pat Smith Jr. of Le Sueur County (retired). A man of integrity, I believe, he was chief deputy and one of the investigators who went to Michigan to learn I was there at the time of Michael Jiminez's murder. In response to reading Stacey's deposition, Sheriff Smith wrote:

> Dear Ed:
>
> I wish I would have had some of this information years ago, instead of now when the two alleged murderers are both deceased.[201]

Thirty five years into my imprisonment, more evidence supporting that Jacobloski and Cook may have ben responsible for the killings:

[T]he Fox 9 investigators looked through hundreds of court documents from Clark's first trial and uncovered several clues that could support his alibi...

Another report says, a farm wife stated that at 10:30 the night Michael Jimenez was murdered, "she noticed <u>two cars</u> in the field right in the area of the crime scene.

But if not Jacobloski and Cook, there is a person of trust: State Patrol Officer Rodney Johnnson who committed horrific acts against women until caught and confessed:

The Fox 9 investigators found a case with eerie similarities: In 1989, a man confessed to killing a female hitchhiker known as "Jane Doe" in southern Minnesota. That was nine years earlier.

He admitted picking up the woman near Interstate 90, then handcuffing her, forcing her to perform a sex act and then strangling her to death with a drawstring from her clothing, He dumped her naked body in a drainage ditch.

At the time of the Jimenez murders in 1974, <u>he was working in the area</u>. He also admitted being <u>involved in other unsolved murders in the area</u>, but has never identified the victims.[202]

Epilogue

Over the years I have been plagued with one question: What evidence did the police and the prosecutors remove from their files before they were subpoenaed for the appellate hearings? They placed no importance on (or ignored or hid) evidence that supports my innocence, including:

- The phone call I placed from Rockford (Belvidere), Illinois, on my drive to Michigan, approximately seven hours before Michael Jiminez was killed in Minnesota.

- The existence of Ernest Ties, another person who observed the Jiminezes at the cafe in Iowa at approximately the same time I made the first phone call home, from the Belvedere, Illinois, area

- The sighting of Barbara Jiminez in a restaurant in Waseca, Minnesota, two days after the discovery of her husband's body

- The fingerprint classification of Barbara Jiminez, indicating that the unknown prints could have been those of the third hitchhiker

- The elimination of my vehicles as having made

the tire tracks at the crime scenes

- The existence of Glen Bjorklund, who identified me and my vehicle and said he saw me alone, in the vicinity of Interstate 90 near the Iowa border

- A former employee of mine seeing me in Michigan, thus supporting my alibi defense

Evidence removed by the police and prosecutors might include the identity of the "three separate persons that may have been in the area or shown to frequent the area" where the body of Michael Jiminez was discovered-the area on which the Blue Earth County Sheriff's Department and the Minnesota Bureau of Criminal Apprehension initially focused. Did those suspects include Jerry Jacobloski or Craig Cook-who, according to Stacey's deposition, had "taken care of business" in regard to the $8,000 in drug money the Jiminezes claimed to have lost?

The solution to the lack of justice that many Americans have experienced may lie partially in these remedies:

- Authorization of judges to exclude the testimony by forensic experts based solely on their conclusions, without evidence to support them

- State forensic/crime laboratories requiring accreditation by an independent organization or federal agency for its technicians; laboratories operating as independent agencies, with loyalty to neither prosecution nor defense, so that their findings are objective

- The videotaping of all police interrogations

- The identification of jurors by number, to prevent jury tampering

- Allowing jurors to take notes and ask questions of witnesses, which is now permitted in a few states, including Arizona, Colorado, Florida, and Indiana

- Cameras allowed in the courtrooms, as some

states already do

- Prosecutors held accountable for misconduct such as withholding exculpatory evidence, eliciting false testimony from a witness, and doctoring documents/court records

- When applicable, compensating defendants who are exonerated or acquitted for their loss of wages and legal fees.

Along with holding accountable the prosecutors who put innocent people in prison through misconduct, so should prison officials answer to the taxpayers and to society in general.

For the past 47 years, through Coalition for Corrections Reform (CCR), I have authored and submitted to the administrative and legislative branches of state government 45 reports, papers, and published articles and essays on the correction system.[203] With public members of the coalition testifying at the Minnesota State Capitol, this work as sometimes resulted in the public scrutiny of corrections officials.

Several legislators have written in response to my input on the correction system, as well as proposals for crime prevention. The Speaker of the [Minnesota] House, Robert E. Vanasek, wrote:

> Thank you for bringing to my attention the reports on criminal justice issues. I appreciate the effort you made in compiling this information.
>
> I would urge you to continue your interest in criminal justice. I want you to know that I appreciate the work you do and that I find your suggestions and insights very useful.
>
> I look forward to your next reports and will be turning them over to a staff member who will be studying the prison system. I'm sure the information will be useful.
>
> Again, thank you for all your efforts. I'm sure there

will be considerable discussion in criminal justice issues this legislative session.[204]

And Senate Minority Leader Duane Benson wrote:

> Thank you for the attention you've given and will be giving to Minnesota's correctional institutions and the programs that make them work. Your personal experience is very valuable to the evaluation of those institutions.
>
> Your preliminary reports were very interesting and I am eagerly awaiting their results in full.
>
> Thank you, again, for your concern in the area of corrections and I hope your passion for these issues will continue. Your work is important to the work of the legislature.[205]

My endeavors in the area of prison reform have, not surprisingly, resulted in my being viewed by prison officials as "contentious". Their animosity has been especially evident when I've sought relief from the conditions and the length of my imprisonment, despite the following positive prison psychologist's evaluation (required upon seeking parole). In part:

> Mr. Clark is serving two consecutive life sentences for first-degree murder. Early this year [1991], Mr. Clark was paroled from the first sentence to the second life sentence. Based on his interpretation of an attorney general's ruling, he believes he is eligible for parole on the second sentence without serving the statutory minimum on a life sentence . . .[206]
>
> Significantly, Mr. Clark continues to maintain that he committed neither of the murders for which he stands convicted. His activities during his [initial] 17 years of incarceration reflect both his belief in his innocence and his desire to contribute positively to society as best he can in prison. Although Mr. Clark appears angry toward

prison officials and toward the court system which convicted him, this writer does not believe that his anger will adversely affect his adjustment were he to be released from prison . . .

While he is viewed by prison officials as contentious and self-seeking, most of his activities reflect a desire to contribute to the welfare of others generally:

Mr. Clark appears to have made adequate preparations for his success in the community once released . . . His plans for his release appear to be consistent with his high level of intellectual and psychological functioning.[207]

Nevertheless, I was denied a parole hearing at that time.

Nine years later, I requested a second evaluation by the prison psychologist, but corrections officials refused to allow it. So, after 26 years in prison, I hired Dennis Philander, a renowned, board-certified forensic psychiatrist, to do a comprehensive, in-depth evaluation. Excerpts from his findings follow:

[Clark's] involvement in the activities of *prison reform* is complete, comprehensive, and extensive . . . Generally, he continues his altruistic commitment to prison reform, and in this regard it sounds extremely *unique*, diverse, sustained (for longevity), timely, successful, and accepted by both sides as a positive, and pro-social venture . . .

His adaption [*sic*] to deal with psychosocial and environmental stressors show that he has dealt with these in the most exemplary of fashions, in the face of the most devastating part of deprivation of freedom, an issue that had collective and progressive stress. He has dealt with this in turn to create the most exemplary behavior, e.g., has shown altruistic concern for significant other, and thus has employed the healthiest of defense mechanisms, i.e., higher adaptive levels of coping . . . He focuses on his mantra, for adjustment in life as a Latin term *inictus manus*.

That basically spells "Never give up. I'm not beaten yet."

> ... No indication of propensity to develop significant psychological or psychiatric condition, despite the fact he has been exposed to the most significant and sustained stressors imaginable, i.e., after losing one's freedom and being incarcerated for two and a half decades-particularly, given his sentiment that he had not been involved [in the murders] at any level.[208]

By society's standards, the psychological evaluations reflecting my exemplary behavior and "altruism" would at least allow me to live in a less restrictive environment. While the evaluations indicate I pose no danger to society and that my endeavors are "accepted by both sides as a positive and pro-social venture", corrections officials don't operate by societal standards, despite what they may project at the prison or agency level.

After 31 years in prison, in preparation for a hearing to determine whether I would be released after another three years, a third psychological evaluation was conducted by a Department of Corrections employee who follows the instructions of his superiors. His "evaluation" consisted of a one-hour interview and questionnaire more applicable to someone on probation or parole than to someone still in prison. Its additional, irrelevant questions such as "What would you change in the judicial system?" and "What is your opinion of this facility?" suggested something more like a survey. And the warden of "this facility" was sitting on the panel determining my fate!

My "exemplary behavior" was ignored in the third evaluation. Instead it claimed that I had had two "major rule violations" six years earlier, for (of all things) not sending out personal property as previously authorized and for having a foam mattress pad (authorized and issued to me years earlier). This underscores the pettiness that corrections officials employ to justify their actions. The evaluations emphasized: "Since Mr. Clark denies committing the murder of Barbara Jiminez, *he expresses no guilt or remorse . . . and has a 31 percent chance of recidivating.*"

Also the policy governing evaluation now takes into consideration whether the alleged crime is a "notorious/highly publicized offense"-in other words, the process and its outcome is political!

The hearing, instead of being conducted by an independent, unbiased parole board, was carried out as an inquisition by the commissioner of corrections-a political appointee-and her "advisory panel" of high-ranking corrections officials who resented my input on the corrections system to the legislature and their agency's resulting accountability. Among those on the advisory panel who should have disqualified themselves from the hearing was a deputy commissioner who argued at the hearing that there are no innocent people in prison. Six years earlier this official expected to be appointed commissioner-until I revealed he was unfit to hold the position. As prison warden, he had abolished community-oriented programs such as the prisons Jaycee Chapter, which raised more than $5,000 a year for medical research and charity, and eliminated successful rehabilitation education and vocational training programs. The official was quoted in the article: "We don't hold ourselves responsible for their rehabilitation anymore."[209]

Further, a wrongful-death lawsuit was filed against him by the family of a mentally ill but non-threatening prisoner who died in the punitive segregation unit. In segregation, he was denied his medication, denied food and water, beaten by guards, stripped naked, and strapped to a board. This resulted in the establishment by the Department of Corrections of prescribed procedures for dealing with mentally ill inmates and establishing a Mental Health Unit in one prison.

Three years before my hearing, the same official canceled a ceremony scheduled for the Minnesota chapter of the National Alliance for the Mentally Ill, to present me with a service award for exposing the mistreatment of mentally ill/mentally impaired prison inmates.[210]

Also on the panel was an assistant commissioner who implemented numerous policies reflecting a punishment philosophy. I believe he was directly involved in intercepting input I had tried to provide to the legislature over the preceding five years. When prison officials stopped issuing "Certified Mail" cards guaranteeing that my mail reached its destination, I filed a grievance; he upheld this unconstitutional restriction.

The commissioner and advisory panel ignored the professional psychological evaluations, my exemplary behavior record, and recommendations from private citizens, including members of a religious community. They also ignored my contributions to society, including:

- Exposing the mistreatment of mentally ill/mentally impaired prison inmates as indicated by the aforementioned service award

- Designing a school-bus-brake-inspection manual for the state[211]

- Preventing a riot by working with legislators (setting a precedent) who authored a bill providing early release for prisoners who deserve it. One reporter noted: "Clark earned a reputation as peacemaker," said Rep. Janet Clark [not related], who worked with him on legislative issues."[212]

Neither did the panel allow me to present the evidence, including forensic evidence, of my innocence. And however the victims' families were informed or misinformed about my prison record, their responses have remained confidential. Finally, the panel banned the presence of media at the hearing.

After going through the motions of making a decision that was predetermined, the commissioner stated that my case will continue for another "ten years" before review, basing the decision on the following:

> The overall accountability time we believe is required as a result of your separate and brutal murders of Michael and Barbara Jiminez, an innocent young couple that you encountered hitchhiking. Although you continue to maintain your innocence, we consider you guilty . . . Acceptance of guilt, as we pointed out, is a first step towards rehabilitation and, without it, there isn't room to consider alternative dispositions.

> You are to be commended for your positive adjustment, and your continued demonstration of it will earn you the opportunity to be transferred to a medium-custody facility in five years.[213]

In other words, as I am now age 82, corrections officials apparently intend for me to spend the rest of my life in prison. Beyond that, the claim of brutality is not supported by the evidence and does not meet its legal definition. Michael Jiminez was shot through the back of his head and probably did not know he was about to be killed. Barbara Jiminez was found in a lake with water in her lungs and no trauma to her body.

When I stated that the decision was a violation of policy and state law in that it had not reviewed the facts and circumstances of my case, the panel responded: "How can we review the case? It's not our job."

Then whose job is it?

With the commissioner, and at least one other panel member acknowledging read the book published under its former title, on the surface it changed from not admitting guilt; but now requiredthrough mandated programming prior to a parole hearing, the official reason for denying the parole is:

> "Not having a comprehensive release plan and not having substantial community support."

This criterion is unrealistic. By this time I had been imprisoned four decades along with an advanced age.

Four years later for the latest parole hearing, emphasizing the reason for keeping me in prison is because of my activities for prison reform, the warden asked, "If released, do you intend to continue your involvement with the legislature?" She recommended I serve another four years before the next parole hearing – the commissioner ruled it is five years.

Along with the other psychological evaluation for that latest parole hearing takes it a step further emphasizing I should be released:

> Mr. Clark is encouraged to continue his pro-social activities,

such as his involvement with his community church, facility religious programming, and working with lawmakers on issues of offemders' well-being. In addition to supplementingthe meaning and prupose he fonds in his writing, these activities demonstrate a commitment to positive change and living…[W]ith his inherent desire to work and to be involved in social justices issues, volunteering with community organizationsmay be a good fit.[214]

One warden, known to be absent from the prison for long periods while drinking his lunch, verbalized the intent to keep me in prison for life. A member of one family that has visited me all the years of my imprisonment signed this statement, in part:

> [The] warden was escorting us on a tour of a portion of the institution. At this time he told us that Mr. Clark was not worth the time we were investing, and he would probably never see daylight.

His prediction came the same year the legislator had encouraged me to continue providing input on corrections.

Now in my senior years, I often think of the Jiminezes, who were denied their future, including perhaps the joy of raising a family, as I once did-decades ago. Out of respect for the memories held by their loved ones, I have only reluctantly revealed that the demise of the Jiminez couple seems to have been drug-related. They are not with us to defend themselves.

And I think often of my children, whom I haven't seen in all these years. No doubt I have grandchildren, perhaps even great-grandchildren.

Appendix

Prosecutorial Misconduct - Harmless Error?

As I (and others wrongfully accused) have experienced, the more serious a charge, the more the accused must *prove* innocence- this despite the U.S. Constitution's promise that a defendant is innocent until proven guilty. The judicial system, technically referred to as "adversarial", is in layman's terms a contest between the government and the accused. The government has available the resources it needs in seeking a conviction and may ignore developments that disprove its case. The lack of proscribed accountability for prosecutors for unethical actions sets the stage for their withholding from juries evidence supporting the innocence of the accused.

A report based on a three-year investigation by the Center for Public Integrity states:

> Most of the nation's approximately 30,000 local trial prosecutors strive to balance their understandable desire

to win-a desire supported by the vast majority of the citizenry-with their duty to ensure justice. There are some prosecutors, however, who have exalted winning and ignored the other half of the equation. Those prosecutors who repeatedly break the rules give *recidivism*-a word usually used to describe those they work to put behind bars-a disturbing new meaning.[215]

The report goes on to reveal:

- A team of 21 researchers, writers, and editors analyzed 11,452 cases in which charges of prosecutorial misconduct were reviewed by appellate court judges. In the majority of cases, the allegation of misconduct was ruled harmless error or was not addressed by the appellate judges, and the conviction stood.

- Since 1970, individual judges and appellate court panels in at least 2,012 cases have cited prosecutorial misconduct as a factor when dismissing charges at trial, reversing convictions, or reducing sentences.

The center's study of criminal appeals from 1970 to the present reveals in Minnesota:

- 240 cases in which a defendant alleged prosecutorial error or misconduct. In 32 of them, the judge ruled that the prosecutor's conduct prejudiced the defendant and would have reversed or remanded the conviction, sentence, or indictment. Of the 32 cases in which courts so ruled, 24 involved improper trial arguments, two involved improper tactics, and six involved the prosecution's withholding of evidence from the defense. In 186 of the cases (including this writer's), the appellate court ruled the prosecutions' misconduct was "harmless error". In the remaining 22, the court did not address the issue.

- Because of the relative rarity of reversals, any prosecutor who has more than one reversal to his or her credit belongs to a select club . . .

At virtually any step in a trial, from the initial questioning of a suspect through the marshalling of forensic evidence and experts to closing arguments and appellate maneuvering, errors by the state-prosecutors and police-can convict the innocent. Prosecutorial misconduct falls into several categories, including:

- Courtroom misconduct (making inappropriate or inflammatory comments in the presence of the jury; introducing or attempting to introduce inadmissible, inappropriate, or inflammatory evidence; mischaracterizing the evidence or the facts of the case to the court or jury; committing violations pertaining to the selection of the jury; or making improper closing arguments)

- Mishandling of physical evidence (hiding, destroying, or tampering with evidence, case files, or court records)

- Failing to disclose exculpatory evidence

- Threatening, badgering, or tampering with witnesses

- Using false or misleading evidence

- Harassing, displaying bias toward, or having a vendetta against the defendant or defendant's counsel (including *selective* or *vindictive* prosecution, which includes instances of denial of a speedy trial)

- Improper behavior during grand jury proceedings.

As revealed in an editorial:

One of the most disturbing tactics that some prosecutors are using today is the use of social services such as child protection agencies as a weapon for the purpose of striking fear into the hearts of defendants and their families. Prosecutors blatantly threaten the defendants' wives and girlfriends with the removal of their children from their homes if they will not "cooperate" with them . . . [Child protection workers have wide-sweeping powers once a mere accusation is levied against someone.]

Some prosecutors not only utilize such tactics to help with their cases, but also use them to help justify their actions. Sometimes, their actions appear to be little more than retaliatory-especially if the case was hotly contested or was highly publicized.

In spite of winning his case, a prosecutor was irate because the defendant's wife took their story to the media He requested that the Child Protective Services remove her child on the grounds that "her continued belief in her husband's innocence demonstrated a gross distortion of reality and posed an undue threat to her child". . . [One of the conditions listed for the defendant's wife to have her child returned was that she must file for a divorce!][216]

A law recently enacted in Minnesota, and in some other states gives prosecutors an unfair advantage in presenting closing statements to the jury. While the defense makes one closing statement, the prosecutor gets the last word with a second closing statement, which goes unchallenged.

As DNA testing has now proven in many cases, crime/forensic laboratories run by governments typically align with the prosecution. Instead of analyzing potential evidence from a neutral and objective position, individuals working within the agency, who portray themselves as experts, sometimes draw the conclusion that law enforcement agencies and prosecutors wish to hear.

A joint investigation on forensic laboratories by CNN and the Center for Investigative Reporting revealed serious flaws in modern forensic work:

> There are no requirements and no standards that must be met [for crime labs]. You can take a two-week course and you could call yourself an expert and get hired and make life-and-death tough decisions . . . The aura of infallibility is a myth. Forensic evidence is subject to human error, and outright egregious claims. Crime labs are unregulated. Standards are ad hoc or even nonexistent.

> The International Association for the Identification tests fingerprint examiners who want to be certified. Nearly half of those who take the test fail it. And those are the ones who take the trouble to get certified . . .

> Once the mindset occurs with the initial examiner, it becomes increasingly difficult for others in the agency to disagree . . . No one knows how often infallible forensic science helps convict innocent people, while allowing the guilty to go free.[217]

The investigation revealed specific cases of individuals (names omitted) who do this forensic testing, including:

> The founder and manager of Montana's state crime laboratory . . . according to his own testimony [in criminal trials] had evaluated hair in as many as 700 investigations. [In] Washington state, where he worked after leaving Montana, the state police had experts review a sample of his work. Their conclusion . . . his methods were badly flawed. The report charged him with neglect of duty, incompetence, gross misconduct, and violation of agency rules.

> Based on their finding that his testimony in Montana was erroneous, the Washington State Patrol dismissed him

. . . He had been a forensic scientist for 30 years before anyone started questioning his methods and results.

In Montana, where his work helped convict three men whose convictions were later overturned, the state's attorney general . . . refused to have the evidence scientifically retested [apparently to avoid both the release of other prisoners wrongfully convicted and possible lawsuits against the state].

In West Virginia, a forensic scientist got away with 12 years of sloppy work and false testimony in a crime lab before DNA testing caught up with him. The state invalidated his entire body of work. His work helped put at least six men in prison erroneously in two states. He was indicted for false testimony but died before he could be brought to trial.

Harold Deadman, a former FBI hair examiner who teaches forensics at George Washington University: "Numerous mistakes in hair analysis have been uncovered around the country . . . There are many laboratories where individuals are put into the position of hair comparisons with very little training.

"Surprisingly, hair examiners, like fingerprint examiners, are largely unregulated. The way we assess professionalism is by having proficiency testing, quality assurance programs and meaningful audits. We don't have any of those in place."

Janine Arvizu, laboratory auditor: "There are no requirements and no standards that must be met. When problems occur in forensic labs, some of the members of the public might just think that it's examples of individual malfeasance or individual problems, but from my perspective as a quality auditor, I look at it more as a systemic failure of the forensic industry in this country.

There are no requirements and no standards that must be met for you to be a forensic laboratory in most parts of the country.

"On numerous occasions, I have approached prosecutors and talked to them about the need for them to assess the quality of their own lab, not simply accept it on blind faith. And almost without exception, the prosecutors say that 'as long as the laboratory results support my theory in the case, I don't want to know if there's any problems.' It is hardly an appropriate response. It's the see-no-evil, speak-no-evil, hear-no-evil approach to laboratory quality."

There is no federal watchdog to make sure that forensics used to imprison people or send them to their death is scientific and accurate. Forensic science has gotten a free ride for the past 50 years, primarily because they made this bogus argument that we don't need to be regulated. Right now, if bad lab work does come to light, nothing requires officials to determine whether it's an isolated incident or part of a pattern.

Only three states require that crime labs be accredited. And about half of the crime labs in the United States have earned accreditation, but critics point out that being accredited by your peers is not the same as being regulated by outsiders. Accreditation is a first step. There needs to be more research, more oversight and more accountability.

Many labs are headed not by scientists but by police officers or political appointees-individuals much too close to the prosecution teams.

A national Institute of Justice report states: "Reasonably credible estimates are [that] up to 10 percent of our national prison population may be factually innocent of the crimes[s] for which they were convicted."[218] Based on a population of two million people locked up in this country, tens of thousands of innocent men and women are behind prison walls. In all but nine states, some face the ultimate punishment-execution!

One example is the conviction and execution of a man in Oklahoma, upon evidence claimed by a police chemist but that did not exist. In other cases in which she gave false testimony, three inmates serving long sentences, one on death row, ultimately obtained release. Four other chemists in the department agreed that no such evidence existed. One of them signed a police memo to that effect, and then resigned from the embattled forensics lab because of a "hostile work environment".[219]

Even when DNA testing proves the convicted are innocent, they are not necessarily free: In one case in Texas, the defense ordered DNA tests that proved a prisoner did not rape and murder a teenager. The State reran the tests, which also proved the man innocent. The appellate court then released him. The state supreme court, however, reinstated the sentence, sending him back to prison. Questioned about sending the man back to prison, the chief of the state Supreme Court, who had joined the majority vote, responded, "The appellant has to prove his innocence."

"How do they do that?" asked the interviewer.

"I don't know, "the judge answered. "It [DNA tests showing the man is innocent] would not have made a difference to the jury."

The prosecuting attorney rationalized his continued opposition to freeing the man: "DNA is not important unless it proves guilt; it is not compelling. It did not prove he is innocent as he could have had an accomplice who actually left the semen in the girl."

In another state, in a case in which a man was sentenced to die, the governor ordered further DNA testing. He also ordered, however, that the result be released to anyone else, including the defense attorney. The tests proved the man innocent, but the governor offered only to commute the death sentence to a life sentence. He gave the defense attorney just two hours to come back with an answer from the condemned man.

The governor, who planned to run for Congress, rationalized: "Well,

I did save his life." The prosecutor's rationale for not endorsing the release of this innocent man: "Individually, there is no harm in releasing a person where DNA says he is not guilty, but collectively there is great harm because it will set precedence . . . How can I go back to the family of the victim and the investigators and tell them that I made a mistake in prosecuting the person?"[220]

According to a study conducted by a Columbia University team of lawyers and criminologists of 4,500 death sentences over a 23-year period, 68 percent of the convictions were thrown out on appeal. Upon retrial, 82 percent of the defendants received lesser sentences, and 7 percent were acquitted. Statistically, since the death penalty has been reestablished, for every eight people executed, one death-row prisoner has been determined innocent.[221]

One strategy used by interrogators and capitalized by prosecutors is the "vision statement". Following hours of interrogation and sleep deprivation, the suspect is given evidence from the crime scene and asked to hypothetically visualize how s/he would have committed the crime, even though s/he professes innocence. The prosecution then uses the vision statement as a confession.

For those executed, the injustice is irreversible. And it is irreversible for some who never reach execution. That was the case for a man convicted by eyewitness testimony in Florida of the rape and murder of an eight-year-old girl. He died of cancer while on death row, where he spent the last fourteen years of his life. Eleven months after his death, DNA testing by the FBI cleared him.[222]

At least 381 murder convictions have been reversed due to police or prosecutorial misconduct since 1963. Not one of the prosecutors who broke the law was convicted or disbarred, and few were disciplined. An unwritten code of silence protects the prosecutors and squelches criticism, encouraging the non disclosure of exculpatory evidence and discouraging the admission of error.[223]

The horror compounds even when clear and convincing evidence of innocence is offered. In almost every case, the system refuses to admit error or to release those who have been unjustly convicted. Everyone agrees it is a terrible thing for an innocent person to be imprisoned. Far worse, apparently, for a politician to take a moderate line on crime and punishment.

There are exceptions: With forensic DNA testing now conclusively determining the guilt or innocence of a suspect, the Ramsey County (Minnesota) prosecutor-an expert in prosecuting cases using DNA evidence-had called for the review of cases prosecuted before forensic DNA testing was available. The prosecutor did this to assure that she had not been responsible for an innocent person going to prison.[224]

And the prosecutor for Hennepin County (Minnesota) convened a conference titled "Protecting the Innocent, Convicting the Guilty". Cosponsored by law schools in the Minneapolis/St.Paul area, it addressed the topic of wrongful convictions, including mistaken eyewitness identification and steps to prevent it. The prosecutor also told the more than 400 conference attendees that videotaping interrogations of suspects, as now required in Minnesota, deters police from coercive tactics that may provoke false confessions. Videotaping interrogations helps prosecutors to secure sound convictions and equips defense attorneys to better serve their clients.[225]

When a bill to reinstate the death penalty was introduced in the Minnesota legislature, a prosecuting attorney among the lawmakers opposing the legislation stated, "I don't want it on my conscience that an innocent person was executed." The bill did not pass.

A bill coauthored by another prosecuting attorney did pass, however; it allows that "a person convicted of a crime may make a motion for the performance of fingerprint or for forensic DNA testing to demonstrate the person's actual innocence."[226]

Finally, in Illinois, when it was revealed that 13 death-row inmates had been exonerated in just ten years, the governor declared a moratorium on executions. He established a bipartisan commission to study the problem and called for a sweeping overhaul of capital punishment in the state. A narrow majority concluded it should be abolished.

The 14-member panel made 185 recommendations to prevent unwarranted executions, including videotaping all interrogations of suspects in capital cases to prevent coerced confessions, submitting all such cases to a state board for review, and establishing a statewide DNA database and independent forensic lab. Because so many cases came to light showing the defendants did not get a fair trial, the governor commuted all 168 death-row sentences to life imprisonment.

These few signs of enlightenment provide a glimmer of hope for the American system of justice, which as, stated previously, may be remedied at least partially through:

- Authorizing judges to exclude testimony by forensic experts based solely on their conclusions and without supporting evidence

- State forensic/crime laboratories requiring accreditation by an independent organization or federal agency for its technicians; labs operating as independent agencies

- Videotaping of all police interrogations

- The identification of jurors by number, to prevent jury tampering

- Allowing jurors to take notes and ask questions of witnesses

- Allowing cameras in the courtrooms

- Holding prosecutors accountable for misconduct (withholding exculpatory evidence, eliciting false testimony, doctoring records)

- Compensating defendants who are exonerated or acquitted for loss of wages and legal fees.

About the Author

Edward Clark has been imprisoned for nearly five decades. He nevertheless has maintained a positive attitude, exhibiting concern for others through his preparation of a school-bus brake inspection manual for the State of Minnesota, his work with legislators for the passage of a law requiring the release of prisoners deserving of a second chance, and his efforts to convince other inmates to seek relief through the legislative process instead of rioting.

He chooses to work outside when possible and is an avid runner, having logged in more than 14,000 miles.

You may share your comments with the author by writing:

Edclarkmn@aol.com

Or

Edward R. Clark #100675

1101 Linden Lane

Faribault, MN 55021-6400

Endnotes

1   Here and following, "Murdered Man's Wife Feared Dead," *Mankato Free Press* (hereafter *MFP*), 24 April 1974.
2   "Only Witness to Murder," *MFP*, 25 April 1974.
3   "Wife of Jiminez Still Missing," *MFP*, 25 April 1974.
4   "Lost Innocence-Slain in Gangland Style" (editorial), *MFP*, 29 April 1974.
5   Here and following, "Sheriff Sees Progress in Jiminez Murder," *MFP*, 29 April 1974.
6   "New Lead in Jiminez Case," *Waseca Journal*, 26 April 1974.
7   "Jury Selection Ends," *MFP*, 20 September 1974.
8   "Brown Shoe May Be Clue in Search for Mrs. Jiminez," *MFP*, 30 April 1974.
9   "Posse Searches for Mrs. Jiminez," *MFP*, 1 May 1974.
10 "Nude Brunette Garroted with Her Own Hair," *Detective Dragnet*, April 1975.
11 "Three Persons Suspected in Jiminez Case," *MFP*, 3 May 1974.
12 Here and following, "Box of Clothing Found Is Clue in Jiminez Case," *MFP*, 2 May 1974.
13 "Police Narrow Killer Search-Single Suspect Now Sought," *MFP*, 8 May 1974.
14 Jon Holten, "Agents Say Local Drug Trade 'Wide Open,'" *MFP*, 4 April 1980.
15 Jon Holten, "Drug Dealing in Kato 'Organized,' Yet Informal," *MFP*, 10 April 1980.
16 Here and following, Jon Holten, "Drug Violence: Complaintless Crime," *MFP*, 11 April 1980.
17 Jon Holten, "Hearing Set in Blue Earth County Drug Bust," *MFP*, n.d. April 1980.
18 Jon Holten, "Mankato Equals Pain," *MFP*, n.d. April 1980.
19 Jon Holten, "Three Lebanese Given Prison Sentences in Heroin Case," *MFP*, n.d. April 1980.
20 Jon Holten, "Grand Jury Indicts Mankato-Area Pair on Cocaine-Related Charges," *MFP*, n.d. April 1980.
21 "Marijuana: Penalties Vary Widely," *Minneapolis Tribune*, 26 July 1977.

22 "Blue Earth County Seeks Early Attorney Election," *MFP*, n.d.
23 *State of Minnesota v. Edward R. Clark*. Appellant's Brief: Appeal from Denial of Post Conviction Relief, Blue Earth County #48668 (hereafter BE Appeal #48668) and Le Sueur County #49974 (hereafter LS Appeal), Exhibit 15.
24 "Appellant's Rights . . . Violated by the Admission . . . of Evidence . . . Obtained in a Search of His Person Conducted during an Illegal Arrest, and (2) . . . in a Search Conducted Pursuant to a Warrant . . . Issued Without Probable Cause." BE Appeal #48668, pp. 97-101, and LS Appeal, pp. 95-99: Exhibit 22.
25 BE Appeal #48668 and LS Appeal, Exhibit 4.
26 California Penal **Code** §863.
27 Here and following, BE Appeal #48668, pp. 97-101, and LS Appeal, pp. 95-99: Exhibit 22. The illegal arrest (minus warrant) was raised on appeal.
28 *MFP*, 8 and 10 May 1974.
29 Ibid., 9 and 15 May 1974.
30 "Adamson Takes Clark Defense," *MFP*, 23 May 1974.
31 Appellant Was Not Afforded Adequate Aid and Representation by Counsel: Counsel's Prejudicial Comments to the Media," BE Appeal #48668, p. 105.
32 *MFP*, 29 May 1974.
33 Ibid., 20 May 1974.
34 Ibid., n.d.
35 *MFP*, 21 May 1974.
36 Ibid., n.d.
37 Ibid., 28 May 1974.
38 *MFP*, 29 May 1974.
39 Ibid., 24 May 1974.
40 "Public Defense Board Stops Budgeting Plans until Its Future's Decided," *MFP*, n.d.
41 "Appellant's Sixth Amendment Rights were Interfered with by an Illegal and Surreptitious Monitoring of His Conversations in the Blue Earth County Jail," *Minnesota v. Clark*, Petition for Post Conviction Relief, Blue Earth County Post Conviction Hearing (hereafter BEPCH), 205-07; BE Appeal #48668, pp. 39-54, and LS Appeal

#49974, pp. 71-87.
42   Here and following, *Minnesota v. Clark,* Petition for Post Conviction Relief, Le Sueur County Post Conviction Hearing (hereafter LSPCH), Exhibit 23.
43   Blue Earth County Jail Log, 30 May 1974.
44   "Appellant Was Not Afforded Adequate Aid and Representation by Counsel: Failure to Argue that Wiebold Statement Was Obtained Involuntarily; Failure to Determine Effect of Monitoring in Blue Earth County and Sacramento Jails," BE Appeal #48668, p. 108.
45   Blue Earth County Jail Log, 30 May 1974, 12:50 P.M.
46   BE Appeal #48668, pp. 11, 104.
47   Rasmussen (evidentiary) hearing, 31 May 1974; "Appellant's Rights . . . were Violated by Admission at Trial of Evidence (1) Obtained in a Search of His Person Conducted During an Illegal Arrest, and (2) Obtained in a Search Conducted Pursuant to a Warrant . . . Issued Without Probable Cause," BE Appeal #48668, pp. 97-101, and LS Appeal, pp. 95-99: Exhibit 22.
48   Here and following, Change of Venue hearing, 7 June 1974.
49   "Lost Innocence . . . Slain in Gangland Style," *MFP*, 8 May 1974.
50   BE Appeal #48668, Exhibit 4.
51   *State v. Thompson*, 273 Minn. 1. 139, N.W. 2d 490 (1966)
52   "Denied Due Process of Law and a Fair Trial Where He was Denied the Right to Change the Venue of His Trial from Blue Earth County" and "Not Afforded Adequate Aid and Representation by Counsel: Failure to Renew the Motion to Change Venue," BE Appeal #48668, pp. 11-27, 104-05.
53   "Appellant was Not Afforded Adequate Aid and Representation of Counsel-Failure to Aid in the Jury Selection," BE Appeal #48668, p.106.
54   BE Appeal #48668, pp. 18-20.
55   "Jury Selection Begins Tuesday in Clark Case," and "Clark Trial Jury Selection Begins," *MFP*, 16 and 17 September 1974.
56   "Jury Selection Toughens Overnight," *MFP*, 17 September 1974.
57   "Selection of Clark Jury Nears Finish" and "Jury Selection

Ends in Murder Trial of Clark," *MFP*, 20 September 1974.
58   BE Trial, pp. 147-48.
59   Ibid., 156-77.
60   "Denied Due Process . . . Juror Intimidated . . . and Not Questioned" and "Appellant was Not Afforded Adequate Aid and Representation of Counsel-Failure to Interrogate Juror David Graham," BE Appeal #48668, pp. 28, 29, 107.
61   Lou Gelfand, "There's No Compelling Reason to Identify Jurors by Name," *Minneapolis Star Tribune*, 19 November 1989.
62   "New Lead in Jiminez Murder Case," *Waseca Journal*, 20 April 1974.
63   Here and following references to second trial, LS Trial transcript (hereafter LS Trial), Vol. 14, pp. 7-80.
64   Denied Due Process . . . Presented to the Jury in Handcuffs," BE Appeal #48668, pp. 28-29.
65   BE Trial, pp. 1-4.
66   LS Trial, Vol. 15, pp. 1-2.
67   Here and following, BE Trial, pp. 2-116.
68   "Three Person Suspected in Jiminez Case," *MFP*, 19 September 1974.
69   "Bringing Evidence" and "At the Scene," *MFP*, 19 September 1974.
70   Ibid.
71   Here and following, BE Trial, pp. 123-67.
72   LS Trial, Vol. 10, pp. 63-73.
73   Here and following, BE Trial, 280-307.
74   "Denied Due Process . . . Admission of . . . Inflammatory and Prejudicial Photographs," BE Appeal #45672, pp. 110-17, and LS Appeal, pp. 39-59.
75   "Colored Photos of Victims among Evidence in Trial," "Jury Hears of 2nd Death," and "Prosecution Attempting Tie-in of Jiminez Cases," *MFP*, 24, 25, and 25 respectively, September 1974.
76   Here and following, BE Trial, pp. 308-46.
77   Ibid., 347-80.
78   Ibid., 481-88.
79   BE Trial, 491-511.

80   Here and following, BE Trial, 519-39.
81   "Landlord, Employer Praise Clark," *MFP*, 28 September 1974.
82   BE Trial, 540-44.
83   Ibid., 544-70.
84   Ibid., 571-609.
85   Here and following, BE Trial, 610-45.
86   Rasmussen hearing.
87   BE Trial, 676.
88   "Constitutional Rights Violated . . . (1) Statements Illegally Obtained, (2) State Introduced Evidence that Appellant Exercised Constitutional Rights, and (3) Court Advised Jury Certain Conversations Suppressed," BE Appeal #48668, pp. 71-87.
89   *Miranda v. Arizona*, 384 U.S. 436, 86 S.Ct. 1602, L.Ed. 694.
90   BE Trial, 610-45.
91   Ibid., 643-52.
92   BE Trial, 610-45.
93   Ibid., 661-70.
94   Here and following, BE Trial, 1067-90.
95   Ibid., 670-81.
96   Here and following, BE Trial, 681-90.
97   Ibid., 690-95.
98   Ibid., 695-754.
99   BE Trial, pp. 754-77.
100 "Denied Due Process of Law . . . Failure to Produce Evidence Vital to the Defense," BE Appeal #48668, pp. 101-02.
101 "Not Afforded Adequate Aid and Representation of Counsel: Failure to Present Certain Favorable Evidence," BE Appeal, p. 111.
102 Here and following, BE Trial, pp. 773-807.
103 BE Appeal, Evidence Insufficient: (1) To Prove Beyond a Reasonable Doubt Appellant Committed Alleged Crime, and (2) Circumstantial Evidence Did Not Exclude Hypothesis of Innocence, BE Appeal #45762, pp. 57-75.
104 Here and following, BE Trial, pp. 808-17.
105 LS Trial, Vol. 7, pp. 12-40.
106 *Austin v. United States*, 113 S.Ct. 2801 (1993).
107 "Defense to Open Friday," *MFP*, 3 October 1974.

108 Here and following, BE Trial, 567-74.
109 Ibid., 870-901.
110 Ibid., n.d.
111 "Denied Due Process of Law . . . by the Failure of the State to Produce Certain Evidence Vital to the Defense: A. The Ed Newberg Statement; B. The Fingerprint Evidence; C. The statement from Glen Fjorlund; D. The Interview with Ernest Ties," BE Appeal #48668, pp. 97-100.
112 BE Trial, 863-70.
113 Ibid., "The Evidence Was Insufficient: (1) To Prove Beyond A Reasonable Doubt that the Appellant Committed the Alleged Crime, and (2) The Circumstantial Evidence Provided Did Not Exclude an Hypothesis of Innocence."
114 BE Appeal #45762, pp. 57-71.
115 Here and following, BE Trial, 837-41.
116 Here and following, BE Trial, 892-1043.
117 BE Appeal #48668, pp. 55-73.
118 Here and following, BE Trial, 1067-90.
119 "Appellant Denied Due Process by Prejudicial Closing Argument of Prosecution," BE Appeal #48668, pp. 96-103.
120 "Appellant Was Not Afforded Adequate Aid and Representation by Counsel," BE Appeal #48668, pp. 104-16.
121 "Clark Salute" (editorial), *MFP*, 16 October 1974.
122 David A. Wood, M.D., to Francis J. Wilcox, Esq., n.d. (Copy formerly in possession of author.)
123 Francis, J. Wilcox, Esq. to David A. Wood, M.D., n.d. (Copy formerly in possession of author.)
124 For example: "Convict Seeks Aid for Long Legal Battle," unidentified St. Paul newspaper clipping, 3 January 1975.
125 Mark Toll, Radio Station KTOB, Mankato, Minnesota, 4 January 1975.
126 "Drug Violence: Complaintless Crime," *MFP*, 11 April 1980.
127 "Bailey a Hypnotic Personality," *The Prison Mirror* (Stillwater, Minnesota), n.d.
128 "Convicted Killer Denies Crimes under Hypnosis," *Minneapolis Star*, n.d.

129 "Clark Denies Killing Couple in Hypnosis," *MFP*, n.d.
130 Robert Bailey, M.D., to *Lie Detector*, 31 March 1983.
131 U.S. Congress (1968) *Title III Omnibus Crime Control and Safe Streets Act.*
132 Hearing to Set Aside the Indictment (hereafter Hearing), 13 June 1975.
133 Lynn Closway, "Clark's Pre-Trial Hearing Closed," *MFP,* 14 June 1975.
134 Here and following, Hearing, 4-468.
135 "Clark Says Sheriff Listened In," "Police Eavesdropped on Talks, Convict Says," and Convicted Slayer Claims His Talks with Lawyer Bugged," unidentified *MFP* and Twin Cities newspaper clippings, n.d.
136 "Illegal and Surreptitious Monitoring of His Conversations in Blue Earth County Jail," BE Appeal #48668, pp. 39-54, and LS Appeal #49974, pp. 71-87.
137 Post Conviction Hearing (hereafter PC), pp. 320-23.
138 "Attorney Says No Eavesdropping Occurred," MFP, n.d.
139 PC. Pp. 114-19.
140 Kenneth F. Schoen, Commissioner of Corrections, to author, 22 August 1975.
141 Edward M. Laine, Special Assistant Attorney General, to author, 27 October 1975.
142 Joseph Michael Hauer statement, 17 May 1979.
143 "Clark Trial," *MFP*, 10 July 1975.
144 LS Trial, vol. 1, pp. 17-25.
145 LS Trial, vol. 1, pp. 34-36.
146 "Appellant Denied Due Process by Admission . . . Evidence relating to Death of Michael Jiminez and Numerous Inflammatory and Prejudicial Photographs," LS Appeal, pp. 39-53.
147 LS Trial, vol. 1, pp. 38-58.
148 Ibid., pp. 33-72.
149 Ibid., pp. 75-124.
150 LS Trial, vol. 3, pp. 97-136.
151 Ibid., vol. 4, pp. 22-57.
152 "Jiminezes Went to Kansas for Car, Sister Testified," *MFP,* 15

July 1975.
153   LS Trial, vol. 4, pp. 58-124.
154   Ibid., vol. 6, pp. 133-39.
155   Ibid., vol. 7, pp. 12-40.
156   LS Trial, vol. 7, pp. 41-81.
157   Andre A. Moenssens, Ray Edward Moses, Fred E. Inabau, *Scientific Evidence in Criminal Cases* (Mineola, New York: Foundation Press, 1973).
158   Keystone Firearms, Philadelphia, related this to the author by phone through a third party.
159   LS Trial, vol. 7, pp. 84-126.
160   Ibid., vol. 8, pp. 10-44.
161   LS Appeal, Exhibit 18.
162   "Failure of the State to Produce Certain Evidence Vital to the Defense," LS Appeal #49974, pp. 113-14.
163   LS Trial, vol. 2, pp. 125-361; vol. 3, pp. 14-19.
164   "Wiebold Bites Bullet in Clark Trial." *MFP*, n.d.
165   "Clark 'Court' in Private Meeting," *MFP*, 21 July 1975.
166   LS Trial, vol. 9, pp. 24-39; vol. 10, pp. 3-25, 40-55.
167   "Court Erred in Allowing State to Read Portions of Appellant's Prior Testimony (A) Prior Testimony Not Admissible at Second Trial (B) Even if Admissible, Manner in which it was Presented so Prejudicial as to Deny Due Process and a Fair and Impartial Trial," LS Appeal #49974, pp. 137-53.
168   Motion for Acquittal, vol. 10, pp. 55-56.
169   LS Trial, vol. 10, pp. 55-56.
170   Here and following, LS Trial, vol. 10, pp. 57-73.
171   Ibid., pp. 74-78.
172   LS Trial, vol. 11, pp. 6-9.
173   Ibid., pp. 40-42.
174   Here and following, LS Trial, vol. 10, pp.79-80; vol. 11, pp. 44-120.
175   Ibid., vol. 11, pp.129-32.
176   Ibid., vol. 12, pp. 2-21.
177   "Marital Privilege Violated when Wife Allowed to Testify Concerning Confidential Communications," LS Appeal #49974, pp.

154-59.
178   LS Trial, vol. 11, pp. 121-28.
179   Ibid., vol. 12, pp. 22-43.
180   "Main Defense Witness Unfairly Impeached," LS Appeal #49974, pp. 160-69.
181   *State of Minnesota v. Edward R. Clark*, 296 N.W. 2d 372 (Minn. 1980).
182   Unidentified newspaper clipping, 24 July 1975.
183   "Final Arguments Today in Slay Trial," UPI, unidentified newspaper clipping, 24 July 1975.
184   Here and following, LS Trial, vol. 14, pp. 76-101.
185   Here and following, "Failure of State to Produce Evidence Vital to the Defense," LS Appeal #49974, pp. 110-22.
186   "Rights Violated through Introduction of Evidence that He Exercised Right to Silence," LS Appeal #49974, pp. 178-94.
187   "Prosecutor's Prejudicial and Improper Closing Argument," LS Appeal #49974, pp. 195-201.
188   "Prosecution Rests in Jiminez Trial," UPI, unidentified newspaper clipping, 23 July 1975.
189   Here and following, LS Trial, vol. 14, pp. 106-31.
190   LS Trial, vol. 14, pp. 133.
191   "Clark Trial Jury to Begin Deliberations," *MFP*, 25 July 1975; "Clark Trial Goes to Jury," *MFP*, 28 July 1975; "Jury Deliberating Clark Case Retires," unidentified newspaper clipping, UPI, 28 July 1975.
192   LS Trial, vol. 15, pp. 1-7.
193   "Michigan Man Convicted in Second Jiminez Death," 30 July 1975, and "Convicted Slayer Gets 2nd Life Term," 30 July 1975, unidentified Twin Cities newspaper clippings; no title, *MFP*, 30 July 1975.
194   "Evidence was Insufficient" (1) To Prove Beyond a Reasonable Doubt that Appellant Committed the Alleged Crime, and (2) The Circumstantial Evidence Proved Did Not Exclude a Rational Hypothesis of Innocence," LS Appeal #49974, pp. 60-70.
195   Le Sueur County Post Conviction Hearing.
196   "Consecutive Life Sentence Constitutes Cruel and Unusual Punishment and Denies Due Process," LS Appeal #49974, pp. 170-77.
197   Minnesota State Supreme Court Syllabus: 296 N.W.2d 359

and 372, *State v. Clark* (Minn. 1980).
198 Here and following, Post Conviction Hearing, pp. 92-94.
199 Post Conviction Hearing, Exhibit 21.
200 Terry C. Stacey Deposition (Attorney Peter J. Wold), 5 December 1984.
201 Sheriff Pat Smith Jr. to Edward R. Clark, 6 January 2000.
202 "Investigator: Reasonable Doubts," FOX 9 26 April 2009
203 (Minnesota) Coalition for Correction Reform, Secretary of State Registration No. 059403.
204 Robert E. Vanasek, Speaker of the (Minnesota) House, to Edward Clark, 19 January 1989.
205 Duane Benson, (Minnesota) Senate Minority Leader, to Edward Clark, 20 January 1989.
206 Minnesota Attorney General's Opinion to the Governor, 15 June 1960.
207 Daniel Paskewitz, M.D., Ph. D., Psychological Services Report, 6 August 1991.
208 Dennis A. Philander, M.D., P.A., Psychiatric/psychological Evaluation, 24 January 2000.
209 "Hard Time or Free Time," *Minnesota Monthly*, June 1995.
210 National Alliance for the Mentally Ill-Minnesota (NAMI-MN) to Edward Clark, "For Outstanding Service to Forensic Alliance for the Mentally Ill-MN," 10 December 1993.
211 C. J. Solberg, Director of Correctional Industries, to Edward Clark, 11 May 1979.
212 "Inmate Charges His Prison Transfer Is Retaliation for Political Activism," *Minnesota Daily*, 30 March 1983.
213 Joan Fabian, Commissioner of Corrections, to Edward Clark, 11 April 2005.
214 Angela Kollman, PsyD, LP Psychologist 3, Lifer Review Psychological Evaluation, 19 March 2019
215 Here and following, "Harmful Error: Investigating America's Local Prosecutors," 4 January 2004. *See* The Center for Public Integrity ,www.publicintegreity.org>
216 "Public Needs to be Aware of Tactics Used by Prosecutors" (editorial), (Stillwater) *Prison Mirror*, 1 February 1995.

217   Here and following, *CNN Presents: Reasonable Doubt*, 13 January 2005.
218   National Institute of Justice, "Convicted by Juries, Exonerated by Science: Case Studies in the Use of DNA Evidence to Establish Innocence after Trial" (NCJ 161258), Washington D.C., n.d.
219   Deborah Hastings, "Capitol Case Involved Tainted Chemist: Man Convicted, Executed for Murder," Associated Press (hereafter AP) clipping, n.d.
220   *Frontline: The Case for Innocence,* PBS Television, original airing January 2000.
221   "A Stronger Case against Gallows Justice" (editorial), *Minneapolis Star Tribune*, 14 June 2000.
222   "Man Who Died on Death Row Cleared by DNA in Murder," unidentified AP clipping, 15 December 2000.
223   Roger Hummel review of Barry Scheck, Peter Neufed, and Jim Dwyer, "Actual Innocence-Five Days to Execution, and Other Dispatches from the Wrongly Convicted," *Prison Legal News*, December 2000.
224   Susan Gaertner, Ramsey County Attorney, to Edward R. Clark, 27 January 2005.
225   "Guilt, Innocence: Seeking True Justice for All," *MST*, December 12 2005.
226   Minnesota Statute §590.01 subd. 1a(a).

EDWARD R. CLARK

www.ingramcontent.com/pod-product-compliance
Lightning Source LLC
Chambersburg PA
CBHW071950070526
44583CB00015B/1135